Citizenship, Faith, & Feminism

BRANDEIS SERIES ON
Gender, Culture, Religion, & Law

Series editors:
LISA FISHBAYN JOFFE & SYLVIA NEIL

This series focuses on the conflict between women's claims to
gender equality and legal norms justified in terms of religious and
cultural traditions. It seeks work that develops new theoretical tools for
conceptualizing feminist projects for transforming the interpretation and
justification of religious law, examines the interaction or application of
civil law or remedies to gender issues in a religious context, and engages
in analysis of conflicts over gender and culture/religion in a particular
religious legal tradition, cultural community, or nation. Created under
the auspices of the Hadassah-Brandeis Institute in conjunction with its
Project on Gender, Culture, Religion, and the Law, this series emphasizes
cross-cultural and interdisciplinary scholarship concerning Judaism,
Islam, Christianity, and other religious traditions.

For a complete list of books that are available in the series,
visit www.upne.com

JAN FELDMAN
    Citizenship, Faith, and Feminism:
    Jewish and Muslim Women Reclaim Their Rights

Citizenship, Faith, & Feminism

JEWISH AND MUSLIM WOMEN RECLAIM THEIR RIGHTS

Jan Feldman

BRANDEIS UNIVERSITY PRESS

WALTHAM, MASSACHUSETTS

BRANDEIS UNIVERSITY PRESS
Published by University Press of New England
www.upne.com
© 2011 Brandeis University
All rights reserved
Manufactured in the United States of America
Designed by Eric M. Brooks
Typeset in Whitman and Mrs. Eaves
by Keystone Typesetting, Inc.

University Press of New England is a member of the
Green Press Initiative. The paper used in this book meets
their minimum requirement for recycled paper.

For permission to reproduce any of the material
in this book, contact Permissions, University Press of
New England, One Court Street, Suite 250, Lebanon NH
03766; or visit www.upne.com

Library of Congress Cataloging-in-Publication Data
appear on the last printed page of this book.

5 4 3 2 1

Rabbi Elazar said in the name of Rabbi Chanina: Torah scholars increase peace in the world, for it is said: and all of your children shall be learners, and great will be the peace of *banayich* (your children). Do not read *banayich* but *bonayich* (your builders). TO MY CHILDREN AND OUR BUILDERS, JEREMIAH, GABE, ZEV, AND LESLY, and with special gratitude, TO MY DAUGHTER DANIT for sharing my travels as a companion and source of insights. The future of Orthodox Jewish women is in the hands and hearts of your generation.

I also dedicate this book TO MY PARENTS, FRANCES AND STANLEY, with unending and bottomless appreciation; and TO SHIRLEY for putting me up and putting up with me, and especially for keeping me thinking and laughing; and TO BETH for her enduring friendship. Finally, thanks and a big biscuit TO SHOMER, for providing tail-wagging constant companionship.

Contents

Acknowledgments

I would like to acknowledge my great debt to
the Taub Center for Social and Policy Research,
especially Laura Brass, for giving me a "home"
in Jerusalem; the Hadassah-Brandeis Institute,
for granting me a generous fellowship and a
very congenial atmosphere in which to work;
and the Women and Public Policy Program
of the Kennedy School of Government for
appointing me as a fellow and showing me
great hospitality. I am particularly indebted
to the Islamic National Consensus Movement
and the Women's Social and Cultural Society
of Kuwait, and all of the women who granted
me the privilege of representing their views
and experiences and thereby broadening my
own. I would also like to express my gratitude
to Suzanne Spreadbury, Associate Dean for
Undergraduate Degree Programs, and Maureen
Worth, Special Projects Associate of Harvard
Extension School, for generously providing me
with a faculty aide. Finally, to Hannah Hoffman
Brion for her help in preparing this manuscript.
For their meticulous reading and insightful
contributions to this manuscript, I want to
thank Professor Lisa Fishbayn and Professor
Amina Wadud, and for her sustained support
and guidance, I want to thank my editor,
Phyllis Deutsch.

Preface

My intent in this book is to reveal commonalities between Jewish and Muslim feminisms. I have no larger agenda. I will not claim that "if only the women ruled the world all would be well." It strikes me that Arabic and Hebrew share the same name for G-d that translates as "the Compassionate One." Still, the cleavages and conflicts between the religions are real: political, historical, and doctrinal. I do not expect the recognition of our shared goals and strategies to result in a grander rapprochement, though, in my dream world, that will occur some day. First, a bit of self-disclosure: I am an Orthodox Jew and a feminist, and, therefore, a participant observer. Muslim and Jewish women are similarly situated with respect to their religious authority. We assume that the sacred texts represent divine self-disclosure and share a strategy that relies on mastering the rules of interpretation and analysis in pursuit of an authentic rather than apologetic, reading of the foundational texts. This, in itself, might constitute the fulcrum of a revolution in the word's original etymological sense—that is to "revolve back to the original," in this case, revealed divine intent. I have no desire to comment on the truth claims of either religion. I take the view that neither religion is inherently and intrinsically misogynistic. But I also take the view that anything that leads to an unjust act is itself unjust. I attribute injustice to humans, not to G-d. That acknowledged, I agree with Jewish and Muslim feminists who deem it critical that women insist on disentangling religion from accrued cultural and traditional attitudes or practices that are hostile to human dignity.

Finally, as with all interpretive endeavors, the interpreter is an ever-present mediator between the material and the reader, and though I strive to accurately represent the voices of the women I have interviewed, I have left my own imprint. That said, any errors in my interpretation of the texts or the views of others are my own. This project took me to Israel, Kuwait, and Morocco, where I conducted open-ended interviews with women activists. I used a snowball sampling method to expand my participant group beyond my original contacts. As a participant observer I brought a certain perspective and self-awareness to my interviews and my assessments, yet, I made every effort to allow my interviewees to speak for themselves in their own voices.

> *The compassion of G-d is not like human compassion. Human rulers favor males over females but the One who spoke and brought the world into being is not like that.*
> ❧ Sifre Numbers 133[1]

Citizenship, Faith, & Feminism

I

Women &
Citizenship

Four Kuwaitis made history in 2009 as the first women elected to the National Assembly. One, who was interviewed for this study, has just challenged an amendment to the 2005 Electoral Law that was introduced by Islamists requiring women to comply with shari'a (Islamic law), specifically by wearing the hijab (head covering). The woman member of Parliament contends that this amendment violates the 1962 constitution. She asserts that religious fatwas (edicts) are not binding and said that she will work to amend all laws passed by the previous National Assemblies that are in violation of the constitution's provisions for equal citizenship rights for women.[1] Additionally, on the heels of this electoral victory, the Kuwaiti Constitutional Court issued a landmark ruling by abrogating an article in the 1962 passport law that banned Kuwaiti women from obtaining their own passport without prior approval of their husbands. The ruling said that the law violates the constitution, especially articles 29, 30, and 31, which guarantee personal freedom.[2]

In March 2010 a group of Muslim American women, who had entered the "national mosque" through the front door to pray in the main hall, were ejected by Washington, DC, police officers in response to complaints by mosque officials. One woman commented, "I thought here we are in a mosque in the United States, and in the nation's capital no less, and the mosque authorities, as self-identified, call in municipal security forces to eject a bunch of women just because they wanted to pray in the main congregational space. . . . Is this where our tax dollars should go? To defend gender segregation? I had thought the days of segregation were long gone in this country. . . . Out in the street I turned to one of the cops, who, like the other policeman, was African-American, and said: 'You know about race and gender in this country. How did you feel about throwing women out? Did you ever think in your job you would be called upon to do such a thing?' . . . He repeated what the other cop had said: 'The mosque is a private place and they have the right to eject you if you do not play by their rules'. . . . All I could say was: 'The lunch counter was also private.' "[3]

Female activists in Iraq, undeterred by the 2010 murder of a female candidate for Parliament in Mosul, continue to challenge Iraq's religious conservatives, claiming that these men are imposing traditional and cultural misogyny, calling it religion. Jenan Mubark is hoping to pull together a slate of women candidates, with the hope of creating a bloc of women activists to fight to uphold Iraqi women's citizenship rights.[4]

These stories illustrate dramatically the potential for collision between civil law and religious law. They also illustrate the determination of feminists to use their citizenship to achieve equality by demanding that all law, including religious law, be made congruent with the constitution and civil law.

Religious women in many regimes are dual citizens, though not in the formal, legal sense. They are dual citizens because of their contrasting status as members of a civic community in which their gender has no impact on their constitutional guarantee of equal rights and their status in a traditional religious community that distributes roles and power based on ascriptive traits, specifically gender. In weak or unstable states, even when women are regarded as equal citizens, women's rights may be bartered away in order to gain support of the religious authorities. In Kuwait and Israel jurisdiction over family or personal status law, which heavily impacts women, has been given over to religious courts. While multicultural democracies such as the United States provide citizens the opportunity to slip the shackles of religion, religious women reject that option. Their struggle to reform their religions from within may be hampered by well-meaning government officials who fortify the gendered power relations of these religious communities in the name of toleration and multicultural accommodation.

The Muslim and Jewish women represented in this study are believers. They are not looking for escape. They are not adopting religion with the intent of subverting it. Their faith belongs to them as much as to men, and they refuse to be forced out. They do not accept that G-d is a misogynist or that G-d is unjust. Their goal is to disentangle Torah or Qur'an from the patriarchal culture that has claimed them. In their view, in defiance of divine intent, tradition and misinterpretation of these scriptures has denied them their equality. The feminist strategies of religious women usually entail a frontal attack on the male monopoly over the right to engage in exegesis of the text and to render legal decisions. Their equal citizenship is critical to their struggle to recover the equal dignity they believe is foundational to their religions.

Social theorists in the West, many feminists among them, have typically viewed religion as an enemy of progress. Some contend that the thinkers of the Enlightenment battled religion and that religion lost. Prominent twentieth-century sociologists and psychiatrists characterized religion as a "pathological flight from freedom,"[5] and others relegated it to the status of slavish and irrational thinking and superstition. Its practitioners are commonly depicted as ignorant, backward, and fanatical. But the predicted demise of religion did not come to pass, and some contemporary sociologists appear stunned by its vitality and current global revival. Despite his merciless critique of religion, Marx ruefully noted in his early essay "On the Jewish Question" (1843) that it was precisely in liberal democracies such as the United States, which legally separated church and state, that religion continued to be most vibrant.[6] Historically, religion has been at the forefront of the fight for civil rights for oppressed minorities because of its close association with natural rights. It would be difficult to understand Abraham Lincoln's Emancipation Proclamation or Martin Luther King Jr.'s "Letter from Birmingham Jail" without invoking religion. It is not surprising, then, that Muslim and Jewish women adopt rather than reject their religion as a vehicle for liberation.

Some liberal feminists doubt that religion and feminism can coexist, sharing Susan Moller Okin's claim that almost all religions are irremediably patriarchal and that women would be better off if religions simply "ceased to exist."[7] But this study rejects the idea of female victimization or passive subordination for which the only remedy is escape from religion. It explores the other option, increasingly embraced by Jewish and Muslim women alike, to deploy their civil citizenship to uproot human injustice and to fulfill their understanding of G-d's justice.

Muslim feminists do not regard themselves as renegades or infidels. These activists differ from those associated with Islamist revival of the 1970s and the political Islamists of the present. While religiously conservative, they do not reject modernity. They do not all want a complete separation of religion and civil law in Muslim countries. The new activists are worldly and pious. They are engaged, in the words of Amina Wadud, in a "gender jihad" or struggle to recover their G-d-given rights.[8]

Neither the prevailing models of normative citizenship in liberal democracies nor feminist theory can account for these women. As faithful, committed members of traditional religions, they are not cowed victims of false consciousness. Rather, they are increasingly deploying their civic citizenship rights in attempts to reform, not destroy, their religions. For them, neither exit nor acquiescence is an option. They are traditional in their faith and contemporary in their autonomous choice to stay, to reclaim, and to fight rather than to retreat. They belie stereotypes of religious women, be they Muslims or Orthodox Jews. This stereotype was succinctly expressed by a blogger who asserted that "Islamic feminists" is a contradiction in terms like a "North Korean tourist."[9]

Many observers see no possibility of reform from within, claiming that Islam and Judaism are too patriarchal and retrograde, and women too cowed or ignorant. To an extent, this perspective seems justified. Religious women may suffer from forced seclusion, illiteracy, and often poverty. They may have no formal education in the primary text of their religion in its original language. They may know little about the rights associated with citizenship. Despite these obstacles, women and girls, at great personal risk, have confronted religious authorities with the laws of the land. In 2008 Nojoud Mohammad Ali, a nine-year-old Yemeni girl, ran away from her abusive husband, thirty-five years her senior, and demanded help from the local police. Her case became an international cause célèbre, prompting a proposal to raise the age of marriage to seventeen years. Protestors, both for and against the proposed legislation, have rallied in front of Yemen's parliament. While Islamic clerics have denounced the ban on child marriage as being opposed to shari'a, human rights and women's rights organizations have turned the issue into one of political and civil rights of citizenship.

It is perhaps surprising that religious feminists are at the forefront of reform movements worldwide, not just in Western liberal democracies. Poverty, war, opprobrium of religious authorities, and even the violent backlash of men in their communities have not deterred women from ownership of their religion and civil rights. Devout Muslim feminists in Muslim states understand that no political reforms are possible if they are seen as incongruent with Islam. Even in theocracies in which gender equality exists formally under civil law, women are increasingly turning to civil institutions to challenge religious personal status law. In Kuwait there is no "exit option"[10] for non-observant or secular Muslims. The same is true in Israel for non-observant Jews. Therefore, theological and political reforms are being undertaken in tandem.

Hossan Banu Ghazanfar, Afghanistan's fourth minister for women's affairs, asserts that change must begin at the cultural level, but when it comes to widespread violence against women, especially honor killings, pointing out that these cultural traditions violate Islam is not enough. "The first step toward improving women's lot in Afghanistan should be to mobilize political will at the highest levels, and pass legislation to safeguard women's rights," according to Helena Malikyar, an Afghani historian. Women's rights must also be incorporated within the judicial system where they are currently treated as the "properties of men."[11] In 2009, after the Afghani government passed a personal status law constricting the marital rights of Shi'a women, their rallying chant was, "We don't want a Taliban law, we want a democratic law and we want a law that guarantees human dignity."[12]

Saudi human rights groups have been pressing the government to ban child marriages, even though the country's Grand Mufti, Sheik Abdul-Aziz bin Baz, asserted that it is permissible for ten-year-old girls to marry.[13] Malaysia's *Sisters in Islam,* an outspoken women's rights organization founded in 1988, has been advocating for women in a variety of areas including polygyny, child marriages, and the caning of Malaysian women for various religious infractions. In retaliation, Muslim conservatives have filed a lawsuit against the well-known organization, demanding that it remove the word Islam from its title. *Sisters in Islam* defends its work as being "driven by the tenets of the Qur'an and Islam."[14]

A twenty-six-year-old Egyptian woman has become an outspoken critic of the genital mutilation to which she was subjected as an eight-year-old child. She has also written and widely distributed an Arabic comic book on the life of Martin Luther King Jr.[15] A Sudanese woman who wore pants in public was fined the equivalent of two hundred dollars, though spared a whipping when a court found her guilty of violating Sudan's decency laws.[16] The law in contention here is article 152 of Sudan's penal code that punishes anyone who commits an indecent act that violates public morality. Mrs. Hussein, the woman on trial, argues that article 152 is intentionally vague, in part, to punish women. Hundreds of Sudanese women, many wearing pants, turned out to protest in front of the court where the trial was to take place. Riot police officers broke up the demonstration and took away more than forty women. Mrs. Hussein contends, "I am Muslim; I understand Muslim law . . . what passage in the Koran says women can't wear pants?"[17] Hussein wants to change the law. She illustrates both strategies that are commonly adopted by Muslim feminists: publicly demanding that the state uphold her rights as a citizen and showing that the interpretation of shari'a that was codified in civil law was actually false. Neither strategy represents a repudiation of Islam or shari'a.

. But these women court danger. The response to feminist activism is often in the form of violent backlash and increased oppression. Women have used global communication technologies to publicize abuse and to support each other's efforts. Interactive media is now seamlessly integrated into global life. Political and religious authorities alike recognize the subversive potential of the Internet. Access to the uncensored, unmediated, and sometimes raw voices of women contributed immensely to this study. Injustice is hard to hide, as was demonstrated when Iranians took to the streets of Tehran to protest the seemingly fraudulent election results on June 18, 2009; women were at the barricades and the forefront of this protest, taking the brunt of police brutality. One young woman, Neda Agha-Soltan, became an icon of resistance when her death was recorded and dispersed internationally on the website Twitter.com. In Afghanistan several hundred women were stoned as they arrived in Kabul to protest a new law issued by the US-supported government. The Afghani marriage legislation, which will apply to Afghanistan's thirty million Shi'a, gives a husband the right to sexual relations without his wife's consent and the right to prevent her from leaving the home without a male protector. Although a mob showed up to throw rocks at protesters, dozens of young women braved the howling crowds to protest the new law. Ironically, among those that surrounded and stoned the women were other women.[18] These events were all caught on film and broadcast worldwide nearly instantaneously. Injustice now has a physical countenance, and no government, even one that claims to disregard world opinion, is truly indifferent to its public image.

Orthodox Jewish women face less dramatic and less harrowing oppression. The largest communities of Jews live in liberal democracies such as the United States, Canada, France, and Great Britain. Israel is its own category. Through progressive legislation, Israeli women have achieved an even greater record of integration in all domains than in most liberal democracies. But in one respect that is critical to feminists, Israel is more like some of the Muslim states (not simply because its legal system was heavily influenced by the Ottoman occupation), as the civil judiciary shares power with the religious judiciary. Without a king or amir to break the stalemate as in Kuwait, a standoff between religious and secular law enforcement is a common result of feminist initiatives.

Citizenship as a Lever and a Lens

The meaningful context for gender reform must be on the national level and take the form of concrete policy. A gender-neutral stance will not necessarily benefit women. Sector-based policy and planning to include women require that analytical data be disaggregated according to gender. In Kuwait, Israel, and the United States, citizenship is the vehicle and the armor that protects the enumerated civil rights of individuals, regardless of gender.

The logic, if not the history, of civic citizenship is irresistibly emancipatory and inclusive. It is based on the natural law of individual equality. Just as women in the United States and England made use of citizenship rights, feminists worldwide use them to campaign for equal rights under the law. Citizenship not only provides protection for rights, but it creates public space for dialogue and a free press to publicize the issues. Global campaigns to reform Islamic family law are often predicated on the rights conferred by citizenship. For instance, Egyptian women pushed successfully for the passage by the People's Assembly of *khula* divorce, which allows a woman to initiate and receive a divorce if she returns her *mahr* bride gift, replacing *talaq* divorce (through triple verbal renunciation by the husband). The language of citizenship rights legitimizes challenges to the leadership of the mullahs, the imams, and the rabbis. But national citizenship has not become a symbol of unity in many countries, particularly in the Middle East. As in Kuwait, national belonging and citizenship must compete with more primal loyalties such as tribe and clan for organizing political loyalties. Citizenship is also intertwined intimately with religion and religious schisms, making it a subordinate organizing principle that has the potential to be used perversely to exclude women and others who are considered outsiders such as *bedoons* (Arab non-citizens in Kuwait), Bedouins, and foreign laborers of ambiguous legal status.

Equal citizenship for women is a means for prodding religious authorities into accepting gender equality in religious life, but it must be demonstrated that equal citizenship is valuable regardless of the structure of the regime. Ironically, in some instances in the Muslim world, women have made greater gains under monarchies than in democracies. Susan Moller

Okin posed the controversial question as the title to her article, "Is Multi-culturalism Bad for Women?"[19] An equally controversial question might be raised: is democracy bad for women? We want to answer in the negative, and most feminists link their struggle for women's rights to a struggle for democracy, on the assumption that democracy is the background condition for the protection of rights. But democracy does not necessarily entail individual rights. Historically, that was the contribution of liberalism to democratic theory. However, if the culture that underlies democratic institutions is not respectful of women's rights, a democratic system may reinforce the unequal status of women. Democracy is theoretically the ideal regime, but ironically, it may not be the first and best hope for women's rights. Israel and Kuwait, unlike the United States, illustrate the problems of democratic politics when it comes to promoting feminist goals. In Israel, despite widespread popular sentiment in favor of women's rights, the deference that the state shows toward the religious elite and the unclear demarcation between civil and religious judicial power is problematic. In Kuwait the amir is more progressive and feminist than much of the population and their elected representatives, not to mention the religious authorities. It is only in the most recent round of elections that the idea of female representatives was democratically ratified (this can just as easily be reversed). In several Gulf States, including Kuwait, the monarch or amir has appointed female ministers. These appointments are exercises of civil authority from above. In Saudi Arabia King Abdullah Bin Abdul Aziz launched the country's first coeducational university. The king is clearly spearheading a program of reform, sending the message to his people that certain social customs, widely supported by clerics and public, are outdated tribal holdovers with no basis in Islam, and that such customs stand in the way of progress and modernity. Though he has met opposition from religious conservatives to whom he is beholden for political legitimacy, he continues to chip away at restrictions placed on women.[20] It is promising that these monarchs have been willing to use their personal popularity to appoint women to ministerial positions, but this victory for women was achieved by short-circuiting democratic processes. Reliance on a progressive monarch is clearly a hit or miss strategy. Women's rights are a demonstration of democratic achievement only when undergirded by popular opinion and imbedded in law and political culture. Perhaps, as John Dewey implied,[21] democracy is the best university for democracy, and there are democratic solutions to democratic problems; feminists might add the proviso that the first task is to forge public opinion and reform cultural obstacles to women's equality.

In countries where shari'a constitutes the law of the land or is the basis of civil law, citizens' rights under nominally democratic constitutions can be problematic. This puts Muslim feminists on a crash course with the partially theocratic state. They may find among their opponents not only government officials and religious authorities but even the majority of their female fellow citizens. In weak states such as Afghanistan or Pakistan, the government may be powerless to enforce civil laws that are protective of women. Whole regions may be under the sway of radical Islamist groups. In failed states such as Somalia the situation is even worse. Women lose even more than men when citizenship becomes virtually meaningless and provides no immunization against the violation of rights.

Even in stable liberal democracies, women historically occupied the intersection of private and public realms and acted as the focal point of religious, social, political, and cultural concerns. In the United States it was a combination of religious and ethno-cultural ideas linked to the American way of life that resulted in the notion of the ideal woman as the "angel in the home." It is about her body and behavior that many social conflicts still arise. The question is whether citizenship in the democratic state mediates between the woman and her religious community or whether the religious community mediates between the woman and her citizenship status. Religion has been both an opponent and an ally in the cause of women's rights and the suffrage struggle in Western democracies. In the United States the liberal propositions in the Declaration of Independence, the Fourteenth Amendment, and the Civil Rights Act and other such legislation were successfully enlisted in the cause of women's rights.

In some settings, however, the association between rights, democracy, and liberalism is viewed as a foreign import that may dilute Muslim or Jewish identity. On the other hand, representatives of the website IslamLib .com explained that the name "Liberal Islam Network" was chosen by their organization because "liberal" citizenship denotes citizens free from tyrannical rule and injustice.[22] The spirit of liberalism is to limit authority and allow individual citizens to enjoy civil rights. This emphasis is not the exclusive possession of Western political philosophy but is also relevant in Muslim society. "Hence, there is no reason in refusing the spirit of liberalism, if we seriously celebrate independence and resist injustice. Freedom? Yes! Liberal? Why not?"[23]

Women who know that the state will protect their civil rights can safely dissent from internal practices of their religious communities. An American imam provoked a storm of outrage when he recommended that men should deal with rebellious wives as suggested in the controversial Qur'an verse 4:34 by " 'Tapping' them as a last resort and done in the privacy of the home to preserve the dignity and honor of the woman and the family."[24] Bloggers not only condemned this interpretation of Qur'an 4:34 but called on the civil state to punish men who use Islam as a cover for domestic violence. One woman responded, " 'Tapping' may work for the woman not for the man. He needs more powerful stroke from the State." Another stated, "a woman must go to the state" for protection from a man who justifies his violence in terms of 4:34. The courts must become the guardians of women. One blogger said, "I pray to Allah that someone soon 'taps' the hell out of you in order that you may observe how much damage 'tapping' can do to the dignity and honor of anyone."[25] These bloggers see the state as the protector of rights for religious women citizens.

Country Case Studies: Kuwait, Israel, and the United States

States are a synergistic mix of culture, tradition, law, and religion and may even have two competing authorities, civil and religious, if that is how the law operates. The state may have a system of power sharing and overlapping jurisdiction as an expedient measure, but this remedy is inherently unstable. Both sides are likely to seek to dominate the other. Kuwait, Israel, and the United States all have a relatively diverse citizenry. The international community recognizes all three as democracies, yet they represent distinct models when it comes to the relationship between civil and religious authority. In Kuwait Islam is the official religion of the state. In Israel Judaism is the official religion of the state, and in the United States the law mandates a separation of religion and state, permits free religious practice by minority religions, and prohibits the formal establishment of the majority religion. Even though religion is formally disestablished, Protestant Christianity is strongly established culturally.[26] The United States is a secular polity superimposed on a religious society.

In all three countries there are links between state and religion, civil law and religious law, and citizenship and personal status law. Dual legal systems pit women's equal citizenship status against their unequal personal status. Civil, political, and social rights of citizenship operate against a backdrop of religious authority that competes with civil law and has jurisdiction over the precise area that impacts women most, namely family or personal status law. In Muslim countries such as Kuwait, governments try to prove their Muslim credentials by appeasing Islamists and conservatives while also backing their democratic constitutions. In Israel personal status law is the symbolic holdout of the religious authorities in their tug of war with the state. It is also the rock on which women activists will either be dashed or make their stand, because it is in this context that crime and heresy are most closely linked.

In Israel, Kuwait, and the United States, the state formally regulates and mediates gender relations, even within the family, and is the final arbiter of law. Religious communities uphold gender-differentiated rights and roles. Civil remedies for gender discrimination exist, but may not be enforced, especially if women seem to voluntarily assent to the rules of their subnational communities. Even when women want the protection of the state, they may be reluctant or unable to access it. In the United States, if the woman is an immigrant, uneducated, or housebound, she may not know that such protections exist. A complicating factor shared by Israel and Kuwait is the legacy of Ottoman colonial rule in their legal systems. Remnants of the Ottoman millet system promote minority group survival, but by permitting religious groups considerable autonomy to apply their own religious laws, this heritage makes gendered power relations more intractable.

Family and Personal Status Law

When states grant religious communities exemptions from civil law, it is often in the area of personal status law or family law. This is no accident. Families are the foundation of both political and religious communities, both of which structure status and membership, which in turn are crucial to demarcating gender boundaries. States regulate membership by determining who is eligible for citizenship or resident status according to principles such as jus sanguinis, jus soli, or jus domicile. Religions define who is eligible for membership according to birth, marriage, divorce, and conversion. Shachar points to the "constitutive, regulative, and sorting functions" of family law.[27] Control over family law is seen by religious authorities to be a crucial boundary maintenance tool. This often appears to the state to be an appropriate arena of religious self-determination, because membership and identity are key to the survival of the group.

As with religion, the state is heavily invested in family life. It has an interest in marriage, divorce, child rearing, and the production of future citizens, all of which have an impact on social welfare and all of which are overseen to some extent by the legal apparatus of the state. Theoretically, the family is lodged in the private realm, but it is not immune from state regulation. Even if it might be detrimental to individual members, families and religious communities are likely to be left alone by the state as long as the law is upheld. In the name of multicultural sensitivity, the state may turn a blind eye to the behavior of religious groups toward their members. As Barbara Swirski notes, "this family is not a free association of individuals but an institution characterized by unequal power relations and governed by rules invented, interpreted, and administered by male communal authorities."[28]

Women will always be central to larger struggles, according to Moghissi, because "the female body is the site of struggle between the proponents and opponents of modernity."[29] Women's rights are not just an issue for half the world's population. As goes the condition and status of women, so goes justice and socio-economic development. Kecia Ali sees women as signifiers in the realms of home, family, and society, which are central to the construction of Muslim identity.[30] Shari'a imposes disproportionate punishment on women in the name of honor and identity. Muslim and Jewish women can become the focal point of what Shachar calls "cultural reactivism,"[31] in which women are harnessed to a backlash against modernity, liberal ideals, and civil society, especially now that secular and nationalist politics have lost their gloss with the failure of Gamal Abdel Nasser, Saddam Hussein, and the Shah of Iran. In their wake, Islamists have emerged as a potent force, with their desire to impose shari'a as the basis of governance.

When the rejection of legal equality for women is entangled with the defense of social and religious traditions (in which women are often made to be the carriers of cultural and religious authenticity), state disruption of social patterns of male dominance is often viewed as illegitimate. The refusal to subordinate religion and culture to secular Western values and laws may be viewed as standing up to outside pressure and, therefore, heroic when practiced by states or even by religious minorities in secular states. In states such as Kuwait and Morocco, the monarch may also be the official head of and defender of Islam in his country. This tacit collusion between state and religion means that women who lay claim to their rights may be unable to count on state support and protection, and worse, find themselves labeled by society as heretics or apostates. The international community may bow to the principle of national sovereignty or to the fear of being labeled culturally insensitive. This applies all the more when an ally is concerned. Nor are officials in secular constitutional governments immune to a personal interest in perpetuating patriarchal power.

This collusion between state and religion means that women who claim their rights may find that these rights have been bartered away. When religious law is integrated partially or fully with civil law, and the separation of religion and state is incomplete, confrontation between civil codes and religious laws are likely to reveal the weakness of the state relative to the religious establishment. In that religious law may form the basis of the socio-cultural norms of the community, it may be perceived as more authentic than the civil law. Both shari'a (Islamic law) and halakha (Jewish law) are understood not just as a body of religious law, but ideally as the framework for political rule. According to the faithful, religious law and religious leaders will ultimately replace civil law and temporal political authorities. Religious law and civil law are competitive, not complementary; the balance of power between theocratization and secularization is constantly shifting.

In both Israel and Kuwait entrenched religious authorities are the most powerful opponents of equal rights for women. In deferring to these religious authorities, the civil governments of Israel, Kuwait, and the United States risk sacrificing the guaranteed rights of their female citizens. In the case of Kuwait and Israel, this may be part of an unspoken deal by which the state sacrifices women's rights to get the backing of powerful religious authorities and their constituents. Israel, unlike Kuwait, has a dense civil society and a strong government, operating as a more or less united front when vying with powerful religious authorities. While usually deferring to religious authorities with respect to family law, the Israeli state can limit the power of religious authorities over women's public and professional lives, but the lack of a clear demarcation between the two categories of law makes conflict inevitable.

Kuwait shares with Israel a foundational commitment to power sharing between secular government and religious authorities. As in Israel, religious authorities control family law, however, the Kuwaiti state is fairly weak. It divides power among three claimants: the monarchy, the secular state, and the religious authority. Kuwaiti feminism is state feminism with a twist. The strongest supporter of enhanced gender equality is the amir, while many members of Parliament are opposed to equality, as are the religious authorities. The phenomenon of the feminist king is not isolated to Kuwait. A similar dynamic currently operates in Saudi Arabia. Muhammad VI of Morocco is a staunch supporter of women's rights and has helped women secure the *Moudawana* (Family Status Law Reform Bill), despite opposition from many legislators and radical Islamists. But the future of women's rights in these countries may depend on generating popular support for curtailing the authority of religious leaders over civil life. This entails the risky expenditure of political capital by monarchs with no proven political payoff.

Kuwait is an important actor in the Gulf region. Although it has a reputation for conservatism, even by Gulf Arab standards, it tends to be a pioneer in democratic rights among other Gulf nations. Although headed by a hereditary amir, Kuwait has a constitution, an elected legislative body, and a judiciary, which have some degree of independence. Political speech and the press are relatively free, there is no mandatory dress code for women, and as of May 2005, in short order, women gained the right to vote, received several ministerial appointments, and won four elected seats in the National Assembly. Women in Kuwait also have achieved a high level of education and literacy and a degree of professional employment in the financial, business, and academic sectors. While these gains were hard fought and are still precarious, they do constitute real advances and put Kuwaiti women in the Gulf's vanguard. Yet the Kuwaiti constitution has a repugnance clause that prohibits any legislation or policy that offends Islam. As of 2009, with Kuwaiti women celebrating the election of four women to the National Assembly, several Islamist members of the legislature have initiated charges against two of these for failing to cover their heads, in violation of an amendment to the election law that requires members (namely women) to adhere to an Islamic dress code. Every step forward seems to elicit its own backlash from powerful religious opponents.

Western liberal democratic regimes provide a different set of opportunities and challenges. Ironically, the greater the hospitality to cultural diversity and sensitivity to minority groups, the greater potential challenges for women in minority Muslim communities. In Germany, France, Britain, Canada, and the United States, many religious women activists have joined their voices with those that condemn some forms of multicultural accommodation for betraying women and even stripping minority women of their core legal protections. In stable liberal democracies with underlying liberal cultures, women can count on their rights as citizens being enforced, but the exercise of multicultural toleration has occasionally created its own hazards for women. In Germany, a woman judge returned an abused Moroccan-born woman to her husband's home after his defense lawyer showed the judge Qur'an 4:34, which can be read to permit corporal punishment of the wife by her husband. The judge, in deference to the religious sensibilities of the husband, accepted this disputed Qur'anic verse and returned the woman to her husband despite police evidence demonstrating extreme abuse.[32] Ironically, the woman might have received better treatment in the courts of her native land, Morocco, than in her adoptive country, Germany.

Multiculturalism: The Enemy of Women's Rights?

In this study, multiculturalism is best represented by the United States and Israel, but the United States is most representative of Western democracies in which a stable unitary government legislates and interprets the law. When Western democracies grant leeway to some sub-national groups to regulate aspects of their members' lives, it is an act of largesse rather than a strategy to garner support from religious authorities. Multicultural accommodation is the recent quasi-official policy of many liberal democracies such as the United States, Germany, Canada, and England. It entails that stable unitary civil secular states with culturally diverse minorities, for principled (if sometimes misguided) reasons, undertake policies meant to give sub-national groups viability in the midst of a dominant majority culture. It is probably more popular with academics and government officials then with the public at large. In the wake of September 11, 2001, countries such as France, Belgium, the Netherlands, Great Britain, Canada, and the United States are experiencing a backlash against Muslim immigrants. Critics of immigration have targeted the principle of multiculturalism. The backlash may be motivated by xenophobia and nativism, but in some instances, the critics are principled and may include feminists. In Canada, the first country to officially declare itself to be multicultural, popular support for multiculturalism is widespread. It was pushed to the limits in Ontario, however, when the formal recognition of Muslim tribunals was proposed. In England furor and resistance accompanied the Archbishop of Canterbury's suggestion to permit the establishment of Muslim tribunals as an alternative for dispute resolution in family arbitration. (This, even though Canada and the UK have Jewish tribunals.) Demonstrators across both countries and in much of Europe included Muslim women, who insisted that any departure from a unitary national system of law would be detrimental to Muslim women as well as other Canadians.[33]

The United States is, in its own popular self-conception, a melting pot by contrast with the salad bowl or mosaic metaphor of Canada. The staunch liberal conception makes the individual the proprietor of rights and is accordingly hostile to the concept of group rights. The United States tends to see groups as voluntary associations rather than as contenders with the state for members' loyalty. Attempts to grant semi-sovereignty to religious groups in the name of the free exercise clause of the First Amendment usually run afoul of the establishment clause of the same amendment. The state cannot be neutral, an inescapable dilemma, even in liberal states that value toleration and pluralism. Sacrificing widely shared norms in the name of compromise may not be a wise choice. The best option, according to Martha Minow, is presented when both the minority group and state find areas in which they can align rather than compromise their norms and interests.[34] Contrast this with the French *foulard* controversy involving the principle of *laicite* (public secularism) in the public schools or Nicolas Sarkozy's public denunciation of the burqa as a symbol of oppression incongruent with French life.[35] Such cases suggest that compromise may be principled as well as strategic. Processes of accommodation may pave the way for peace, social integration, and stability, but it must be peace without appeasement. In the United States, the typical resolution is actually a minefield of exceptions. Jonathan Sacks, chief rabbi of the United Hebrew Congregation of the Commonwealth, advocates the application of one law of the land.[36] He maintains that religious law is best treated as private and voluntary.

Multicultural accommodation is particularly problematic for Muslim and Jewish feminists. On the one hand, they benefit as members of religious minorities, but on the other, their denomination may call on the state to underwrite manifestly unequal systems of personal status law that would not be legally permissible if practiced by other associations. The liberal state can justify this stance on three grounds: (1) treating religious and cultural subgroups as voluntary associations, in which case the state is only responsible for insuring the right of members to leave the group; (2) granting partial sovereignty to subgroups under the rubric of liberal toleration, respect for diversity, and a strong reading of the principle of freedom of association; and (3) stressing the free exercise clause to protect minorities and their religions.

For the United States, which struggled to enact the Fourteenth Amendment, the Twenty-first Amendment, and the Civil Rights Act and other such legislation, vestiges of partial citizenship lingered into the twentieth century. Any departure from gender equality in the name of religious freedom creates a potential for what Shachar has termed the "paradox of multicultural accommodation," whereby grants of exemptions or partial sovereignty to religious groups further entrenches, with the state's unwitting imprimatur, the internal patriarchal hierarchy of the group's status quo.[37]

Gender equality is a norm of liberal culture and is widely accepted in most American religious communities. But communities that do not accept gender equality create a tension between liberal democracy and group-differentiated politics of identity. When groups are seen as vehicles for political recognition and intergroup equality, four concerns arise: (1) laws of the group replace civil law, asking the government to relinquish its monopoly over legal/constitutional interpretation; (2) it threatens to lend the state's seal of approval to establishment clause or civil rights violations; (3) it implicates the state in entrenching the existing power structure, which almost always excludes women; (4) acknowledging groups as bearers of rights ossifies identity and makes women or other reformers appear to be disloyal or heretical.

The identity of the group as defined by the elite, may constrain women rather than emancipate them. In the United States the government hesitates before catering to groups that are internally undemocratic, non-individualistic, hierarchical, and patriarchal. This hesitation is also expressed in religious communities when reformers perceive the unfair advantage given to community elites recognized by the state in preserving the status quo and silencing dissent. For example, while some first generation immigrants may have brought patriarchal traditions from various Muslim communities overseas, other first generation immigrants are highly educated professionals and progressive in their religious views. The younger generation of Muslims, whether the children of immigrants, members of the domestic Black Muslim community, or converts, are often well-acclimated to American liberal norms and, therefore, well-positioned to engage in reform from within. Multicultural accommodation, then, would make the government party to actually amplifying the power of a patriarchal elite.

In Kuwait the term "multicultural" is of limited use, ironically, since Kuwaiti citizens are a minority group in their own country. The cleavages are largely between Kuwaiti citizens and non-Kuwaiti guest workers, which outnumber Kuwaitis almost two to one. The population, nearly entirely Muslim, is about 70 percent Sunni and about 30 percent Shi'a. There are also Arab non-citizens or *bedoons*. Kuwaitis proudly consider themselves ethnically and culturally Bedouin, and while the majority is urban, Bedouin tribes still inhabit rural areas. Kuwaitis are still very conscious of their clan and tribal affiliations, which are often the basis of political participation and loyalty.

Kuwait is not truly multicultural in that almost all citizens are either Sunni or Shi'a Muslim. Social cleavages have to do with tribes, rural and urban distinctions, and origins, as almost everyone but the Bedouins is a fairly recent arrival, mostly from Iraq. Even the *bedoons* are ethnic Arabs. The only truly multicultural variations are presented by the expat foreign workers, who have no status and are considered beneath the notice of the Kuwaitis they serve. While Kuwait's constitution does not declare that all law will derive from shari'a, it does say that no law can be made that is repugnant to shari'a. This removes family law at least partially from the purview of the state and permits violations of domestic law and international legal codes. The government is understandably hesitant to rile religious constituents. Political democracy in Kuwait is precarious, and the National Assembly, which is constantly at odds with ministers appointed by the amir, has been dissolved with almost predictable regularity, precipitating new elections every few years.

Israel embodies elements of the multicultural model and the nationalization model. Israel is a liberal democracy by most measures and has a fundamental commitment to the equal rights of women that goes back to the *yishuv* pre-state era. The government has protected minority rights (even if these are sometimes respected in the breach), most of which can be considered both ethnic and religious in nature. For instance, Israeli Muslims comprise several distinct cultural, religious, and ethnic groups. Israeli Jews encompass distinctive ethno-cultural and racial groups originating in Ethiopia, Europe, the Levant, Russia, India, North Africa, Iran, and North America. More recently, a growing number of foreign workers are in the mix. These groups all represent identities and political cleavages. While Israel has affirmative-action style policies aimed at ethnic minorities, the state officially shares political power with religious authorities.

Israel demonstrates the downside of multicultural accommodation and shared legal jurisdiction, for women and for the state. Non-Jewish religious courts (designated for Druze, Muslims, and at least ten Christian denominations) are granted even more leeway and less interference than Jewish courts. While all residents have access to civil and criminal courts, it is only with great caution that the Israeli state involves itself with infractions by the religious authorities.

Theocratization

Theocratization is ominous and possible through conquest or even through democratic means. (The Algerian and Egyptian governments have tried to keep elements such as the Muslim Brotherhood from competing in elections as legitimate democratic parties for fear that they might actually win.) Theocratization is a less ambiguous case and is not currently a salient threat in Kuwait or Israel. Nonetheless, both Israel and Kuwait have factions that would choose to return their civil states to religious rule. In Kuwait, Dr. Badr al-Nashi, president of the Islamic Constitutional Movement (ICM), which is close to the Muslim Brotherhood and the Salafi (meaning the original forefathers and followers of the Prophet) perspective, asserts that the goal of his party is to replace civil law with shari'a.[38] While the Salafis experienced a setback in the most recent election, they remain an active and significant political force. Nations that have shared civil and religious legal jurisdictions run the risk of slipping into this model. In such cases, women lose the ability to use their civil citizenship as a lever for wresting rights and protections. The cautionary tale is Iran, which was proclaimed the Islamic Republic in 1979; Shi'a Islam is the official religion and basis of law. The legislature is an Islamic consultative assembly modeled after the traditional *shurra* or consultative council of early Islam, while members of the council of guardians ensures that laws are in keeping with Islam. The supreme leader is an ayatollah. While Iran seeks international applause for the staged visibility of women in public roles, actual feminists, and other critics of governmental policy, have been persecuted, jailed, and censored for drawing attention to domestic violence and repressive aspects of family law.

Pakistan is undergoing a tacit Islamization of the legal system, which began with Zulfikar Ali Bhutto in mid-1970s and intensified under the military coup led by General Zia ul-Huq in 1979, who, as Sadat in Egypt, was courting support among the otherwise unpopular Islamist parties. So great was ul-Huq's need for religious approval, among his first policy initiatives was the reversal of virtually all of the reforms that had helped women in the previous thirty years.[39] The current government recognizes its own precarious position and attempted to mollify Islamists by handing them the Swat Valley. This led to a debacle and a half-hearted military attempt to reclaim this area. There are currently at least a dozen Middle Eastern states that are increasingly unstable as Islamic forces contend for power, chiseling away at the territory bit-by-bit and setting up sub-governments under strict shari'a codes. The first casualties in these struggles are often women.

The International Human Rights Regime

Feminist strategies are not limited to the nation state. International organizations, particularly the United Nations, have put women's rights on the human rights agenda. The discourse on women's rights has become truly global and has been imbedded in all recent economic, educational, and political development programs. A plethora of documents and resolutions have been passed since the United Nations proclaimed its first Decade for Women and held its first international conferences. While powerless to force compliance, the routine country assessments give women the moral high ground because they can point out that their countries are signatories to the principle of human rights and women's rights.

The UN Charter (1945) and UN Universal Declaration of Human Rights (1948) assert the principle of gender equality. The recognition that political and legal equality still eluded women called forth gender-specific policy approaches. The welfare approach and the development approach in the 1970s called attention to the plight of women in poor nations. The UN designated 1975 the International Women's Year and the period 1976–1985 as the Decade for Women. Around 1980, the word sex was replaced by gender to reflect the academic emphasis on the social as opposed to biological construction of gender roles. Attention turned to understanding why women in most cultures did not benefit equally from development and were assigned secondary roles in society. The gender approach led to the women empowerment approach, as operationalized by UNIFEM, the UN Development Fund for Women. The goal was to generate resources, access, and bargaining power, or empowerment (also called gender mainstreaming) and was formally adopted by the Beijing platform for action at the 1995 UN Fourth World Conference on Women.

Perhaps the most significant United Nations response was in the form of the CEDAW (Convention on the Elimination of All Forms of Discrimination Against Women) treaty, adopted by the UN General Assembly in 1979. CEDAW is often referred to as the bill of rights for women. It is the second most widely ratified human rights treaty, but it is also the one with the most reservations. By UN agreement, countries may sign treaties but enter reservations to provisions that are found unpalatable for cultural or religious reasons. Through these endeavors the UN has established an international legal framework for women's rights but with no guarantee of enforcement. Critics claim that international human rights standards are culturally specific. They therefore may reject as cultural imperialism political and civil rights, especially for women. But no UN member nation wants to openly defend gender violence or other forms of human rights violations, even if this means engaging in human rights double-speak and tacit acceptance of the international human rights treaties. The downside of these treaties and their provisions for mandatory public reporting of violations is that any whiff of compulsion may provoke retrenchment of shari'a-based governments' repression of women activists.

International accords remain merely symbolic in the absence of member states' commitments to legislate and enforce their provisions. The state is still the most important actor when it comes to mediating between religious and other bodies of law. Tort law is the meeting point between civil rights as expressed in CEDAW and domestic religious law. While states have an internationally recognized responsibility to comply, including policing domestic human rights violations and protecting equality regardless of gender, the state may lack the will or the power to do so. Both Israel and Kuwait have signed CEDAW and both have entered reservations pertaining to religion and culture, in which they assert that religious law and tradition trump CEDAW provisions. This means that these two governments will not override offending family law because it falls under the jurisdiction of religious authorities. Nonetheless, the state has inescapable commitments created by its own constitution to address rights deprivations of its members.

The discrepancy between a country's international commitments and its domestic stance, specifically its unwillingness to take on religious opponents, has enormous repercussions for women. The balance of power may be shifting in favor of religious authorities. Israeli women talk about covert gender war while Muslim feminists call for gender jihad against religiously endorsed abuse.[40] Preferential treatment of religious authority gives the imprimatur of the state to gender discrimination. Therefore, the citizenship status of women takes on a renewed importance, and the state must address the rights deprivations of its members. Accordingly, the focus of this study will be the nation state, because it remains the primary locus of citizenship and the only entity that can enforce international commitments.

The strategic and sophisticated approaches to reform adopted by Muslim and Jewish women are striking. Both focus on scholarship and reclamation, based on their confidence in the justice of G-d, which implies subordination of humans to G-d but expressly forbids subordination of humans to other humans. They share a willingness to take on male authority in both the religious and civil realm. We can summarize the agenda of Jewish and Muslims feminists:

1. Gender justice should be considered part of social justice.
2. Women's rights should be considered part of human rights.
3. Religion should revert to its earlier inclusive and respectful treatment of women.
4. Religion should be understood as living and evolving. The gates of interpretation are never closed.
5. Religious women should be permitted to speak for themselves, free of externally imposed stereotypes and agendas.
6. Citizenship within a rights-protective regime can be used to persuade or even force religious authorities to adopt a more women-friendly interpretation of divine texts, particularly with respect to the application of family or personal status law.

2
Feminisms

ISLAM AND JUDAISM

> *And among His signs is this, that He created for*
> *you mates from among yourselves, that ye may dwell*
> *in tranquility with them, and he has put love and*
> *mercy between your hearts.*
> ◆ Qur'an 30:21

> *G-d is never unjust in the least degree*
> ◆ Qur'an 4:40

> *The daughters of Tzlafchad, Mahlah, Noah, Hoglah,*
> *Milcah, and Tirzah stood before Moses and the entire*
> *congregation saying, "Our father died in the desert and he*
> *had no sons. Why should our father's name be eliminated*
> *from his family because he had no son? Give us a portion*
> *along with our father's brothers." So Moses brought their*
> *case before G-d. G-d spoke to Moses, saying: "Tzlafchad's*
> *daughters speak justly. You shall certainly give them a*
> *portion of inheritance."*
> ◆ Numbers 27: 1–7

Tzlafchad's daughters understood that prevailing social arrangements are not necessarily eternal or immutable. To believe that they were would underestimate G-d's love and mercy, which extends to women as well to men. Accordingly, if G-d supported the daughters' demand for justice, then why assume that contemporary injustices are of no concern to G-d?

Feminism, like the wheel, may be a product of simultaneous invention. It is certainly a product of global cross-pollination. While there are a multitude of offshoots and divergent branches responding to geography, culture, race, class, ethnicity and religion, there is a shared core idea among all feminists that human rights and dignity apply to both men and women. However, many Muslim and Jewish women cringe when the term feminist is applied to them, probably because they reject the connotation that they are then harnessed to Western or secular ideals. Feminism is a set of norms and principles, a set of concrete policy proposals, a call to unity and action, a mode of analysis, an ideology, and an identity. The birth of feminism in non-European settings was often simultaneous with episodes of resistance to colonialism and the repudiation of Western influences. Veiling was adopted in some cases, where it had hitherto been on the wane, as a protest against Western mores that were becoming prevalent in colonized cities. In Egypt, in particular, where feminist theorists arose at the end of the nineteenth century, they were already distinguishing their program from that of Western feminists. These indigenous Muslim feminist movements arose in tandem with nationalist movements. These modernizing movements were discriminating and selective about which aspects of modern life they promoted, while simultaneously resurrecting fading, even defunct traditions and putting them in the service of national liberation. Detaching feminism from its Western moorings has continued to be essential to feminist reforms in many Muslim settings. "The women's liberation movement, as it was lived in the West, was perceived as part of the colonial project, therefore opposed with fervour to remain faithful to the Muslim identity. . . . this explains the social diversity of these women who far from forming a monolithic bloc of women 'victims of all misfortunes' . . . emerged in each country with original ideas to counter the traditional social ruling without imitating the Western model."[1]

Western feminism has been affected by Western culture and is strongly individualistic and occasionally anti-family and adversarial in its language and goals. It is seen as advocating gender-blurring equality that simply does not fit religious and cultural sensibilities of Jewish and Muslim women. The agenda of liberal feminism has been largely accomplished in the West. Legal discrimination, at least formally, is ended, and any further advances will require deviations from the liberal model of equal treatment under the law. Muslim and Jewish women have generated their own theoretical innovations and have forged their own credentials as scholars, theorists, and activists. They have not rejected all elements of liberal feminism. Many are suspicious of the word liberalism, but embrace the word freedom. In the 1990s several Muslim women scholars discovered that they were engaged in a reinterpretation of Islamic texts and laws from a gender perspective. Writers and academics such as Fatima Mernissi and Asma Lamrabat recognize the usefulness of liberal concepts of rights to the critique of traditions responsible for keeping women in an inferior position.[2]

Among devout feminists, both Jewish and Muslim, there are many voices, yet it is possible to distill a few common themes. They might send a joint message that:

1. Liberalism is not the only source of human rights, and even in classical liberal theory, the original source of rights was divine and natural law.
2. Injustice is forbidden, therefore any laws or policies that contradict G-d's justice must be inauthentic. G-d's justice does not prefer men. Men and women were created as partners of equal moral worth and dignity.
3. Feminism is not merely about the hijab or sheitel. It is not just about the extent of coverage of the body. Clothing is not necessarily emblematic of women's oppression.
4. It is essential to differentiate between religion (divine will) and cultural overlays.
5. The sacred texts represent divine self-revelation and are living.
6. Humans were created with reason and intended to apply it. Any laws or practices pertaining to human interactions that cannot be justified by reason are inauthentic.
7. The sacred texts may give rise to multiple and evolving interpretations, and the best interpretations are those that serve the welfare and dignity of the community.

Margot Badran offers this definition: Muslim feminism is "articulated within an Islamic paradigm. Islamic feminism, which derives its understanding and mandate from the Qur'an, seeks rights and justice for women, and for men, in the totality of their existence."[3] At the core of Islamic feminism is the spiritual equality of men and women *nafs* (souls) as stated in Qur'an. Islamic and Jewish feminism share the aims of feminism in the West. Believing feminists put their feminism in the service of G-d. Devout Jewish and Muslim feminists recognize a connection between theology and politics. When possible, both groups have harnessed their quest for their G-d-given rights to their acquisition and deployment of citizenship rights and democracy. This chapter will examine their project of theological reclamation and, at the conclusion, some practical policy applications.

Research has taught Muslim feminist scholars that women's rights have a long history in Islam but were eclipsed by erroneous and misogynistic interpretations of the texts. Ironically, Muslim women had more rights under early Islam than they do now; Muslim feminism is, therefore, an act of recovery. Muslim feminist scholars do not see misogyny as intrinsic to Islam. Jewish feminists, like their Muslim counterparts, want to refocus on the foundational text: Torah, which is, for them, the source of divine self-disclosure. Having been forced into Diaspora and therefore historically having no state to rely upon to enforce Jewish law, communities had only their portable government, the Torah, as the basis of rule. Rabbis and scholars were default political authorities, but had no power of enforcement beyond the freely given respect of the Jewish community. Historically, these communities in Diaspora tended to be isolated, and communication was difficult. The development of differing interpretations and practices was inevitable. Just as one Qur'an produced many Islams, one Torah gave rise to a variety of interpretive communities.

Both Islam and Judaism were influenced by their neighbors, the former because of its rapid conquest of other cultures and the latter because of forced Diaspora. Many of these influences became the unacknowledged traditions that account for the variations in practice and have become so intertwined with religion that they are no longer distinguishable from it. This blurring of boundaries between law and custom is of particular importance to feminists, who assert that the religion is more hospitable to gender equality than is the overlay of interpretation and tradition. For instance, Orthodox Jewish woman are now being trained and hired in the role of *mashgiah* (kashrut supervisors), a job that has traditionally been performed by men. In the United States, where there is a shortage of qualified men, women have stepped in to perform this essential role insuring the laws of kashrut are upheld. While there may have been scant historical precedent for women filling this role, there was never a religious law against it, even though many Jews wrongly concluded as much based on the absence of women in that job. This example demonstrates the importance of distinguishing between religious law and tradition.[4]

On February 25, 2008, an Egyptian woman, Amal Soliman, was appointed as a *mazouna* (marriage registrar), a position that had traditionally only been filled by men. The chair of the committee of Egyptian *mazouns* said, "the Ministry [of Justice] should refuse the appointment, because it is unacceptable that women should work in this occupation." But Soliman argued, "legally, there is no reason why a woman can't do the job, and the Mufti (Islamic scholar and interpreter of Islamic law) said it was religiously acceptable." After delays and attempts at intimidation, Soliman took up her position when the Egyptian minister of justice officially authorized the appointment.[5]

While religion supports human rights and dignity, it may become an obstacle to both when traditional gender relations are confused with religion. In such cases, any challenge to the political, social, economic, and legal structure is likely to be depicted by its opponents as a challenge to religion and G-d. It is also likely to elicit a dramatic and even deadly response in the name of G-d. When Saudi Sheikh Ahmed al-Ghamdi recently asserted that it is not Islam, but tribal custom that prevents men and women from mixing in public, supporter of the status quo, Sheikh Abdulraham al-Barrak declared that "anyone who permits men and women to work or study together is an apostate and should be put to death unless he repents."[6] This kind of response is based on tradition, not religion, and should be understood as an attempt to uphold male privilege rather than to serve G-d. In both Judaism and Islam, religion is *din*, an all-encompassing way of life. There can be no change in one area that does not affect another aspect of life. The central proposition in both religions is that G-d cannot be the author of injustice; therefore, Muslim feminist thought is prefaced by the claim that *zulm* is *haram* (injustice is forbidden by Islam).

Regaining rights is complicated because women are seen as cultural signifiers and symbols of either cultural dignity and integrity or cultural degradation and capitulation. Personal status law is the area of law that is most strictly enforced, most static, most politically and ideologically resistant to change, and most likely to be enforced stringently by states, even those that are nominally democratic and secular. Women have figured centrally in anti-colonial and nationalistic movements in Israel and Kuwait. When the day has been won with their help, women's rights are often taken off the table, as was discovered by Kuwaiti women who believed they had won the right to vote through their heroic resistance to the Iraqi occupation in 1991.

Islam and Judaism must be disentangled from accrued tradition when that tradition is unjust to women. The first step requires mastery of the texts. For women in some Muslim countries, education must begin with literacy; their lagging literacy rates as compared with men's are well documented.[7] Authoritarian rulers and conservative scholars obstruct lively and vigorous thought and stifle progress under the shroud of authenticity and tradition. In many Muslim countries men as well as women are unable to read Arabic. Even native Arabic speakers may be deficient in their grasp of classical Arabic. This situation reinforces the monopoly of the religious elites. For instance, Saudi Arabia is a significant source of translations and publications of Qur'an, exporting the distinctive and conservative brand of Wahabi Islam worldwide. The audience for these versions of Qur'an may have memorized large portions of the text without understanding what they are repeating. They may not know, for example, that there are 750 verses of the Qur'an that enjoin Muslims to seek knowledge, reflect, and reason. As one feminist said, "What I am proposing here is to empower Muslim women. I'm not a Western feminist. I'm not proposing that Muslim women bare themselves and burn their hijabs. I'm proposing that we change statistics which show that half the women in the Arab world are illiterate and in all but four Arab countries less than 80 percent of girls go to secondary school."[8] She concluded that if you "educate a man, you educate a person. Educate a woman and you educate a family. Educate a family and you educate the *ummah* [worldwide community of Islam]."[9]

The United States upholds the right of religious individuals to free thought and inquiry, public discourse, and access to texts. This sits well with American Muslims, who do not feel bound by the cultural preferences of other Muslim communities worldwide. It is also in keeping with the North American style that Islam has no universally accepted clergy or ecclesiastic institutions. Mosques reflect the congregational style of many other American religions. American Muslims choose their mullah, imams, mosque, sources of fatwa, and *fiqh* (Islamic law). They have established a variety of advocacy organizations and educational institutions and a multitude of Internet accessible sources. There are online muftis, websites, and blogs on every subject related to religion and life. Muslims in the West are free to retain or discard their heritage. They can adopt and adapt from the life and culture around them. "Unlike their brothers and sisters abroad, they do not have to be concerned about either political censorship or retribution."[10] Democracy and freedom of expression facilitates exegesis without fear. Women's equal citizenship rights are acknowledged and enforced by the government.

In other societies, disentangling religions from culture is more complicated. Liberal democracies based on cultures of gender equality and equal rights will produce different outcomes than democracies superimposed on conservative, particularly religious Catholic, Jewish, or Muslim traditions. Democracy may be an ally in the pursuit of gender equality, but only in states where there is an underlying culture that is supportive. This supplies even greater urgency to the project of recovering sources of equality in the sacred texts themselves. No substantial reforms will be possible in many communities unless they can be squared with shari'a.[11] A backlash against a liberal cultural backdrop may occur when the culture's values seems to be rapidly shifting, especially away from acceptance of political and religious authorities. In such instances religious authorities may suddenly call for "a return to purity."[12] This is the case in Aceh, Saudi Arabia, Sudan, tribal areas of Pakistan, Afghanistan (under the Taliban), and Nigeria. In each case, *fiqh* has been used as an instrument of social control, and women are often its targets. Feminists' reforms are likely to be considered especially dangerous in that they imply a dramatic overhaul of the status quo, even if the proposed reforms represent a potentially superior reading in terms of justice for all.

Hermeneutics and Exegesis as the Foundation of Feminist Politics

The core of the feminist program is really about who has the authority to interpret the foundational texts and who can claim to speak for G-d. What is wanted is a fresh perspective that treats Qur'an as living, or as one rabbi put it with respect to Torah, "it must be seen as a tree not a building."[13] Yet in both religions by some religious authorities claim that "the gates of inter-pretation are closed."[14] They maintain that only a small elite, almost entirely male, meets the stringent credentials that allow them to "reopen the gates." Conservative authorities in Islam and Judaism are likely to fix on texts that support a limited public role for women or demonstrate supposed deficien-cies of women's character in order to hold women and even justice at bay. But the interpreters and decisors who harness their position to the most rigid or ancient readings do not necessarily have the best readings. For progressive feminists, the prophet Micah's admonition (Micah 6:8) that "you shall act justly, love mercy, and walk modestly with your G-d" should be a watchword of men and women who engage in exegesis—to do so with intellectual humility in the service of the entire community.

Rabbi Shai Held argued, "The time is long past for Jews to assume that the forces of reaction are somehow 'more authentic' or 'more religious' than the forces of dynamism, responsiveness, and creativity. For generations now, those arguing against *Chiddush* (innovation) in halacha have prided themselves on their insistence that conservatism is just about always the (only) authentic position . . . It was Rabbi Chaim David Halevi, the late Sephardic Chief Rabbi of Tel Aviv, who insisted again and again in his Teshuvot (responsa) that *Chiddush* in every generation is not just permitted, but actually required. And it was Rav Chaim Hirschensohn, legendary scholar and prolific *posek* (legal decisor) who two generations earlier emphasized that there could in principle be no contradiction between Torah and the progress of civilization. Needless to say, not everyone will agree with eminent figures such as these. But they were not somehow 'less religious' or 'less authentic' than those who argued against any evolution or development in gender roles."[15]

In states where religious and political authorities intertwine, the feminist project is both political and theological. While feminism may strike some as novel and unprecedented, it is really conservative, aiming to restore rather than dismantle. It is radical in the true original meaning of the word—to go back to the foundation, in this case, the sacred texts of religion as a basis for challenging later accretions. Women are seeking to attain a level of religious scholarship and interpretive expertise that will allow them to challenge centuries of a male exegesis.

In Kuwait, Israel, and the United States, the *midrasha* and *madrasah* (schools of higher religious learning in classical Hebrew and Arabic respectively) have opened their doors to observant Jewish and Muslim women, allowing women to possess their own sacred texts through deep scholarship and exegesis. The critical return to the texts marks what may be the most intellectually vibrant and open period of Islamic and Jewish ferment since the early Middle Ages, when both religions experienced a golden age of rationalism and openness. This is a project that ought to be of equal concern to all the faithful, not just women. They undertake their project with humility, with the attitude deemed proper by both religions: *Abd* and *Islam* (in Arabic) and *ibd, avodah, mesiros nefesh, kabbalat ol malchut shamayim* (in Hebrew) express self-abnegation and submission to G-d.

Language: The First Hurdle

The first problem encountered by would-be exegetes is that both Hebrew and Arabic are polysemic and gendered languages, based on a three letter root system that yields a multitude of flexible and nuanced constructions, even if meanings are not entirely fungible. In Weir's Arabic dictionary there are twenty translations totaling more than six pages for "*daraba*," most often translated as "to hit." The interpretation of this word is critical to making sense of Qur'an 4:34, which appears to give husbands the right to strike disobedient wives. The interpretation of this word crystallizes all of the problems determining the precise meaning of Hebrew and Arabic words.

In gendered languages, G-d is commonly discussed in male terms. In Arabic and Hebrew there are many names for G-d associated with divine traits. Orthodox Jews commonly use *Hashem* (the Name) to avoid characterizing, and thereby limiting, G-d in any way. Some of G-d's traits are considered masculine, and some feminine. Some are gendered and some are not. When people are habituated to a gendered language, gender is less likely to seem significant. In English, however, gender becomes noticeable and inevitably politicized, as a marker of inferiority or exclusion. Language intimately reflects of the culture around it. In Judaism, while most references to G-d contain anthropomorphic and male gendered language, it is forbidden to attribute human characteristics, including gender, to *Hashem*, because of the prohibition against idol worship or *avodah zara*. For finite humans to conceptualize G-d in terms that a human mind can understand, such as male or female, falls under this prohibition. (When humans are described as having been created "in G-d's image" this refers to their capacity to make moral judgments, not to anatomy.) Differences in interpretation cannot be settled by words alone. Reliable authoritative texts are available in translation from classical Arabic and Hebrew, however, unreliable texts also abound, creating yet another mediating layer between the would-be exegete and the original text.

Feminist Exegesis: Arguments for the Sake of Heaven

Is G-d a misogynist? If each individual has an unmediated relationship with G-d in both Islam and Judaism, how did women lose their agency? How can laws presumably derived or deduced from G-d's commands be unjust? How did rigidity and hierarchy enter Jewish and Muslim history? How did the idea of male superiority and female inferiority emerge? How did Islamic and Jewish women respond? Is there an emancipatory reading to be reclaimed in Jewish and Muslim sacred texts? One of Muhammad's first communications with the Angel Jibril took the form of a command: "*Iqra!*" (read and proclaim),[16] a directive aimed at women as well as men. But who has the authority to read and proclaim after the prophets? The word Torah means instruction, and the community that received Torah at Sinai included both sexes. Engaging in daily Torah study is a requirement for men and highly commendable for women. But can anyone interpret the texts if they approach them with knowledge, desire, reverence, and recognition of human fallibility? Feminists recognize that no real progress can be made without reopening the gates of interpretation. They are unwilling to challenge divine authority, but they are willing to challenge men who claim to be speaking for G-d. This warrants a return to the basic texts such as Torah or Qur'an. The idea of reviving a faithful reading of the basics texts is not new. In the United States, legal theorists and constitutional scholars often divide on the issue of judicial activism versus judicial self-restraint, whether judges should faithfully adhere to the original meaning of the framers in the context of the eighteenth century or whether they should factor in changing historical circumstances.

Some feminists see Torah and Qur'an as inherently and irredeemably misogynistic. Some are not interested in the project of feminist exegesis. Political scientist Chantal Mouffe acknowledges that she is more concerned with gender justice than maintaining the integrity of the traditional interpretations. She asserts, "the pursuit of feminist goals requires the transformation of all the discourses, practices, and social relations where women are construed as subordinate."[17] But devout feminists favor a return to the foundational texts that reflect divine justice, including gender equality, blaming male exegetes for the anti-woman attitudes that have crept into religion.[18]

While many feminists agree that the gates of exegesis are never closed, this does not settle the issue of authority. Does each individual have the authority to interpret? While human interpretation may well have been part of divine intent, how far can interpretation stray from earlier exegesis? How can the sacred texts be protected from becoming an accessory of a political agenda? Both Torah and Qur'an enjoin each individual to read and study. Does this count as permission to come to one's own understanding? What counts as expertise and credentials? This is not a new conflict. It is reminiscent not only of the Protestant Reformation and the Chassidic challenge to highly-intellectualized, elite-dominated Judaism of its era, but also of the "red versus expert" debate that raged in China under Mao Zedong and in the Soviet Union under the Bolsheviks. Intellectuals became suspect in these settings in which authority was associated with support for the ancien régime. Contemporary Islamists reject scholarly credentials. Bin Laden and his cohorts are largely uneducated, but claim the right to issue judicial rulings. They reject the credentials of the *ulemma* (scholars) as well as their monopoly on individual interpretation. They blame the *ulemma* for supporting corrupt, Western-style governments. Islamists, despite their claims of absolute subservience to Allah, freely impose their own supposedly pure interpretations of shari'a, exhibiting stunning self-confidence about their infallibility and loyalty to Qur'an. Rules and standards are required to avoid the danger posed by political activists who harness their campaigns of hate and bloodshed to religion. The rules and standards must include justice as a criterion of reliability.

Is Reinterpretation a Possibility? Is Revelation Ongoing?

Did the first generations of sages fully explain the sacred texts and are the gates of exegesis permanently closed? For those who hold that the sacred texts were issued by G-d in a finished state, these texts are trans-historical and universal, applying to all people at all times and in all places. History and context are irrelevant to the process of interpretation. Jewish feminist scholar Tamar Ross suggests a strategy for searching for authentic divine intent that has been obscured by generations of male interpreters. Ross assumes that G-d never intended the Torah to be treated by humans as immutable or trans-historical. She claims that revelations are ongoing, forever calling forth new interpretations taking into account the progressive developments in morality. If humans have reached a new level of moral understanding, say, about the injustice of slavery or the injustice of gender inequality, G-d intends us to revise our interpretations of Torah accordingly. Permission to hold slaves or multiple wives and concubines may have been based on the level of human moral understanding at the time that Torah was conferred. For Ross, second order interpretation is a response to the dynamics of history, but does not contradict claims of divine authorship.

In this view, there is no reason to reject contemporary exegesis in favor of past scholarly exegesis. Ross sees contemporary feminism as just such a revelation, intended by G-d to be communicated to the community now that humans have reached a level of moral development and receptivity. Ongoing interpretation, taking into account history and context, is a divine mandate. Her view seems to be ratified in principle by several respected

Orthodox rabbis, "A Torah at once vibrant and worldly, a Torah that can speak G-d's word in every time and place, a Torah that believes that women's emergence into positions of leadership and equality is a redemptive process of G-d's image becoming more manifest in the world—let's call is what it is: Torah-true Judaism."[19]

Exegesis Is Always an Act of Reform

Among progressives, reform is built into the divine plan. It is part of a process in which humans continually search for guidance in their ongoing process of moral evolution. Others claim that while eternal, these texts are also living. As they see it, it is part of divine intent that humans respond to novel historical circumstances in keeping with divine justice. All reinterpretation is an act of reform, not only reinterpretation that appears to be progressive or innovative. Therefore, Islamists are also reformers. They reject aspects of modernity such as secular government and democracy, and seek to reinstate a mythical, unified caliphate that never existed. A self-proclaimed imam such as American-born al-Awlaki, who has repeatedly called for the murder of civilians, simplifies the world considerably by dividing it into *dar al-harb* (the world of war or enemies of Islam) against the *dar-al-Islam* (the Islamic world). They criticize Western social mores, particularly greater gender equality and they condemn governments, Muslim or secular, despotic or democratic, as impure. Yet they are just as selective and agenda-driven as the entrenched *ulemma* that they seek to supplant. The Islamists' call for authenticity actually yields a novel reading, whether it is based on the ideology of Abd-al-Wahab (the founder of the Saudi Wahabi movement) or Ayman al-Zawahiri, al Qaeda's so-called chief theologian. While they reject the authority of credentialed scholars or *ulemma*, they are not returning to anything original. Their ideologies represent novel renditions, more political than theological. It is a reform movement struggling for credibility by claiming that it is the sole heir of the original pure Islam.

Among Jews, the debate about reform is similarly related to the question is Torah fixed and transcendental or are interpretation and reform inevitable? Even among those who claim that they support the original and suprahistorical meaning of the text, almost every act of interpretation has an element of novelty. In Judaism, those who are against *chidush bahalacha* (innovative ways of understanding the classic texts and traditions) must recognize, "every contemporary halakhic decisor [must] examine the tradition and the text based on his (or her) own understanding: 'l'fi r'ot eini hadayan'—according to the way the judge—of any era—sees it. . . . When it comes to understanding the infinite word of G-d, especially in the world of Halacha . . . that understanding cannot be based on 'status quo,' . . . but, rather, by the most contemporary understanding of the halakhic decisor who is examining it."[20]

As Rabbi Lopatin argues, the Vilna Gaon, the great Torah luminary of the eighteenth century, "regularly disagreed with Rishonim and Gaonim, authorities of the centuries and millennium before him. He had no choice: he had to be honest, and if he felt they didn't read the tradition and the texts (Talmud and Midrash) correctly, he had to disagree with them. . . . In the end of the day it doesn't matter: halakhic decisions are not just copied from the past, they are based on the latest, freshest thinking of the individual halakhic authority. Independence and, yes, innovation, where it is called for to bring out the truth of the Torah, are the hallmarks of the Orthodox halachic process. . . . Orthodoxy believes in a divine, infinite and eternal Torah that was revealed to Moshe at Sinai and through the 40 years in the wilderness. . . . these new and innovative understandings . . . are celebrated as the contribution of each individual mind, in every era, to give us a better understanding of what G-d commanded Moses and the Children of Israel in the written and oral law so many years ago. It is ever fresh, ever eternal, and ever open to debate and new challenges."[21]

Pedigree and Lineage:
Broken and Unbroken Chains of Transmission

Some contemporary religious authorities, both Muslim and Jewish, counter women's efforts to participate in exegesis with the claim that the interpretive enterprise is now complete. They claim that earlier, more able scholars accomplished most of the work, and contemporary scholars simply fine-tune their work without straying far. The further removed in time from G-d's original self-disclosure at Sinai, the easier it is to claim that human subjective and agenda-driven interpretation tainted G-d's actual meaning. While this very admission might support feminists' charge that past scholars have erred, and that exegesis is never complete, authorities draw a different conclusion from the same idea. They treat as self-evident that the earlier exegetes were superior to the later ones. In Judaism, this is expressed by the adage that contemporary scholars are "dwarfs standing on the shoulders of giants." Contemporary exegetes cannot attain the status of their forebears, and any innovative interpretation is likely to be wrong. Privileging the earlier over the later exegetes does not, however, silence would-be reformers. This attitude of deference toward the earlier scholars is challenged on many grounds. If the sacred texts are living, then today's complex world demands fresh perspectives. The more history passes, the more it distances us from the ancient sages and their world. Human interpretive agency is needed now more than ever.

According to Rabbi Shai Held, head of Yeshivat Hadar, "We shouldn't be slaves to the present. There is much to criticize and even condemn in contemporary society, and Torah offers crucial correctives to much that ails us. But neither should we be slaves to the past, as if ancient social arrangements were the heart of G-d's message to our broken world. The Torah has thrived in countless social and political settings, and it can continue to do so today. So let's not apologize, but understand who we are and where we fall on the crucial question of *Torat Chaim*, a living Torah, a Torah of life."[22]

Islam and Judaism both, throughout their histories, embraced a spectrum of reformers. Both religious traditions have shared a number of crucially important theological debates including the question of human free-will versus determinism, G-d's justice in relation to G-d's mercy, cosmology, ontology, the nature and source of evil, and the relationship between reason and faith. Both scholarly traditions have produced those who believe that human reason is derivative and therefore congruent with divine reason, so that reason and revelation can both lead to knowledge of G-d. Both religious traditions have seen periods in which the rationalists seemed to hold sway and periods of backlash against human reason and free will. During historical periods when Muslims and Jews lived in close proximity, both religions produced scholars that have been cognizant and respectful of each other's theologians and philosophers. Cross-pollination from other traditions and receptivity to surrounding cultures has been a hallmark of both Islamic and Jewish history. Every act of interpretation created an opening for reform. Feminists treat as far-fetched the claim that a pure, historically transcendent, and complete understanding of divine intention has already been achieved. The so-called discourse of authenticity really represents a profound anxiety about the ability of religion to answer or reconcile with the forces of modernity, especially gender rights.

The Elite Official Scholars and Jurists:
Is Expertise the Sole Qualification of the Exegete?

In Islam and Judaism, mindless submission to authorities has never been the ideal. In both religions the act of study is an act of prayer, worship, and obedience demanded by G-d "until the day before death." "Learn it and learn it [Torah], for everything is in it. Look deeply into it; now grow old and grey over it"[23] There is no reason to think that this ideal applies only to men. While individuals are enjoined to study, they are cautioned not to settle issues of law on their own. This seems contradictory, but it is based on the recognition that wading through the thicket of possible interpretations runs the risk of arriving at a faulty conclusion and that one should therefore at least consult if not defer to a legal expert. While scholars may have an edge when it comes to discerning the proper interpretation, this very injunction contains an acknowledgement that the text itself does not yield straightforward answers. It is not only the uninitiated who may err in interpreting text. Erudite and pious Muslim and Jewish scholars have spent lifetimes in contention over the true meaning of a text. For the average Muslim or Jew, study is intended to direct one's focus to G-dliness and right actions. Among Islamist reformers, al-Mawdudi holds that Islamic law is subject to evolution and must respond to changing historical conditions. He also accepts that Muslims jurists are called upon to rule according to their best judgment of the requirements of the case. The four rules of legislation provide guidance for the jurist. *Ta'wil*, interpretation, allows jurists to use their insight into Qur'an and Sunnah. *Qiyas*, the application of deductive logic, allows jurists to reason from analogous cases when no clear precedent can be found. *Ijtihad*, individual, rigorous judgment, is applied to cases in conformity to shari'a's general principles when no like cases can be found, and *istihsan* allows jurists to establish rules in areas that are not explicitly prohibited by Qur'an. Yet al-Mawdudi is just as cautious as any member of the *ulemma* when it comes to creating openings for a free-for-all of individualized judgment. While arguing for the intrinsic vitality and adaptability of Islamic jurisprudence, he quickly extinguishes any hopes that ordinary, or even extremely pious, people can adopt these four rules. He limits their application to only the educated elite with a thorough knowledge of classical Arabic and the vast literature of Islam.[24] One elite may be replaced with another, presumably Islamist elite, but the guidance by an elite is still required.

The holy texts were never intended to become the sole province of an elite caste of decisors. Muhammad was an illiterate orphan when he was singled out. Jewish history is full of upstart sages, such as Hillel and Akiva, who came from a lower, uneducated stratum of society and, in some cases, were even converts to Judaism. David was pulled from his father's sheep-cotes ahead of his older, stronger brothers to become king. The entire community that fled Egypt was present at Sinai, including women and children. Judaism and Islam are emphatic that each person is equally responsible for their actions and is directly answerable to G-d. This idea is embedded in the foundational idea of humans as free-willed. Islam and Judaism are both at odds with a professionalized clergy. Moral praxis and judgment are attributes of both men and women. Barlas claims that Qur'an does not bind us to the interpretations of previous generations. Nor should we confuse communal norms with Qur'anic norms. "To me, this norm [bowing to patriarchal authority] is a heresy even if it is masquerading as orthodoxy because it subordinates the Qur'an [the universal] to males, Arabs, and scholars [the particular]."[25] "Qur'an belongs to all Muslims," as does the freedom to arrive at one's own understanding.[26] But this is not a haphazard or purely subjective exercise. There are guidelines. The best exegetes have the self-awareness and integrity, as did Abu Hanafah, who specified his cultural assumptions and how they shaped his understanding. There are rules for interpreting the *fiqh* in light of the environment and culture and even when Muslims constitute a minority in a society.[27]

To counter the monopoly of a self-proclaimed elite, "Ordinary Muslims around the world who have concerns, questions and considerable moral dilemmas about the current state of affairs of Islam must reclaim the basic concepts of Islam and reframe them in a broader context. Ijma must mean consensus of all citizens leading to participatory and accountable governance. Jihad must be understood in its complete spiritual meaning as the struggle for peace and justice as a lived reality for all people everywhere. And the notion of the ummah must be refined so it becomes something more than a mere reductive abstraction."[28]

"The process of reduction started with the very notion of the *alim* (scholar) itself. Just who is an *alim*; what makes him an authority? In early Islam, an *alim* was anyone who acquired *ilm*, or knowledge, which was itself described in a broad sense. . . . But after the gates of *ijtihad* were closed during the Abbasid era, *ilm* was reduced to religious knowledge, and the *ulama* came to constitute only religious scholars. . . . But over time the clerics and religious scholars have removed the people from the equation and reduced *ijma* to the consensus of the religious scholars. Not surprisingly, authoritarianism, theocracy, and despotism reign supreme in the Muslim world. . . . Obscurantist mullahs, in the guise of the *ulama*, dominate Muslim societies and circumscribe them with fanaticism and absurdly reductive logic."[29]

Reformers in all three Abrahamic religions have usually drawn their bead on the religious elite. Just as Martin Luther challenged the Catholic hierarchy, Islamists such as al-Banna, al-Mawdudi, Sayyid Qutb, Bin Laden, and theorists of Hamas and Taliban have all challenged the authority of the *ulemma*. If interpretation is no longer the exclusive arena of the entrenched scholarly elite, and no other standard of qualification is generally accepted, why exclude women exegetes? Why would gender matter at all in either Islam or Judaism, in which women are increasingly becoming masters of the texts?

Preventing an Exegetical Free-for-All:
Who Has Credentials to Interpret?

In Judaism, the first recorded instance of a man interpreting G-d's word was when Adam misreported the divine injunction against eating from the tree of knowledge to Eve, inaccurately including his added personal admonition against even touching the tree. When the serpent pushed Eve against the tree and she did not die, the serpent was able to easily convince her that Adam had got the eating part wrong too. From the point of view of many religious feminists, this marked the beginning of a long history of male-dominated exegesis gone wrong. Humans do not share the inerrancy of G-d. Muslims hold that the transmission of Qur'an from Allah through the angel Jibril arrived intact to Muhammad. Even if Muhammad transmitted it to his companions without injecting anything of his own in the process, humans intervened in the reporting of Qur'an, even during Muhammad's lifetime and certainly in the first generations after his death. The accepted version of Qur'an did not take its complete written form until years after the death of the Prophet. It was revealed through the Angel Jibril to Muhammad in a piecemeal fashion over a twenty-three-year period until his death in 632 CE. During his lifetime, portions were memorized and transmitted, and portions were recorded by various scribes on a variety of surfaces. Muhammad shared his very first revelations with his first wife, Khadijja, and later, after her death and his marriage to Aisha, he shared his revelations, teachings, and example with her. Aisha was perhaps the source of the largest collection of *ahadith*, as well as enjoying the most proximate and intimate relationship with the Prophet. Abu Bakr, a close companion of the Prophet and the first caliph after the Prophet's death, gathered, transcribed, and recorded many reports, passed them to his son Umar, who in turn, passed them on to his daughter, Hofsa. The third caliph, Uthman, issued the first authoritative copy of the Qur'an in 653 CE. Subsequently, Muhammad's sayings and actions were narrated, recorded, and passed down in the form of *ahadith* and, along with the Sunnah, or reports about Muhammad's ways, became, in addition to Qur'an, the basis for shari'a. Qur'an, accepted by the majority of Muslims as divine self-disclosure, is considered inerrant. However, Muslims are divided as to the inerrancy of the humans who recorded and interpreted it.

The Good of the Community Is the Best Meaning

The quality of the interpretation is related to the moral quality of the interpreter. Education may have been a male monopoly in earlier times, but good character and piety is not an exclusive male province. An equally important standard against which to measure the accuracy and reliability of an interpretation may be the probable social impact of the ruling. Is the interpretation that produces the most salutary social outcome the best interpretation? Qur'an reports that G-d enjoined Moses to "hold fast by the best of the precepts."[30] The ability to discern the best precepts in turn favors a political backdrop of democracy, freedom of debate, and dissent. Coercion in religion, even by a scholarly and pious elite, is expressly forbidden, not just because it destroys human freedom and dignity but because a repressive atmosphere does not encourage the pursuit of unpopular, but perhaps accurate interpretations. Judgment must be guided by good character. Qur'an states "take and hold these with firmness, and enjoin thy people to hold fast by the best in the precepts."[31] Yusef Ali said, "This principle is repeatedly emphasized: Those who listen to the Word and follow the best (meaning); those are the ones whom Allah has guided, and those are the ones imbued with understanding."[32] When comparing meanings, "listen closely to all that is said, and follow the best of it." This describes people who examine every religious proposition in light of their own reason, accepting that which they find valid or possible. Honesty and good character are required to discern truth. "The people of knowledge [scholars] document all of the evidence [on the matter] whether pro or con. The people of whim, however, document only evidence that supports their position." Interpretation will always be required. The best meaning of the text is the one that conforms to evidence and one that, when applied, yields a just outcome. It is inconceivable that the best interpretation could be at odds with justice. In addition to privileging good character of the exegete over formal credentials, this strengthens the claim by feminists that if the social impact of gender discrimination is injustice, than the best reading will be the one that supports gender equality and dignity. Muslim and Jewish feminists argue that since interpretation is unavoidable and all readings are mediated by subjectivity, why not interpret in light of the best, namely the most just meaning and return to the communities' most ethical vision?

Rules and Methods of Exegesis

Both Judaism and Islam represent comprehensive ways of life. Torah and Qur'an, according to their followers, were transmitted by G-d, through Moses and Muhammad, respectively, directly to a community of recipients, not to a handful of scholars or elites. While ancient Israel had a tribe of priests, and kings were obligated to copy at least one Torah scroll during their rule, Jews quickly established yeshivas and attained near complete male literacy, even before the second Diaspora. Throughout Jewish history, every male was expected to be something of a Torah scholar, and the obligation to study and learn Torah everyday was as important as prayer.

While the Prophet was himself illiterate, the injunction to learn Qur'an applied both to men and women. Learning implies interpretation, under the tutelage of a scholar or on one's own. Yet interpretation could not be allowed to descend into a purely subjective free-for-all. Various interpretations inevitably arose early on, even among sincere and pious scholars. Each page of Talmud consists of often-conflicting commentaries by several authoritative sages surrounding a *mishna* (Torah law). Early exegetes and jurists recognized this problem and in both Judaism and Islam took steps to establish rules of interpretation based on logic and intellectual humility. For instance, while shari'a constitutes divine law and ethics, the various contending *madhabs* (five major schools of *fiqh*) are approximations of shari'a arrived at through *ijtihad*, the interpretive exercise aimed at discovering

shari'a. The epistemological methods of *ijtihad* draw on textual and interpretive resources called *usul al-fiqh*. *Ibadat* (laws of worship) and *mu'amalat*
(laws of human interaction) are subsumed under *furu al-fiqh*, the content of
shari'a as derived by scholars using *ijtihad* or interpretation. Feminists may
rightly point out that opportunities for men to err are plentiful and that
jurisprudence, rife with human interpretive judgments, can hardly be
treated as unalterable, eternal, or perfect. Yusef Ali takes a fairly conservative view of how much latitude an interpreter is permitted. "I think the art
of interpretation must stick closely to the text. Every serious writer and
thinker has a right to use all of the knowledge and expertise he possesses in
the service of the Qur'an, but he must not mix up his own theories and
conclusions."[33] Does the "he" in Yusef Ali's category of serious thinkers
include women?

Islam: Vetting for Authenticity

Feminist historians claim that the women of the Prophet's time "enjoyed
the full range of rights and freedoms that Allah and the Prophet allowed
them. There were many prominent Muslim women in that generation,
who were outspoken and contributed to building Islamic society, whose
names have been recorded. But after that, notable women rapidly drop out
of Islamic history. What happened?"[34] Can the cause be found in Qur'an, in
the later compilations of *ahadith* and Sunnah, or in the absorption of alien
ideas and customs during the rapid spread of Islam? Did the intertwining
of political and religious elites undermine women's authority, rights, and
participation in their religion? In the early centuries after the spread of
Islam, rulers were called upon to improvise and supplemented Qur'anic
principles with laws, customs, styles of rule, and political institutions of the
peoples they had conquered. This meant that as early as the seventh century, Islam began to display regional differences in political, social, and
economic spheres, as well as in religious practice. As a result of conquest
and the contact between Islam and the Mongols, and later confrontations
with the Christian armies of Europe, a retreat into conservatism, retrenchment, and maintenance of the status quo on the part of Islamic leaders and
religious authorities may have brought a halt to the open, rationalist, creative evolution of Islam. The absorption of non-Islamic practices and the increasing resistance to scholarly innovation had a stultifying effect on schol-

arship. A return to the rationalist tradition and a humanistic *fiqh* would revive the spirit of inquiry represented by the great philosophers, scientists, and jurists of the golden age such as Ibn Sina (Avisenna), Ibn Rushd (Averroes), al-Farabi, al-Biruni, al-Haytham, and Ibn Khaldun. This spirit of reason is no more foreign to Islam than opposing traditions of interpretation that seek to stifle reason.

Qur'an, Sunnah, *Ahadith, and Shari'a*

The Qur'an is complicated, extensive, often repetitive, in places highly poetic. Like the Torah, it does not adhere to a strict chronology. In the case of Qur'an, the verses do not follow the time-line of revelation, rather the length of the revelations from longest to shortest. Qur'an is laid out in the rough equivalent of 114 chapters called *suwar* (sura, singular) that are subdivided into *ayat* (*ayah*, singular). There is a pronounced difference between the revelations of the Meccan (610–622 CE) and Medinan (622–632 CE) periods. The Qur'an, in addition to laying out the stories of creation, includes rules of social relations and etiquette as well as rules of prayer and religious observance. Earlier verses from the Meccan period tend to be more poetic and cosmological, while later verses after the *hajira* (flight to Medina, 622–632 CE) tend to be more specific and prescriptive. Qur'an contains topics such as the nature of G-d, tales of the prophets, human creation, human nature, human relations, descriptions of the afterlife, and the pillars of faith—the basic doctrines, tenets, and ethical prescriptions that serve as the basis for Islamic law or shari'a. There are many parables and metaphorical stories that give rise to a wealth of implications and interpretations. The case for gender equality can be made directly from Qur'an. The principle of equal worth and responsibility is stated many times. The principle of human dignity applies to both men and women, and both sexes are imbued with ethical qualities, charity, chastity, honesty, and piety.[35] To be *mu'min* (a believer) one is responsible for and judged by one's actions, regardless of gender. Ontological and moral equality must, therefore, be intended in all of its social and economic dimensions.[36] There is as much variation among individuals of the same sex as there is between the sexes. G-d is the source of rights for all, and mothers are to be honored by their children. "O mankind! Reverence your Guardian-Lord who created you from a single soul/self. He created humans of like nature, and from them twain scattered (like seeds) countless men and women; reverence G-d, through whom ye demand your mutual (rights), and (reverence) the wombs (that bore you); for G-d ever watches over you."[37]

Almost all Muslim religious duties are incumbent upon both men and women, with time-honored exceptions for women, as in Judaism, who are considered weakened by menstruation and childbirth. It is repeatedly emphasized that the relevant distinction among humans is based on goodness and evil of characters, regardless of gender. Similarly, rewards and punishments in the afterlife are distributed on this basis: "Whoever works righteousness, man or woman, and has faith, verily to him will We give a new life"[38] and "Never will I suffer to be lost the work of any of you, be he male or female; ye are members one of another."[39]

Women are full partners of men in terms of moral potential, and couples should be paired according to shared moral attributes or lack thereof. "For Muslim men and women, for believing men and women, for devout men and women, for men and women who are patient and constant, for men and women who humble themselves, for men and women who give charity, for men and women who fast, for men and women who guard their chastity, and for men and women who engage much in G-d's praise, for them has G-d prepared forgiveness and great reward"[40] and again: "Whoever works righteousness, man or woman, and has faith, verily to him will We give a new life."[41]

Again, moral parity between the sexes is emphasized: "G-d has to punish the hypocrites, men and women, and the Unbelievers, men and women, and G-d turns in mercy to the Believers, men and women."[42] Rewards will come to both men and women if they are devout. "One day shalt thou see the believing men and the believing women—how their light runs forward before them."[43] Further, "For those who give in charity, men and women . . . they shall have a liberal reward."[44] The same punishments are to be meted out to men and women for adultery (the unequal punishment for adultery meted out in many shari'a-based communities arises from an ambiguity in Qur'an in which 4:15 (that decrees that lewd women be confined to their houses until death) is posited by Yusef Ali to refer to lesbian acts, whereas 4:15 is overridden by 24:2, which prescribes whipping as punishment for adultery for both men and women.[45]

Qur'an: Text in Context

Context is significant for progressive exegetes. In Islam as in Judaism, the institution of marriage is built on the idea of equal moral worth and complementarity. Harmony, it was recognized, requires that partners have similar characters, as is stressed in many Qur'anic verses. The principles of moral equality and complementarity of men and women go a long way toward making sense of the troubling Qur'anic verse featuring the claim that men are *qawwam* over women. "Men are the protectors and maintainers of women, because G-d has given the one more (strength) than the other, and because they support them from their means."[46] The word *qawwam* is often translated as superior but may also be translated in a more protective way connoting reciprocity and mutuality, the more appropriate translation in light of the verse that states that men and women are "garments to each other."[47] Protection here would signify mutual rather than unilateral. This still leaves unsolved the meaning attached to male superiority, which must then be understood according to the context and intent of the verse. The word appears in the sentence, "because they spend on them from their income," referring to men being obligated to meet the financial needs of the family. For feminists the notion of superiority is quite specific and applies only to the man who is supporting his wife, mother, daughters, or sisters and then only in terms of his financial leadership.

The error, according to many feminists, is that this specific sense of superiority has been generalized by male commentators to indicate an overall superiority of men over women. Superiority is narrowly construed by feminists such as Barlas, Engineer, and Wadud, and related to a particular social role and not to anything innate or biological. Men are only superior to the woman they support, but not in an absolute sense. If a wife is working, even that notion of superiority collapses.

The most felicitous translation of the troubling word and verse reads *qawwam* as mercy or solicitude toward the weak. But even if weakness is defined as a temporary condition, applying to pregnancy and post-partum periods, it runs the risk of becoming the stereotype of male-female relations, as in Yusef Ali's respected translation, "and as woman is the weaker vessel, that tenderness may from a certain aspect, be likened to the protecting kindness that the strong should give to the weak."[48] But Islamists such as Abu'l al-Mawdudi call the principle that men are in charge of women one of the unalterable and unambiguous laws of Qur'an (along with the laws and punishments related to adultery, divorce, and inheritance).[49]

Another particularly controversial Qur'an verse, 2:223, says, "Your wives are as a tilth unto you; so approach your tilth when and where you will; but do some good act for your souls beforehand and fear G-d." Yusef Ali treats the comparison of wives to tilth as literal, explaining that men, just as they cultivate their fields or husband their property, are free to choose the time and manner in which they approach their wives. This is generally interpreted to mean that wives must be available to their husbands on demand. Her refusal puts her in the category of *nushuz* (a rebellious woman), and husbands can use sura 4:34 as justification for imposing physical punishment. The second part of this troubling sura seems to undermine the principle of humane treatment. "Therefore the righteous women are devoutly obedient and guard in (the husband's) absence what G-d would have them guard. As to those women on whose part ye fear *nushuz* (disloyalty and ill conduct), admonish them (first), (next) refuse to share their beds, (and last) beat them (lightly); but if they return to obedience, seek not against them means (of annoyance)." The respected translator of Qur'an, Yusef Ali, adds his own comment, "Some slight physical correction may be administered. . . . It is inadvisable though permissible and all authorities are unanimous in deprecating any sort of cruelty."[50]

Some apologists suggest that in the context of the times, this was a humane recipe because it made beating a last resort only after the first two steps failed. Or apologists select the least offensive translation for *daraba*, rather than "beat," "hit," "strike," "scourge," "chastise," or "flog," they choose "make an example of," "spank," "pet," "tap," and "seduce." But the fact remains that the right to admonish in whatever form is restricted to husbands, and that it is inconsistent with Islam that G-d would sanction one person harming another, even if harm took the form of humiliation. Laleh Bakhtiar, in her controversial 2007 translation of Qur'an, decided that the word should be translated as to "go away," because that is how the Prophet responded to his rebellious wives. The behavior of the Prophet takes on more significance than the word used. Arabic grammar and G-d's revealed word cannot simply be dismissed, and she has many critics, many of whom she suggests will "oppose the idea of an American, especially a woman, reinterpreting the prevailing translation."[51] Her detractors on both sides of the question have accused her, and commentators like her, of trying to make the verse palatable, bowing to pressure to make Islam seem modern and western.

The Qur'an also states that excessive punishment is unjust. Sura 58:1 called *Mujadila* (the woman who pleads) proclaims that "G-d has indeed heard (and accepted) the statement of the woman who pleads against her husband and carries her complaint (in prayer) to G-d: and G-d (always) hears the arguments between both sides among you."[52] Sura 4:40, which says G-d is never unjust in the least degree, can only be used to prove that G-d would not permit physical punishment, if physical punishment of women can be demonstrated to fit in the category of what Allah considers unjust behavior. Many male commentators believe that physical punishment of women under some circumstances is justified in Qur'an, and therefore must signify Allah's acceptance of it as a just act, making it fully compatible with sura 4:40. This error has been perpetuated throughout Islam's history.

The significance of context is also revealed in contemporary feminists' attempts to overturn laws permitting up to four wives. The origin of this permission is tied to historical circumstance. After the battle of Uhud in 625 CE, in which many companions of the Prophet were killed, surviving companions were encouraged to take the widows and orphans of their fallen comrades so that they might be provided for. Yet men are warned that they must do justice (treat equally) each of their wives and that men who cannot fulfill this obligation should refrain from marrying more than one woman. Many feminists argue that the intent of the sura was to oppose polygamy in that it is a logical impossibility that any man could treat all of his wives with justice and equality. The same can be said about slavery, divorce by triple proclamation *(talaq)*, captives, and concubines, all of which institutions may have been appropriate in an earlier time, but are forbidden today even in many predominantly Muslim countries. Both the context and the specificity of the sura suggest that it was not intended to apply in contemporary settings.

Context can make sense of the issue of the Muslim dress code for women, which is treated as emblematic of women's position in Islam by many Muslims and non-Muslims alike. Variation has been pronounced throughout Muslim history and in different communities as to the necessity and extent of covering. Muslims are divided over whether Qur'an demands coverings for all women or just for the consorts of the Prophet.

There are many Qur'anic admonitions directed at men as well as women believers to dress and behave modestly. Instructions directed at the consorts of the Prophet specifically, emphasize that they are not like other women and must follow more stringent rules related to attire.[53] The problem is that men are susceptible to "dazzling displays" and that according to Yusef Ali[54] because of conditions in the Prophet's contemporary Medina, hypocrites (men who pretended to be Muslims, but whose behavior did not accord),[55] made it necessary to give women this protection in terms of dress, and it was never intended to restrict women to their homes. Hence, Qur'an admonishes, "O Prophet! Tell thy wives and daughters, and the believing women, that they should cast their outer garments over their persons (when abroad)."[56] This is meant to protect women by identifying them as Muslims. For those who read the covering as a commandment, opinions are divided over the extent of the coverage. Facial covering is not commanded, but some Muslims feel it is implied (although it is prohibited when on pilgrimage to the holy cities). The great variety of Muslim women's garments across the globe attests to the variety of possible interpretations by sincere people. Contemporary Muslim women who have recently donned the hijab cite a variety of reasons, not all related to religion, including identity, politics, dignity, and the ability to move freely in the public sphere. Hijab, polygyny, and wife beating are a few of the flashpoints that clearly illustrate the differences between Islamists and progressives regarding interpretation of scripture.

Sunnah: The Way of the Prophet

In addition to Qur'an, Muslims have the Sunnah, the accumulated behavior and actions of the Prophet during his lifetime, based on first-hand accounts of his companions. Many Muslims treat the Sunnah as reliable information about how the Prophet conducted his life and as a model for his followers. Muhammad never physically punished his wives, which would challenge the legitimacy of physical punishment of wives in the troubling passage of Qur'an 4:34.

Ahadith: The Broken Chain of Transmission

The *ahadith*, the various reports about the sayings of the Prophet, are of a later vintage. Therefore, it is particularly important to understand them in their historical and syntactic context. The two most authoritative collections are those of al-Bukhari and al-Muslim, who died in 870 and 875 CE respectively, more than one hundred and fifty years after the death of the Prophet. One of the largest compilations of *ahadith is* attributed to Aisha, making it the first in the chain of transmission and theoretically the most credible, yet ironically, the majority of it has been widely dismissed by male scholars. There were thousands of records compiled by dozens of followers, some regarded as more verifiable and, therefore, more reliable than others. Some have been challenged because of the flawed character of their purveyors, some because they represent only a single example of a particular anecdote or quotation, some because there is a physical and temporal gap in transmission between the conveyor and other links in the chain back to the Prophet. The wealth of conflicting *ahadith* invites selectivity among interpreters, particularly in support of a political agenda. Even among the sincere transmitters, as in the children's game gossip in which one child initiates a message that is communicated around the table, becoming more and more garbled the more ears and mouths it passes through, feminists can contend that the original divine message has passed through a similar process of obfuscation. Most believing feminists favor a return to the foundational texts, which reflect divine justice including gender equality, blaming male exegetes for the anti-woman attitudes that have crept in.[57] Many progressives and feminists hold that if a narrative contradicts reason and *fitra* (the natural order), it should be rejected. These exegetes give primacy to the Qur'an as the original and, therefore, reliable source of divine self-disclosure, trumping any hadith that may contradict a Qur'anic passage.

Feminists and progressives challenge some of the offensive *ahadith* as fabrications, even among those collected by al-Bukhari and al-Muslim. They are more easily dismissed when they can be shown to be weak in terms of their pedigree, reliability, or some other rule of exegesis. Since they were collected one hundred and fifty years after the Prophet died, they are not thought to be of divine origin by Muslims. Their main currency lies among the scholars of Islam, while many feminist exegetes reject any *ahadith* that does not conform to the Qur'an or the example of the Prophet. Reliability of a particular hadith is ascertained in part by the use of *ahl al-ra'i* (reason and opinion) of the interpreter to distinguish the *sa'hih* and the *hasan,* the authentic and the good.

The notion of dismissing some *ahadith* out of hand may be radical, but progressive Muslims can draw on historical precedent, pointing to examples of pious imams who revised their jurisprudence in accordance with evolving notions of justice or to protect divine intent. "The divine purpose behind every law is *maslahat al-ibad . . .* the well-being of people . . . G-d is repeatedly referred to in the Qur'an as *al-rahman al-rahim* (compassionate and merciful)."[58] "Hadith which states that the jurist who engages in *ijtihad* and reaches the correct conclusion receives two rewards [from G-d], while the jurist who engages in *ijtihad* and reaches an erroneous conclusion nevertheless receives one reward."[59] This hadith yields a remarkably similar conclusion to that of the Talmudic recounting of the adversarial rabbis deducing divine law even when the interpreter falls short. The message is that engaging in independent, rigorous thinking is laudable. An earlier scholar does not necessarily hold the best interpretation for today.

Amin Ahsan Islahi, an Islamic scholar from the Indian Subcontinent, suggests four rules for understanding *ahadith*. These rules can provide guidance for feminist and progressive scholars when confronted with post-Qur'anic texts that suggest the subservience of women.[60]

1. The Qur'an is the measure of truth and guidance in shari'a and all matters. *Ahadith* provide the details and explanation. *Ahadith* that conflict with Qur'an must be treated as inauthentic and rejected as fabrication or distortion.
2. The language of the *ahadith* matters to interpreters. While many of the *ahadith* were orally transmitted, and while Arabic language evolved over time, language that is closer to the classical Prophetic Arabic is likely more authentic.
3. Context is important. The interpreter must be able to differentiate *ahadith* that refer to specific situations from those that are meant to be universal in application.
4. The religion is created with the whole of human life in mind and cannot contradict the dictates of reason and *fitra* (human nature).

Shari'a

Shari'a is a system of derivative laws that rely heavily on Qur'an, Sunnah, and *ahadith* as well as the practical needs of rulers in different times and places. Different *fiqh*, subsystems or schools of legal reasoning, sprang up very soon after the death of the Prophet. Derivation requires both *ijtihad* and *tafsir*, a rigorous, rule-bound methodology combined with logic, sincerity, and personal judgment. There are four sources of shari'a—Qur'an, Sunnah, *qiyas* (analysis), and *ijma* (consensus), and, according to Abul A'ala Maudini, "there is hardly a command with an agreed interpretation."[61] According to Ziauddin Sardar, while most Muslims consider shari'a to be divine, it is a human construction, an attempt to understand the divine will in a particular context. This is why the bulk of the shari'a actually consists of *fiqh* (jurisprudence), the legal opinion of classical jurists. When we describe shari'a as divine, we actually provide divine sanctions for the rulings of bygone *fiqh*. The elevation of the shari'a to the divine level also means the believers themselves have no agency. Their role is to submit and follow rather than to think and interpret. Shari'a is best understood as rules for guidance that are as dynamic as the changing world around them. "The only thing that remains constant in Islam is the text of the Qur'an itself, its concepts providing the anchor for ever changing interpretations."[62]

Progressive Islam: Holding Fast to Revelation and Reason

Muslim jurists have had to confront alien background cultural influences, deciding how or if religious precepts should be maintained or adapted. There is a grey area between behaviors that are clearly *haram* (forbidden) and those that are *ihalah* (permitted). Jurists have historically considered the special compromises that must be practiced by Muslim communities in non-Muslim nations. Islamic law has long recognized that Muslims living as minorities may exercise some flexibility with respect to adherence to Muslim law. Debates are ongoing over the status of *fiqh-al-aqalliyat* (more lenient jurisprudence for Muslims when they live as minorities in non-Muslim society), and *maqasid-al-shari'a* (the objectives of Islamic law), the desirability of *madhab al-tafsir* (the way of seeking ease or latitude in religious rulings or practice), and whether to emphasize *rikhsa* (legal dispensation) or *azima* (the strongest, strictest legal ruling). Unlike the more formalistic, traditional branches such as Salafism and Wahabism, which emphasize *tarbiya* (strict moral rectitude and stringency in behavior), a majority of Muslims live outside the Arab world and outside shari'a-based governments. In a widely dispersed situation, these forms of Islam can be difficult to practice. The intense historical preoccupation with positive regulations, the development of a scholarly elite, and its entanglement with political rule sparked a contemplative, individualistic, and often woman-friendly response in the form of mystical Sufi orders, which are increasingly popular in Western nations and highly attractive to converts raised in a liberal culture.

Progressives emphasize individual moral sovereignty and the flexibility of Islam, allowing Muslims to adapt more easily to conditions of liberal democracy and tolerance for pluralism. They also emphasize the continuing evolution of Islam in accordance with the best of contemporary social values. Without holding fast to revelation, Muslims will lose their connection with the divine, which for many would cause life to lose meaning.

Progressive Muslims are particularly sensitive to the entanglement of religion and culture. A Muslim, says feminist scholar al-Hibri, "is bound by every word and letter of Qur'an, but she is not bound by her cultural values."[63] The biggest problem for al-Hibri is that culture masquerades as religion. For instance, democracy and women's rights are at odds with culture but not religion. In the case of inconsistency between customs embodied in legal codes and Qur'an, *ahadith*, and Sunnah, offending laws must be rejected. Lack of religious education, says al-Hibri, is a problem. Globally, Muslims are largely illiterate in classical Arabic language and have acquired Qur'anic knowledge through memorization. Muslims are often unable to discern the cultural sources of objectionable laws. Pakistan's *zina* (adultery) laws, and honor killings are considered by their perpetrators to be in keeping with Qur'an though they are really products of culture. The Prophet himself modeled this approach. Muhammad made it a point to distinguish Islam from the cultural milieu of the Quraisha tribes, which regularly practiced female infanticide, by revealing though Qur'an, "when the souls are sorted out . . . when the female (infant) who was buried alive is questioned—for what crime she was killed," there would be no answer acceptable to G-d.[64]

"The challenge for Muslims today is to latch on to the currents of democracy, modernity, and globalization without cutting the umbilical cord to the heavens." When it comes to *ijtihad*, American Muslims are "miles ahead of other Muslim communities." An example is the adoption of guidelines for women-friendly mosques by many Islamic communities in the United States, Europe, and Canada. This can also be seen in the progressive role that women play in the Muslim community, in keeping with their public achievements and the principle of gender equality in the West. Western Muslims and their organizations express their commitment to democratic rules, civil rights, pluralism, political participation, and solidarity with their non-Muslim fellow citizens.[65]

The Islamist Backlash:
Women as the Source of Fitna *(Social Chaos)*

Muslim progressives and feminists recognize the need to counter the of-fending passages and hold them to the best meaning in light of the princi-ple of divine justice and contemporary moral standards. They must be prepared to face their most dangerous adversaries, Islamists. The agenda of Islamists is political, and they are involved in a highly selective exercise rather than an objective search for divine truth. Both the *ulemma* and Islamist exegetes reject explanations that render Qur'anic verses congruent with contemporary norms, but they both engage in interpretive acrobatics to support their agenda. They are hyper-literal yet highly selective in their interpretation and application of these verses. This is a hallmark of the Islamist revival worldwide. Islamists want to unite politics and shari'a under one government. They attack democratic as well as despotic regimes as corrupt and immoral. Western culture fares poorly in their estimation. They treat Western norms as debased and use gender equality as their prime example of moral decay. They bow selectively to modernity, enlisting modern technology to their cause. Particularly peculiar is the attempt to harness what they purport to be the findings of biology and psychology to buttress traditional female roles as ordained by nature as well as G-d. Most disturbing is their cynical enlistment of the vocabulary of women's rights to justify male dominance.

It is worth quoting at length from Islamist treatises: "A woman just can't do anything about the billions of cells (of which she is made of), genetically stamped with X&Y chromosomes. And it is this genetic coding which makes her a different entity from the man. No amount of education, train-ing, or change in attire can do away [with] this natural difference. And hence Islam provides reasonable allowances for these traits while deciding rights and obligations for women. . . . Considering her physical weakness & vulnerabilities, Islam frees women of all financial obligations and places the responsibility squarely on the shoulders of man, as the protector & provider for his family. . . . As regards the social status of women in Islam; it should be noted that as a mother, Islam raises women to such an exalted position in the society, which no man can ever imagine to reach."[66]

Science is invoked to make the Islamist point: "The woman is different from the man. . . . Allah's wisdom has also ordained that the physical and psychological construction of the woman should carry elements that enable her to attract and be attracted by the man."[67] For this reason, Allah has equipped her with characteristics for wifehood and motherhood. "Islam disapproves of systems that clash with this instinctive nature. . . . Islam protects femininity to keep the stream of tenderness and beauty running. . . . Islam supports femininity . . . placing it in the hands of a supporting man, securing the costs of living and the provision for her needs . . . as an obligation under the Shari'a. No basic need should compel her then to wade in the unexplored stretches of life with its conflicts, within the hustle of competitive men to win her bread—something that has befallen the Western woman." Similarly, "Allah's religion protects her morals and decency, guards her reputation and dignity, and defends her chastity against evil thoughts and tongues, and tries to foil tempting hands that seek to harm her. . . . Islam makes it incumbent on women to lower the eyes . . . and protect their private parts from illegal [unmarried] sexual acts etc. . . . At the same time Islam protects man from anxiety and aberration, the family from disintegration, and society from collapse and decay."[68] "The cunning and slyness is frequently shown in not declaring outright what is wanted is woman to rebel against her nature, exceed the limits of her femininity and make use of that femininity for illicit pleasure or illicit earning. . . . It is not in the interest of the woman to force her out of her nature . . . and force her to do a man's work. Allah has created her a female. To do a man's work, then, is cheating her nature and reality. . . . If it works in the West, it does not work for us as Muslims. . . . It is harmful for the woman herself because she loses her femininity and her distinguishing characteristic and is deprived of her home and children. Some become barren and some are like the 'third sex' . . . and causes imbalance, disorder, and chaos."[69]

Leaving pseudo-scientific arguments aside, Islamists condemn gender equality as a deliberate Western plot against Islam. "The craftiness of western culture is its ability to make dangers look attractive to unwary Muslim women through the pseudo-arguments for unrestricted mixing. . . . 'Intellectual imperialism' has managed to create in our countries people who turn a deaf ear to the ruling of Allah and His Messenger. These people call on us to give the woman free reign to assert herself, promote her personality, and enjoy her life and femininity. They want her to mix with men freely, experience them closely where they would be together alone, travel with them, go to cinemas or dance till midnight together. . . . In answer to this line of reasoning, we must say that we are Muslims first and foremost. We do not sell our religion in imitation of the vagaries of West-erners or Easterners. . . . The effects of promiscuous mixing . . . have borne its bitter fruit. . . . Moral decay . . . unlimited rein given to desire . . . illegitimate children . . . The Spread of Lethal Diseases . . . neurotic, mental and psychological disturbances . . . have filled hospitals and asylums."[70]

Islamists try to demonstrate that Islam creates an enviable life in the "great kingdom of women" (the home). "In spite of such status of honour and privilege conferred on women by Islam, if our sisters still like to get fooled by the West promoted feminist movement, we have nothing more to say. It is there for everyone to see, how women are being exploited and abused as objects of sex in the name of 'gender equality,' by those very people who claim to fight for women's rights."[71] Muslim women have been enlisted as the symbol, even icon, of Islamist purity campaigns. Policing their behavior, especially sexual behavior, is considered paramount. More rides on women than on any other single item of the Islamist agenda. Enforcing and punishing women who deviate from Islamist gender princi-ples will be called by the name liberation rather than oppression.

As these passages express, Islamists regard the modern world as full of dangers awaiting unprotected, naïve Muslim women. If women fail to take on their primary roles and duties under the protection of a man, they pose a danger to the social order and thwart the divine plan. Women are in danger, and they are a danger when they step out of prescribed roles. Many devout Muslims, adopting contemporary feminist terminology, will claim that Is-lam was the first system designed to promote women's rights, and that it continues today to be the true gender-friendly religion that liberates and respects women by protecting their inherent difference and their wellbeing.

Judaism: Progress and Backlash, Vetting for Authenticity

For Jews, G-d's decision to convey His laws to humans was the central event in Jewish history. At Sinai G-d did things differently than in Eden. He first called on the House of Jacob (the Jewish women) and then upon the men.[72] Women heard directly from G-d without male intermediaries to listen and interpret. Mosaic code as revealed to Moses at Sinai is the basis of Jewish life and law in the days of the judges and the first temple (950–586 BCE).[73] Written Torah (*Torah-she-bi-khtav*) is accompanied by the oral law tradition (*Torah-she-be-al-peh*), which is understood by Orthodox Jews to have been given at Sinai but not written or redacted. "Talmud is a summary of Oral Law that evolved over centuries of scholarly effort by sages who lived in Palestine and Babylonia."[74] Talmud has two components: Mishna (a book of halakha [law]) in Hebrew, and commentary on Mishna, called Talmud or Gemarah (discussions and elucidations of Mishna in Hebrew and Aramaic).

Talmud provides the basis for halakha, Jewish law, which would be roughly analogous to the relationship of shari'a to Qur'an and *ahadith*. For Orthodox Jews, the oral Torah was also conferred at Sinai, but with a prohibition against writing it down. It was intended to be transmitted from one generation to the next aurally from teacher to student as it was from Moses to Joshua. When the Jewish community was dispersed, along with its scholars and *yeshivot* (schools of higher learning), the oral Torah was committed to writing. Talmud was written in Babylon and in Jerusalem in different forms. If the oral Torah was conferred in its completion at Sinai, future interpretations would have already been anticipated by G-d. This attaches a great deal more authority to the commentaries than if they were simply thought to reflect fallible human reason and, therefore, suggests to some that there is little room for further innovation.

The use of legal reasoning and precedent as described by the oral Torah, Maimonides, the Rishonim (medieval interpreters), Joseph Caro's Shul'han Aruch, Moshe Isserlis' Mapah, and the Responsa tradition establishes how and if to accommodate to changing times, but does not give much credence to pure creativity or human influence. Yet, there is still room for interpretation, especially because Torah is acknowledged by many Orthodox, particularly Chassidic, Jews to contain an inner, hidden dimension.

Whether one subscribes to the view that the whole of the Talmud was handed down along with the written Torah at Sinai, including all future commentary, the Talmud has always been a living document because it records disputation, much of which is still unresolved, among sages and scholars throughout Jewish history. Talmud was never envisioned as complete. What would justify a claim that the age of interpretation is over? Marriage laws are a particularly good example. Reforms were periodically proposed over the centuries, all of them motivated by a desire on the part of rabbis to improve the situation of women in marriage and in divorce. The reforms being suggested today fit into this context, yet the pretext of the finished state of halakhic discourse has been raised as an obstacle to the urgent quest to ameliorate the unnecessary injustice of the *agunah* (woman chained to a dead marriage). Just as Qur'an 4:34 focuses the minds of Muslim feminists, the divorce issue is a common denominator that focuses the minds of Jewish feminists.

R. Samuel Eliezer Edels (Maharsha)[75] ended many of his commentaries with the word "*vadok*" (look into it), meaning that the last word on the text in question had not been uttered, and more investigation might yield a different, if equally provisional, conclusion. The gates of interpretation have never been shut, though no new commentary on the whole Talmud has been offered in several generations. Exegesis proceeded for thousands of years despite turmoil, war, and exile, so there is no reason why it should not continue with contemporary scholars, continuing the direct line transmitted to Moses, then to the leaders of the generations, the heads of the academies, the heads of the exile, and the members of the Sanhedrin. Maimonides accepted that laws developed over time, based on a process that began at Sinai. According to Maimonides, the three important exegetical principles of the halakhic process were established by G-d:

1. Not everything has been written down. There is a process of unfolding that reaches back to Sinai.
2. Rabbinic authority is essential to the process and Moses was the first rabbi. (Here, Maimonides is using the word rabbi in its meaning as teacher, not as it is frequently used today to denote a male leader of a congregation. This rule speaks to the issue of credentials and expertise, which in his world, would have been limited to men. Would he find a role for erudite and pious women in communal leadership today?)
3. Human involvement is essential to the development and transmission of the law. Laws are determined through the application of hermeneutical principles and logical methods, otherwise, circumstances would have left the law silent on new developments. "G-d takes the dramatic, revolutionary step of handing divine law over to man for interpretation and application. Using rules of study rabbis are entrusted with the analysis of the text and the laws."[76]

What about the inevitable conflicting opinions? How do we know which opinion is correct? The astounding claim that "these and these are the words of the living G-d" held that conflicting opinions can both be true.[77] This suggests that once the Torah is given over to humans, contradictory answers are not only inevitable, but potentially correct. Does this elevate the rabbi above Torah? Is truth within the halakhic process determined by loyalty to the process itself? The methodology of interpretation contains a principle similar to the Islamic concept of *ijma* (consensus), in which the majority opinion rules. Deference to the majority may be expedient, but it is not a very reliable indicator of the truth. Even when the majority produces an erroneous assessment[78] the error may be outweighed by the benefit of having authorities able to make halakhic decisions. Could G-d possibly approve of such hubris?

The Gemarah (Bava Metzia) relates a remarkable tale involving a debate among great sages. Rabbi Eliezer was being challenged by his colleagues for a lenient ruling of which they disapproved. Rabbi Eliezer called for support from heaven. First he asked that if his interpretation was correct, let this carob tree move from its place, which it did. Having failed to convince his opponents with this dramatic sign from above, he asked that the water in the canal flow in reverse, which it proceeded to do. His opponents similarly rejected this as proof, and so Rabbi Eliezer asked the walls of the study hall to collapse if heaven approved of his position. Immediately Rabbi Yehoshua rebuked the walls saying to them "if rabbis vie with one another over Torah laws, what business is it of yours?" In deference to Rabbi Yehoshua, the walls did not fall, but in deference to Rabbi Eliezer, they did not resume their normal posture. Rabbi Eliezer than said, "if the Halakha accords with me, let Heaven prove it" and a response was heard, "what argument do you have with Rabbi Eliezer whom Halakha follows in all places?" At this Rabbi Yehoshua stood up and answered, "The Torah is not in Heaven," because it had been given into the hands of man at Sinai. It is then recorded that one of the sages later met Elijah the Prophet and asked him what had been G-d's response to R. Yehoshua's declaration. Elijah reported that G-d had laughed and remarked that "my children have prevailed over me."

One of the lessons of the anecdote is that G-d allowed contradictory individual opinion, majority opinion, and even erroneous opinion (not to mention chutzpah) to stand, signaling that Torah was now in human hands and open to human interpretation. This anecdote is related by men and involved only men. Nonetheless, this tale provides an opening for feminist scholars. If the transmission and exegesis of texts is still ongoing and human intelligence is adequate to the task, the work of the sages is not complete. The debate about whether humans have divinely-granted authority to interpret and whether the Torah is intended to be reinterpreted in each era seems to be resolved in the affirmative.

If G-d is not a misogynist, how did the domination of the female by the male come to be prevalent in the Orthodox Jewish worldview? The three renditions in Torah (Genesis) of the creation of humans are suggestive of simultaneous creation of an Adam who is originally an androgyne. Torah is full of powerful and assertive women. Midrashic and Kabbalist texts emphasize the intense spiritual contribution of the feminine principle from creation to the ultimate redemption of humanity. It is in Talmud that the idea of Eve's guilt and the punishment takes shape. When critics want to illustrate the irredeemably patriarchal nature of Orthodox Judaism, they invariably refer to the ancient, troubling passage in the *siddur* (prayer book) that is recited daily during morning prayers. In it women give gratitude to G-d for "making them as they are" while men give gratitude to G-d for not making them women. In isolation, this prayer would seem to be damning evidence against women's rights, especially the contemporary model of liberalism with its focus on individual rights and gender equality. Against this standard, these exemptions from obligations appear to be exclusions from the enjoyment of rights. These exclusions, in turn seem to put women in a category with slaves, the disabled, and minors, who are excluded from the performance of certain mitzvot. Many Biblical exclusions were based on some sort of incapacity or deficiency, including "the deaf, the imbecile, men with defective facial characteristics, genitals, and those with, *tsara* [skin diseases often mistranslated as leprosy]." Boys can become men, slaves (male) can become free, sick people can be cured, but women remain women, which leads Baskin to read woman as a category of permanent disability, much in the way that Aristotle saw women as defective men.[79]

However, almost all of the 613 mitzvot are incumbent upon both men and women. In a duty-based religion refracted through contemporary rights-based individualism, women's exclusion from a mitzvah is troubling because mitzvah is misunderstood as a right rather than an obligation. Being excluded from a universally applicable right is correctly interpreted as an offense against human equality and dignity. Yet obligations, particularly time-bound performances, may exclude any man or woman who is not available when the mitzvah is required. The Chabad Chassidic interpretation of the blessing in which man thanks G-d for creating him a man, is actually an acknowledgment that G-d imposes upon men an extra burden of public prayer as a form of discipline to bring men closer to G-d, for which they must be grateful rather than resentful. Women are excused, not only because of their time-bound duties to children, but because they do not require the strict discipline and watchful eye of the public in order to cleave to G-d. These exclusions are not necessarily prohibitions. Women are free to commit to daily attendance at the synagogue, daily Torah or Talmud study, and daily donning of tefillin. The prohibition is against committing to the performance of a mitzvah or taking any vow which one is not able to consistently fulfill. For this reason, the majority of Orthodox feminists do not read this blessing as paradigmatic of Judaism's irremediable misogyny.

Baskin finds the greatest support for the claim of misogyny in Talmudic and *Midrashic* (non-legal, informal texts) portrayals of women. She finds that the construction of female otherness has an overwhelmingly negative tone, which not only sets women apart but justifies their exclusion from public life, not merely on the basis of their intellectual inferiority but because of their suspect morality and unbridled sensuality. What do we make of Ben Sira's claim, "from women, sin had its beginning, and because of her we all die"[80] or "better is the wickedness of man than a woman who does good; it is a woman who brings shame and disgrace."[81] Scholars such as Ross Shepard Kraemer and Bernadette Brooten[82] demonstrate that the views expressed by some rabbis did not necessarily conform to prevailing popular norms. The many recorded instances of women's participation in public and religious life raise the possibility that the rabbis of that era may have constructed this putative subservience as a backlash against practical reality.

Talmudic scholars drew upon Torah, if selectively and out of context, to demonstrate that the daughters of Zion are vain, have roving eyes, and, in counterpoint to their virtues, even the mothers had feminine flaws: "Sarah listened at the entrance of the tent," "Leah was envious of her sister," "Rachel stole her father's household G-ds," and "Dinah went out to visit the daughters of the land," for which she was subsequently raped by the prince of Shechem.[83] Her rape is explained in terms of her resemblance to her mother Leah, who had brazenly gone out to confront her husband Jacob. The covenant between Israel and G-d is likened to a husband and wife. Israel is the bride who followed her bridegroom into the wilderness, strayed like an unchaste wife, and then returns once again. The unflattering construction of the fallen woman provides a justification for patriarchy according to Boyarin. Talmudic sages reconstructed the three specifically feminine and empowering commandments as three eternal punishments (niddah, challah, candles).[84] Menstruation is viewed as a punishment for costing Adam eternal life, candles are to rekindle to light of holiness that she extinguished for Adam, and the like.[85] The view of menstruation as a punishment was prevalent in folk culture of Jews and other cultures. These prohibitions reflect cultural prejudices, and, in the context of the Torah portion, also cover other conditions that create a state of ritual impurity for both men and women. (Many observant men make weekly, if not daily, trips to the mikvah for purification. If the Torah expresses distaste for bodily fluids, it is certainly not limited to menstrual blood.) It was asserted in Talmudic discourse that women receive ten curses as punishment for Eve's transgression, of which the following are the last three according to this Midrash: "She is wrapped up like a mourner, she is banished from the company of all men, and confined within a prison."[86]

Repenting for Being a Woman

The ideal woman who emerges in Talmudic depictions must repent her nature by embodying the trait of *tsniut* (modesty), an umbrella for many traits pertaining to hair covering, clothing, voice, walk, inwardness, domesticity, discretion bordering on silence, passivity, and subservience to her husband in repentance for her harm to generic man. It permits a rereading of the principle of modesty, which actually applies to both men and women, into a gender-specific justification for the seclusion of women in the private realm.[87] This is reinforced by the interpretation of a line in Psalm 45:13: "All of the glory of the king's daughter is within," which is taken as G-d's will that women should remain in the inner confines of their father's or husband's house and go about in public as little as possible. Ancients and modern men seem to share a peculiar anxiety about women and sexuality, a simultaneous attraction and repulsion. Women can be the of cause individual and social depravity, even when their actual comportment is blameless. Their mere presence can create irresistible temptation, even without intention or consciousness of their influence. Restricting women to the private realm is not based solely on oft-cited fear that they will neglect their household duties, but that they will be a negative influence in the public sphere. Restriction to the private realm has a dual purpose—to serve the family by her presence and to preserve social order by her absence. This attitude is also found in the Islamic claims about women introducing *fitna* (chaos) into the world. Both religions find adherents who justify female seclusion not in terms of provocative behavior of women but in terms of their mere presence. Women exude innate seductive powers that men are not responsible for resisting and can only be disarmed by keeping women under strict supervision.

Yet there is no mention of obedience or seclusion in the Jewish marriage contract. The *kettubah* (Jewish marriage contract; B. Kiddushin) outlines ten obligations of the husband that make it clear that marriage was envisioned as comfort and companionship, support and love, and improvement of character. Talmudic rabbis spoke with great solicitude and respect about women in their lives. The *kettubah*, however, does not innumerate the duties owed by the wife to her husband. Either she had no corollary duties or her duties were so well known that they did not need to be written. Men could divorce their wives, and there was much rabbinic debate about what constituted just cause. The trend from the first century CE onward with respect to modifying marriage and divorce laws was always to strengthen women's rights by encumbering a man's ability to divorce capriciously.

In both Judaism and Islam, marriage is contractual, not sacramental, though it is a blessed and natural state, designed to secure companionship, mutual support, and joy, in addition to children. R. Hanina said, "All the days of a poor man are wretched [referring to the man with a bad wife] but contentment is a feast without end [referring to the man with a good wife]."[88] "He who has found a wife has found happiness."[89] But "mercy upon the man whose wife is a *moredet* [rebellious wife]." The text is unclear about what constitutes her rebelliousness. The balance between positive and negative references to women and wives favors the positive. It would be appealing to dismiss the negative on grounds of cultural context, personalities of the commentators, influences from neighboring cultures, or the comparatively good treatment of women compared to the treatment of women in surrounding communities. But some of these troubling passages simply cannot be dismissed. We might regard the offending passages as misinterpretations or representative of the commentators' character or social context. This debate must remain inconclusive, as rabbis wrote most of what we know about women from the era. We do know that in the wider world, Jewish and gentile, there were traditions of women's autonomy, communal leadership, and religious participation as well as subservience.[90] The real question is whether we must be guided today by male musings from earlier generations.

Progressive Judaism

Orthodox Judaism is no more of a monolith than is Islam. There is no unitary response to feminism. Orthodox Judaism is sometimes divided into Haredi (ultra Orthodox) and Dati (modern Orthodox). These groups differ in doctrine and attitudes toward the modern world, reflecting their different historical responses to the Enlightenment, citizenship in secular, liberal states, the creation and status of Israel, and women's roles. What they share is the hallmark of Orthodox Judaism: the divine origin of Torah and the centrality of halakha as codified through the generations. The differences have less to do with doctrine than with *minhag* or *hashkafa* (practice and customs of different communities). Modern Orthodoxy attempts to bridge religious and secular life for both male and female adherents. Modern Orthodox Jews are typically involved in public life and professions. Modern Orthodoxy registers the disparity between women's public roles and achievements and their more restrictive roles in their religious communities. While there is a great deal of variation among modern Orthodox communities as to how they distribute roles, the issue is salient and discussions ongoing.

Historian Jonathan Sarna regards Orthodox Judaism as the "great success story of late 20th-century American Judaism."[91] Despite predictions that Orthodoxy could not retain its grip in the face of the seductive secular culture, Orthodoxy has been tenacious and is experiencing a renewal.[92] Some scholars identify what they see as a trend toward "Haredization." While this trend would be seen as a step backward for gender equality, one branch of the Haredi community, Lubavitcher (Chabad) Chassidim, have a novel perspective on women's roles. The founder of Chassidism, Israel Ba'al Shem Tov (born in 1699 or 1700), countered the hyper-intellectualism and elitism of prevailing Judaism by introducing joy, emotion, and *devekus* (personal cleaving to G-d) into Jewish observance. He also revived interest in the hidden inner meaning of Torah found in Kabbalistic texts. The significance of this for feminists is profound. If an exegete assumes that there are deeper meanings beneath the words of Torah, it allows one to interrogate the text and delve beneath the apparent meaning of the component words. It allows one to take into account context and symbolism. In searching beyond the revealed or apparent meaning, Chabad scholars, most notably the Rebbe Menachem Mendel Schneerson (z"l), have been able to reconcile some of the more controversial passages involving women.

This permits Chabad feminist Sara Esther Crispe[93] to argue that we have reason to doubt any interpretation when it is insulting or demeaning toward women. She also contends, "The majority of statements which appear to negate the importance or power of women . . . often are due to being read literally, with the simple translation leaving out the esoteric and deep underpinnings." Revealing a deeper, mystical meaning in the text is an interpretive method used by Chassidic scholars who hold that there are *nistar* (hidden) and multiple dimensions in the texts. Lubavitcher or Chabad Chassidim reject apparent misogyny in the texts and search for the deeper woman-friendly meaning beneath the words. The ambiguity of the Chabad position on women lies not in the wording but the temporal application. Does this feminine principle apply in concrete and practical ways to the daily lives of modern women or is this an ideal associated with the post-Messianic future?

The Feminist Agenda

In addition to the recovery of the right and the skills of exegesis, Muslim and Jewish feminists are actively engaged in several policy initiatives that are intended to create a practical reality of gender equality. For both Muslim and Jewish women, family or personal status law is crucially connected to gender equality and justice. Feminists of faith use their citizenship rights as leverage against intransigent religious authorities. The issue of a male-dominated prayer space is an additional agenda items shared by both Muslim and Jewish feminists.

Prayer Space, the Architecture of Exclusion, and the Mosque Movement

The issue of women's near exclusion from public prayer is a significant one for Muslim women outside of the Arab Middle East. (Many Arab women do not attend mosque except on major holidays and have not made this a central agenda item.) But in Asia, South Africa, Europe, Australia, and the United States, the architecture of prayer spaces has been challenged. Muslim women call on authoritative injunctions such as "Do not stop the maid-servants of Allah from going to the mosques of Allah."[94] Earliest history suggests that women prayed in the mosque and may have also led prayer. In the mosque of the Prophet in Medina, men and women have always prayed together, and face coverings are prohibited. This, ironically, has caused some Saudi families to avoid the hajj altogether because of gender mixing. In Morgantown, West Virginia, journalist and Professor Asra Nomani raised eyebrows by entering the mosque by the front door and taking her place in the main prayer space. Now in her mosque, women can not only pray in the same prayer space but can run for elected office and hold leadership positions in the community. The incident in which an eighteen-year-old girl in a conservative northern town on India's Independence Day (August 15) prayed in the mosque was apparently inspirational. The next day one hundred and fifty other women followed her example. The mosques in Delhi and Calcutta have since seen many women offering *namaz* (prayers). Challenges such as these to the status quo are beginning to proliferate and CAIR, one of the major national Muslim organizations in the United States, has gone on record supporting inclusive mosques.[95] Women and their supporters are holding firm to their belief that "gender equality is central to Islam. The prohibitions arose only among Muslims who apply the most restrictive interpretations and adopt archaic positions."[96]

Most Orthodox Jewish feminists accept, even value, separate prayer space but insist that their space permit them to see and hear. Traditional synagogues were constructed so as to eliminate the distraction that women can create for men at prayer and vice versa. The architecture of prayer space often left women struggling to follow the service. In mosques, the architecture may not be conducive to women's spiritual involvement. In some smaller mosques women may be told that they cannot be admitted due to space constraints, or they may be given some small sequestered space out of hearing or sight of the service. The rationale behind removing women from the sight of men in both Islam and Judaism was to protect women's modesty and protect men from distraction. While one can well understand why having women in the front row prostrating themselves would be embarrassing to both the Muslim man and woman, there are several options when it comes to constructing a prayer space that would allow women to participate without such problems. For instance, in Orthodox synagogues there are many variations on the styles and materials used in the construction of the *mehitsa* (partition) that conform to the principle of gender-segregated prayer while allowing women to participate more fully.

In Jerusalem, the controversial group, Women of the Wall, continues their attempt to gain the right to conduct prayer using the Torah in the women's section of the Western Wall. Each time they gather, usually on *Rosh Chodesh* (the new moon that marks the beginning of the month in the Hebrew calendar), which has traditionally been a day of particular importance to Jewish women, they are met with derision and often violence from Orthodox men and sometimes women. Attempts to gather followed by dispersion by the police have become something of a monthly tradition.

Communal Leadership

The demand for positions of communal leadership is a natural response to the disparity between women's public professional and academic accomplishments and their exclusion from similar roles in their religions. Some women find it insulting to have their spiritual commitment and intellectual competence challenged, especially when it is based on the claim of female inferiority.

Qur'an permits women to lead other women in prayer, and some claim, to lead men, as well. In South Africa and in London, American professor and imama, Amina Wadud, led Friday prayers. In March 2005, now in New York, Amina Wadud, though supported by one hundred and fifty activists, was refused permission by three mosques to lead mixed prayer. She officiated, instead, in prayer space offered by the Cathedral of Saint John the Divine. Though applauded by many, Wadud's actions nonetheless caused an immediate and vociferous backlash. Fatwas were issued across the Muslim world, as were death threats. The event crystallized the issue of women's rights, and it continues to generate intense worldwide debate. Many women consider the articles, blogs, and book devoted to the dialogue as a positive response, regardless of the positions taken by their authors.

Umm Yasmin of the Centre for Muslim Minorities and Islam Policy Studies at Monash University, Australia, defines a Muslim feminist as "one who adopts a worldview in which Islam can be contextualized and reinterpreted in order to promote concepts of equality and equity between men and women; yes and for whom freedom of choice plays an important part in expression of faith."[97] For her, "This is the issue at the heart of the women led Friday prayer controversy and until that prejudice is erased, women will never experience or enjoy the 'unprecedented rights' that Islam once granted them long ago."[98]

Orthodox Jewish women who call for full-blown, official rabbinical ordination for women are a still a minority, though Reform and Conservative Jews have been ordaining women rabbis for years. Among the Orthodox, there is no specific prohibition against women serving as rabbis, but the traditional reference to "dignity of the community" or the "modesty of women" is seen as sufficient to prohibit women from leading prayer for a mixed congregation. A workable option for some Orthodox Jews is for women-only prayer and study groups that would permit them to read directly from the Torah in each other's presence. New roles for women that mirror many functions of the congregational rabbi have been created. These measures are intended to heighten women's spiritual life, not to usurp roles specified for men under religious law. The Jewish Orthodox Feminist Alliance (JOFA) has focused on women's education with the goal of empowering women as lay leaders. The group became embroiled in the controversy over the conferral of religious leadership status on women. They have particularly rallied behind Sara Hurwitz, who has been designated as rabba, having completed the equivalent of rabbinical studies and passed the rigorous examinations. JOFA members see as inevitable the move toward women as full-fledged spiritual leaders and devoted a great deal of attention to this issue at their March 2010 conference in New York. While JOFA is optimistic that women are on a path toward full rabbinic ordination, many Orthodox Jews regard this prospect with alarm, seeing titles for women as just the narrow edge of the wedge. The RCA (Rabbinical Council of America), the largest organization of Orthodox rabbis, met behind closed doors with no press admitted in order reach a consensus statement for publication at the conclusion of their April 2010 convention. JOFA, just prior to the convention, issued its own statement to the RCA and campaigned by email for women to approach their own rabbis on the subject of ordination for women. The vague resolution fell far short of satisfying JOFA's ideal, but nonetheless acknowledged that the expanding educational attainments and quest for commensurate roles could not be ignored.[99] RCA's announced its commitment to women's Torah education and scholarship at the highest levels."[100] While the RCA's consensus resolution was wishy-washy, it still produced a backlash. Rav Hershel Schachter, Torah scholar and leading figure at Yeshiva University, offered the most vociferous and strident comments. He denounced the ordination of women as rabbis as a violation of halakha, and as falling under the ancient and narrowly defined category of *Yehareg Ve-al Ya'avor* (behaviors or actions that one should sooner be killed than engage in). While this was probably intended as a rhetorical flourish, he represented a powerful category of rabbis for whom the ordination of women is and always will be out of the question.

Rabbi Lopatin noted that Rav Schachter invoked the ruling of his rebbe, Rav Yosef Dov Soloveitchik, that it was "halakhically impermissible for a woman to be a rabbi." Many of the speakers at the convention, some of whom are poskim, halakhic decisors such as Rav Schachter, disagreed with this understanding of Jewish law. Even Rav Schachter, to the best of my understanding, is in favor of women's Torah learning and teaching on the communal level; everyone at the convention, including Rav Schachter, would agree with Rabbi Held's view that "one of the crucial mandates of the hour is to create more opportunities and contexts [within halacha education] for women's voices to be heard in Jewish life."[101]

Decades ago Rabbi Joseph Soloveitchik embraced secular studies, especially science, women's learning, and Zionism, in the face of criticism from many traditionalists. Many of his views, controversial when presented, are now widely accepted, keeping alive the potential for a continuing progressive dynamic.

Public Roles and Political Leadership

In Western democracies and in Israel and Kuwait, women eventually won the right to hold elective or appointed governmental positions. Some Muslim states permit and even encourage women to take public offices and political roles. Others prohibit this. In her research on Islam and women's political participation in Kuwait, Khadijah al-Mahmeed concludes that Islam does not forbid the political participation of women.[102] As a devout Shi'a feminist, she shares many principles with Islamists. For Instance, she hopes ultimately to see the establishment of a caliphate, but one with democratic overtones. She is also a staunch defender of women's political rights, asserting that "Women demand political rights but do not want to violate Shari'a."[103] She analyzed three major Islamic schools of thought: liberal Islamic school, Salafi school, and Muslim Brotherhood against her understanding of Islam to determine whether Islam prohibits women's political participation. She found that Kuwaiti liberals do not necessarily link women's political rights to Islam while Salafis prohibit women from all political roles and rights. The Muslim Brotherhood contends that Islam permits women to exercise all political rights and roles with the exception of leadership of the state.[104]

Most jurists agree that women lost their distinct political role after the early Islamic era due to environmental, political, and social factors, as well as to a narrow understanding and wrong interpretations of the Qur'anic verses. Sunnis tend to emphasize women's duties to the family. Shi'a balance woman's contributions to the community and to the family. The Islamic juristic schools differ in methodology, use of science, and inference from the texts. Most Sunnis accept the *ahadith* on female deficiency, while most Shi'a do not. They also differ in manner in which they check the authenticity of a hadith. Both use deduction and analogy from evidence in different directions: Sunni to oppose women's political role and Shi'a to accept it. Shi'a are approving of quick moves to get women into politics, while Sunnis are opposed. The trend is toward greater acceptance of women's political rights. While previously the Salafi school had banned all political roles, many contemporary jurists now approve of some posts. Also the Muslim Brotherhood has changed from disapproval to approval. The Salafi school published its support for a woman's right to nominate and vote, relying on general texts of Islamic shari'a and opinions of contemporary scholars.[105]

Al-Mahmeed's results reveal that contemporary Islamic juristic opinion responds to the social environment and is increasingly congruent with women's political rights based on Islamic evidence from Qur'an and Sunnah. The arguments forbidding women to participate in politics seems to hang on one hadith. In it the Prophet responded to news that the daughter of Kisar, king of Persia had taken power as queen, saying, "Those who entrust their affairs to a woman will never know prosperity."[106] Accordingly, the Muslim Brotherhood prohibits rulership or elective office for women, but allows voting rights within the confines of Muslim morals and behavior.

The variety of contradictory interpretations of the same text, according to al-Mahmeed, is the result of the piecemeal and selective use of evidence. It is also the result of confusing tradition with religion.[107] For instance, in a 1995 survey, 84.1 percent of the students at the College of Shari'a and Islamic Studies, Kuwait University, opposed granting women the right to be elected and 81.7 percent justified their view on grounds that it conflicted with cultural traditions. Salafis use the *ahadith* that states "women are of deficient mind and religion" to deduce that women are unsuited to political life.[108] According to al-Mahmeed, this is a faulty deduction from a questionable hadith. She argues for the inclusion of women in political life[109] and that while the constitution in Islam is shari'a, G-d is the guarantor of human rights.

Al-Mahmeed does not see any reason in Islam to bar women from these rights and responsibilities. She argues that women are not precluded from political activism by the Islamic sources that enjoin women to stay in the home, not to display themselves, and to submit to male guardianship because of supposed male superiority. Al-Mahmeed finds no textual evidence within the parameters of Islamic dress and behavior barring women from public life. She represents a minority voice among feminists in her desire to instantiate a caliphate as well as her confidence that Islamists are amenable to women's political equality. She should not be dismissed. If reform comes to the unwavering Salafi and the Muslim Brotherhood, it will be because of women such as al-Mahmeed, working from within, wielding the credentials of a believer and scholar.

Orthodox Jewish Women in Israel, Europe, and North America face no overt religious prohibitions regarding political and public roles, and many Orthodox women have held a range of elected and appointed political positions. Orthodox women have made their way into all professions in Israel, Europe, and North America. Therefore, Jewish feminists are more focused on issues within the community of believers such as the elimination of the *agunah* (chained woman) status and the expansion of women's education and communal offices.

Orthodox Jewish feminists have been active on many fronts, from offering women's prayers and creating women's prayer groups, to producing scholarly treatises on religious subjects. They are taking on new roles that were hitherto reserved for men, whether it is as congregational leaders and consultants or as kashrut supervisors. But no issue evokes more passion than the problem of the *agunah*, a problem limited to the Orthodox community because other denominations have settled on remedies that many Orthodox Jews regard as non-halakhic. For Orthodox Jews, dismissing inconvenient halakha is not an option even when it creates injustices; it must be reformed within halakhic parameters. Even though relatively few women have been *agunah*, the issue crystallized all of the ills attributed to misogyny rather than Torah properly understood and applied. The Jewish Orthodox Feminist Alliance (JOFA), along with similarly oriented groups in North America and

Israel, has been in the forefront of attempts to remedy this problem. More rabbis are directing brides and grooms to the prepared versions of prenuptial agreements now available on websites such as JOFA's and the RCA's. And more states in the United States are willing to enforce such prenuptial agreements under civil contract law. This topic will be discussed more fully in the chapters on Israel and the United States.

❧ Both Jewish and Muslim women believe they can demonstrate that Muslim and Jewish women had more freedom, equality, access to public life, scholarship, and leadership roles in the past than now. There is no reason to uphold unjust practices in the name of piety. Recapturing the promise of gender justice embedded in Judaism and Islam is an ongoing struggle. Essential to this endeavor are the emerging feminist scholars who are mastering exegesis and thereby highlighting the textual sources that affirm the equality of humans. Prominent Jewish and Muslim exegetes claim that revelation is ongoing, the foundational texts are flexible and responsive to cultural context and historical circumstances, and that G-d cannot be unjust, specifically, cannot prefer one sex over the other. This is likely to be a protracted struggle. Evidence of a backlash against greater gender equality is palpable and is likely to increase in tandem with every forward step that women take. Regardless, Jewish and Muslim women will continue to pose their simple question: Why privilege a degrading interpretation over an available just interpretation?

3 Kuwait

MONARCHY, THEOCRACY, AND DEMOCRACY

Situated at the intersection of politics, identity, gender, religion, citizenship, and human rights, women are the best test of the emancipatory power of citizenship. Kuwait's commitment to democracy and civil rights is being tested by its women citizens with mixed results. The development of feminist activists' political strategies and agendas must be framed within supranational, national, and sub-national contexts. In a country in which the theological is political and women are at the center of national and religious identity politics, Kuwaiti feminists must confront both religious and political authority in order to achieve their goal of full and equal citizenship. The constitution grants women full and equal citizenship, but in order to appease religious authorities, the courts and the government simultaneously upheld the election law that prohibited women from voting until 2005.

What impact will women's suffrage have on women's lives? Kuwaiti feminists range across the political and religious spectrum from Islamist to liberal. Islamist feminist activists see the vote as empowering, as do liberal or progressive feminist activists. But Islamists intend to use their votes to secure an ordered society eventually governed by shari'a, in which women and men will have different, rather than equal, responsibilities, while fulfilling their duties to G-d, family, and society. Progressive feminists see their vote as a means of achieving the unfulfilled promise of the constitution, civil equality of men and women in all areas of law and life. Yet most Kuwaiti women are unlikely to use their votes to upend or radically challenge social and religious norms.

Women in Kuwaiti Political Life

The May 2009 elections, which put four women in the National Assembly for the first time, took everyone including the candidates by surprise. With

Islamists dominating the Parliament since 1992 and coming on the heels of the 2008 election, which produced another Islamist majority in the National Assembly, it seemed unlikely that a woman could be elected. Frequent elections are common in Kuwait and these four women could find themselves voted out in short order, but there is no minimizing the significance of their feat. Kuwait, like several Gulf States, has seen women appointed to ministerial or other government positions. Freedom House has rated Kuwait as "partly free" and finds that Kuwaiti women enjoy the second highest degree of freedom in the Gulf Arab countries, second only to Bahrain.[1] The novelty of this election is that women were democratically elected without resorting to a quota system (which had been vociferously debated by Kuwaiti feminists), meaning that a substantial portion of the voting public has ratified the idea of women representatives. But before the newly elected MPs could take their seats in Parliament, they experienced a setback at the hands of their Islamist opponents, who invoked the condition attached to the 2005 election law, requiring that all women voters, candidates, and officials cover their heads in accordance with shari'a. Two of the women MPs covered their heads and two, plus the education minister, did not. In response, Rola Dashti, one of the four women elected, submitted an amendment to the election law that sought to revoke the provision. She claimed, "The fatwa is not binding. . . . The only reference for us is the constitution. . . . Including Shari'a regulations in the electoral law is a breach of the constitution. . . . The regulations clearly violate articles in the constitution which call for gender equality and make no reference to Shari'a regulations."[2]

The matter is still unresolved but women see it for what it is—a diversionary tactic by opponents of women in politics. MP Maasouma Mubarak understands the goal of the opposition, which is to make it appear that the newly elected legislators are incapable of getting down to the business of introducing women-friendly legislation. "The question they pose is, 'what have you done so far? You have not participated in bettering the situation; you have failed.'"[3] Yet, Rola Dashti already sees a positive impact on Parliament and Kuwaiti politics created by the four newly elected women MPs. They have learned the ropes and have become active on a range of committees including finance, health, foreign affairs, education, social affairs, and labor. Dashti says, "men have started complaining that 'you women are taking over the committees.'" Dashti claims that "women members have also brought discipline to the parliamentary system. We attend committee meetings and do our homework, which embarrasses some of the male members who do not attend. We don't engage in the mutual flattery which is traditional among male parliamentarians."[4]

But the integration of women into political institutions has not been without setbacks, whether they take the form of attempts by Islamist MPs to ban women's longtime participation in sports as un-Islamic[5] or to impede the progress of political, economic, or social reforms. The main tool in the limited arsenal of women activists is being consistently deployed: holding offending laws and religious edicts up to the standard of equality set by the constitution.

The evolving trend is that the Constitutional Court is responding to women's demands that all Kuwaiti law be brought into congruence with constitutional law that upholds women's equal rights. On October 20, 2009, the Supreme Court issued a non-revocable ruling abrogating an article in the 1962 passport law that banned Kuwaiti women from obtaining their own passport without the prior approval of their husband. Female MP Aseel al-Awadhi welcomed the ruling as a victory for democracy, adding that she will work to amend all laws passed by the previous National Assemblies that are in violation of the constitution.[6]

Though the women's movement has the support of the former and current amir, the secular and religious head of state, Kuwait is not really a model of state feminism. Women's rights advocates are locked in battle with democratically elected conservative elements, which are willing to use democratic methods to roll back nearly forty years of hard-fought gains by Kuwaiti women. Citizenship's emancipatory potential was a lever for achieving women's suffrage, but engaging religious opposition and an unconvinced electorate will be paramount if these gains are to become permanent. Especially important will be persuading women voters, whose turnout has remained low and sentiments about women in official positions, mixed.[7] Women activists continue to lobby for broader and more equal participation of women in the labor market, greater cultural and educational opportunities, greater legal equality in access to housing, the right to pass their nationality on to their children and foreign husbands, and greater equality in areas of personal status or family law, social security, pensions, and working hours. Women are still prevented from being judges and from joining the military. Islamists' attempts to make shari'a the basis of legislation have succeeded in passing bills that limit the number of hours women may work and restricting them from working at night. They have also imposed gender segregation in post-secondary education, though this measure has been particularly contentious and not uniformly enforced, in large part because of its financial implications. Equally important is the effort to square equal citizenship of women with shari'a by wresting the interpretive monopoly from men, particularly Islamists. If women thereby find themselves accused of politicizing religion, they can point out that opponents of women's rights have already rendered Islam a political weapon in an ongoing battle to preserve their prerogatives.

It is difficult to characterize the Kuwaiti regime in the usual categories of political science. It is a theocratic democracy, a democratic theocracy, and of course, a hereditary monarchy, in which the head of state and many key political actors are members of the al-Sabah family. The self-perception of the amir may be that he represents a mock-up of the ideal caliphate and Parliament represents the principle of *shurra,* consultation, as laid out in early Islamic texts. Perpetual rule by the al-Sabah family is ensured by the Kuwaiti constitution. The very structure of the regime creates convergence between state and religion, civil law and religious law, and citizenship and personal status law. The construction of civil rights, political rights, and social rights of citizenship has taken place against a backdrop of religious authority, which competes with civil law and has jurisdiction over the precise area that impacts women most, that is personal status law or family law.

Many nations have attempted to merge, blend or create a division of labor between religious and secular authorities. India, Israel, and Nigeria all follow a strategy similar to the Ottoman millet system, in which the state grants near autonomy to religious authorities when it comes to family matters. However, these states govern commercial and criminal matters under civil law. Even liberal democracies that separate religion and state are looking for ways to respond to minority groups that are challenging the state's monopoly over the construction and enforcement of family law. But more often than creating separate and uncontested realms, the policy of granting partial sovereignty results in overlapping sovereignties that only muddy the lines of authority.

Kuwait has a three-tiered judicial system. Personal law, however, which covers marriage, divorce, and inheritance, falls under the aegis of religious law, though handled within the state's court system. Sunni and Shi'a Kuwaitis each have their own family law courts, based on their own schools of shari'a. Unlike the civil and criminal courts, a woman's testimony in family law courts counts for half that of a man's.

The division of authority is complicated by the rising popularity of Islamists, which can be attributed in part to the growing frustration of voters over the tendency of democracy to produce endless gridlock. While corruption has plagued Kuwaiti society since before the introduction of democracy, public opinion suggests that Kuwaitis are likely to lay the blame on public officials rather than operatives in civil society. Many of the Islamist candidates made anti-corruption the centerpiece of their campaign platforms, making good use of the general perception that religious figures are less corruptible. Associated with religious authenticity, Islamists enjoy popularity among many Kuwaitis, even women, who are increasingly donning Islamist-style garb. The flaws of democratic government are exacerbated by the traditional clan and tribal rivalries, personal politics, and the pervasive *wasta*, the Kuwaiti brand of corruption. The National Assembly has the power to grill ministers, and this has become a way for Islamists to bring government to a halt, with the predictable result, the dissolution of the National Assembly and call for new elections by the amir.

Kuwaiti politics is further complicated by the government appearing to be a moderate international political actor, but at the same time appearing as the protector of Islam at home and abroad. This is a difficult task in light of the increasing salience, domestically and globally, of Muslim identity politics and calls for resistance to Western influence and presence. This requires that the government seek alliances with conservative elements, as they lend it needed legitimacy. Women unavoidably find themselves at the center of this conflict, as the delegated standard-bearers of Islam, culture, national independence, and tradition. The government tends to emphasize a republican motherhood model of national development, while the conservative religious elements stress the role of women under shari'a and Islam. The behavior and attire of women becomes a measure of the sanctity, power, and purity of the family, the religion, and the state. This is a big burden for women.

When religion and tradition provide a cultural and legal backdrop, as well as the normative model of human relations, gender will almost always be forced onto center stage. Any challenge to the political, social, economic, and legal structure can be recast as a challenge to religion and G-d. This makes even the most trivial of reforms appear radical—in the true sense of the word—meaning going to the very root and foundation of the divine order, rather than simply challenging patriarchal privilege. Kuwait is a model of the syncretic combination of law, custom, religion, and tradition. That means that "in Muslim societies where shari'a constitutes the framework for family law, the possibility for reform is contingent on a serious and respectful engagement with religious beliefs and practices."[8]

The Kuwaiti state, as a democracy and as an international actor and signatory of major UN rights documents, cannot fail to address the rights deprivations of its citizens. Nor can it follow the path open to liberal states, wherein the government can exonerate itself in two ways: first, by treating religious communities to as voluntary associations in which the presumption is that entrance and exit are freely available to the individual member; and second, by granting partial autonomy to gender-discriminatory groups under the model of multicultural accommodation. Both approaches assume background conditions of free individual choice for women to exit their cultural or religious group, without taking into account that exit may be unrealistic and the costs prohibitive. In Kuwait neither option is possible in that religion and state are completely intertwined. For Kuwaiti women, exit is not an option, nor would most Kuwaiti women choose a secular or alternative religious life if they could. They are no more inclined to repudiate Islam as inherently oppressive than American suffragists in the nineteenth century were to repudiate Christianity.

Two questions arise, one religious and the other political. The right question, as Judith Plaskow said, is theological.[9] Does Islam forbid women's participation as full citizens in the public realm? Another question is political. Does citizenship in the democratic state mediate between women and their religious communities or conversely, does the religious community mediate between the woman and her citizenship status? Which membership has priority, her Kuwaiti citizenship or her ascriptive role as woman in her religious community? I will address the political question first by looking at the supranational, national, and sub-national political forces and actors in the gender rights movement. I will then argue that part of the failure of Kuwaiti women to elect female MPs in either the 2006 or 2008 elections can be attributed in part to a failure to attend adequately to the religious opposition to women's political rights. Without convincingly demonstrating that Islam is compatible with women's rights and demarcating the difference between tradition and religion, interpretation and divine self-revelation, *ahadith* and Qur'an, women may remain stymied in their quest for equality in Kuwait.

Why Kuwait?

Kuwait has many features that make it worthy of note. Freedom House has rated Kuwait as "partly free" and finds that Kuwaiti women enjoy a high degree of freedom in the Gulf Arab countries, second only to Bahrain.[10] It combines elements of modernity with elements of tradition. With a population of just under one million, it has a slight majority of women as both citizens as eligible voters (50.9 percent women and 49.1 percent men).[11] Education is guaranteed to all citizens, male and female, by article 40 of the constitution. Illiteracy rates are low, though not the lowest in the Muslim world: 10.2 percent for women as compared with 2.1 percent for males. Yet, in terms of academic achievement beyond high school, women surpass men both in terms of percentages and performance. Women constitute about 70 percent of the total student body of Kuwait University. In 2000 a law demanding gender segregation in private post-secondary institutions was passed, but due to the controversy it provoked, had lain dormant until it was announced in 2008 by the then minister of education that it would be implemented. This has revived the controversy between liberal and conservative members of the National Assembly. A similar law was applied to public universities in 1996 and more rigorously enforced because Kuwait has only one public university, making the logistics of implementation less complicated.

Under article 27 of the Labor Law, men and women performing the same tasks in the private sector must be paid the same wages. A similar law applies to the public sector. Economic and labor indicators suggest that women constitute about 40 percent of the workforce distributed in terms of (1) professional and technical, 59.2 percent; (2) executive and clerical, 35.2 percent; (3) service occupations, 13.7 percent. Men predominate in the upper-level and management positions and their salaries reflect this fact. Customs and traditions, as well as law, determine what professions are considered suitable for women. The biggest employer for both men and women is the public sector. The government wage bill has little relationship to productivity. Most positions are overstaffed and heavily subsidized. The expectation of constant wage increases or cost-of-living bonuses is translated into political pressure on the government and seems to be one of the chief political agenda items.[12] If a woman feels that she has been the victim of wage discrimination, she may file a complaint with the administrative court. The effectiveness of the court in such cases is low, with only 42 percent of complaints resolved as of 2010.[13]

Kuwaitis, despite their frustration over the deadlocks and confrontations that democratic governance inevitably creates, are proud of their democracy. Kuwait gets high ratings for democracy and human rights, as well as women's achievements compared to the other Gulf States and is one of only two that have fully elected parliaments in which women have the right to vote and stand for elected office. Kuwait's democracy is both similar to and distinct from the liberal model. The amir is widely respected and admired and is one of democracy's biggest boosters (it was a previous amir who created Kuwaiti democracy after independence from Britain).

The Ottoman Empire ruled what is presently Kuwait as part of Iraqi Basra province from the late-seventeenth to the late-nineteenth centuries, when the Treaty of Protection put Kuwait under British control. Kuwait proclaimed its independence from Britain in 1961, instituting a constitutional monarchy. Its legal system was heavily influenced by Egypt's French-inspired system. Most of Kuwait's commercial and civil laws, codified in the 1960s and promulgated in 1980, were based on Western codes, but personal status and family laws are derived from the Maliki *fiqh* of Sunni shari'a. The Kuwait Code of Personal Status was promulgated in 1984. The status of Islam is stipulated in the constitution, which was adopted on November 11, 1962. Article 2 states, "the religion of the State is Islam, and Islamic Shari'a shall be a *main source of legislation*" (emphasis mine). Article 1 (2) of the Civil Code directs that in the absence of legislative provision, judges are to adjudicate according to custom, and in the absence of applicable custom, according to appropriate principles of Islamic jurisprudence (in this case Maliki *fiqh*). Kuwait has a tri-level court system covering all areas of legal disputes: personal status, civil, commercial, and criminal. Courts of the First Instance have several divisions, including personal status; the High Court has five divisions, including personal status; and, the Supreme Court has of two divisions, High Appeal and Cassation. For ruling on personal status, the courts are divided into three sections: Sunni, Shi'a, and non-Muslim.

Provisions for freedom of expression and freedom of the press exist but can be suspended if deemed necessary. The amir appoints the ministry and many ministers (five in the current government) are members of his family. The prime minister is his nephew, and the important ministries such as security, foreign affairs, and the like, are under family control. The amir has the power to suspend or dissolve the Parliament, which he has done many times, for instance, in both 2008 and 2009, when he perceived a deadlock between government and Parliament. There has been periodic criticism directed at the amir's monopoly over power to make ministerial appointments, and accusations of family in-fighting with politically destructive consequences. The amir has weathered each storm and seems genuinely popular among average Kuwaitis. The constitution ensures that a male member of the al-Sabah family will always hold the reigns of government.

The political structure creates near dual citizenship for Kuwaiti women in their own country: treated equally under civil law but unequally under shari'a. Many strictly observant Muslim women are quite comfortable with the position they occupy in Islam and believe that it confers on women many rights and privileges unavailable to Western women. What many reject is the eliding of religious law and civil law so as to deprive them of political rights. They hold that Islamic law does not prohibit women's participation in public life and politics. They do not want their quest for their political rights to be regarded as a sin in one sphere and a virtue in the other.

So what is the relationship between shari'a and civil law in Kuwait? As in many countries with Muslim minorities or majorities, the government is structured so as to create a division of labor between religious authority and secular authority. In liberal democracies, this grant of power by the state is one of largesse or accommodation. Sometimes power-sharing is the condition of a government's very existence (as seems to be the case with respect to the Wahabis and Saudis). Even if the state does not depend on the religious authority for its survival or stability, it may derive essential legitimacy from religious authority, both in the eyes of its own citizens and in the global Islamic community. The lesson has not been lost on Kuwaitis. There are benefits and costs to alliances, particularly with radical Muslims, or any group whose ultimate agenda may be the dismantling of democracy and monarchy. Kuwait has delicately combined elements of hereditary monarchy with elements of theocracy and elements of democracy. This compromise was necessary in order to secure approval for many aspects of Kuwait's program of economic modernization. The government compromised by delegating control over family law to religious authorities. This trade-off leaves the Kuwaiti government relatively free to pursue its agenda of rapid economic development and partial democracy without interference. But it has done so by sacrificing women citizens, depriving them of full public participation under protection of the law.

The amir was the most important single actor behind the revised election law. Whether his support for women's suffrage was part of a larger political agenda, a reward for the universally recognized heroic role of Kuwait women under Iraqi occupation, or a personally held principle, without the amir's support, the goals of Kuwaiti women might have been stalled indefinitely. Other Muslim leaders have not given in to international or domestic pressure, and it is plausible that the amir could have responded similarly. That he became a champion of women's suffrage, even in the face of opposition from Parliament, Islamists, and civil society, is to his credit. However, there are downsides to having rights granted from above, particularly if the recipients have received them through largess rather than hard work or if these gains fail to percolate throughout civil society.

Kuwaiti women have paid for these grants from above. They have been fighting for rights, though not always in unity, for forty years. To the extent that women have served in official political positions, it has been exclusively through appointment by the amir, not by election. This suggests that opposition to women's political participation is still pervasive. Without grassroots support, women's achievements will be only as durable as the generous will of the amir and his successors. Kuwaiti women, in the aftermath of the recent electoral debacle, will have to evaluate their strategies for the future.

Kuwait combines a strong social traditionalism with an equally strong program of modernization. Kuwait's experience of colonialism under the British was relatively benign and not very disruptive of the existing social fabric, so Kuwait retains strong clan and tribal structures that often define political interests and loyalties. This is an obstacle to social solidarity and the attempt to foster shared national ideals and projects. While Kuwait's population is almost entirely Muslim, it is not free of religious conflict. Sunni Muslims are the vast majority and predominate in the economy and politics. Shi'a constitute between 25 percent and 30 percent of the citizenry, but further religious divisions have become increasingly prominent. The big winners in the 2008 election were the most conservative elements of Kuwait society: Salafi, Muslim Brotherhood, and Bedouin. As a bloc, they now exercise majority control of the Parliament and veto power over proposed liberal reforms.

If liberals and moderates were big losers, the biggest losers were the women candidates who did not even manage to achieve one seat, even though women constitute a slight majority of eligible voters. While this outcome was not unforeseen, an alarming result was that the most recent election replicated social divisions very closely. It is as if proportional representation of all factions was an actual goal, except that women did not count as a faction worthy of representation. Kuwaiti politics are not driven by individual interests, and voting does not typically represent aggregated individual preferences. While political parties are banned, as are electoral primaries, and civil associations of a political nature are closely scrutinized, the government has not been able to prevent bloc voting along traditional group loyalty lines. The recent election was the first conducted under the newly reformed district lines, which combined and reduced the previous twenty-five districts into five districts. The intention was to consolidate districts so as to create in each a more diverse mix of citizens and thereby reduce the salience of tribal or religious affiliations. This did not, as far as post-election analyses reveal, interrupt the tribal, religious, and ideological basis of voter loyalty, though it cost candidates who have formerly engaged in vote-buying a much larger outlay of money. Despite government attempts to ban them, unofficial primaries and pre-election campaigning took place at *diwanyis* (traditional male meeting places) and even in parked cars.

Many women candidates had believed that the redistricting reforms would give them a better chance at success, but for a variety of reasons, if there were benefits, they were not apparent in terms of electoral outcomes. In municipal elections several weeks after parliamentary elections, female voter turnout was stunningly low. This may be evidence of the seeming futility of their efforts in the preceding major election.[14] Kuwait may be headed for more stalemate because the "line-up of Islamists, liberals, Shia and tribesmen was more a reflection of political and social quotas than a programme for the future."[15] Kuwait and Gulf newspapers have expressed dismay, calling the election results a "national frustration government" as in the headline in the newspaper, *Alam Alyawm*. The new government was characterized as being "one of appeasement rather than caliber" by analyst Ayed al-Mannah.[16]

Supranational Norms and Conventions:
The International Human Rights Regime

International human rights organizations and NGOs have put women's rights at the top of their agendas, subsuming them under the umbrella of human rights. The current approach of the UN instrumentalities is to understand discrimination against women as contrary to the dignity of women, and as an obstacle to family wellbeing and national development including human capital, economic prosperity, and the social and cultural life of the community. Comprehensive development can only be achieved with the full unleashing of women's contributions in all fields.

Women's rights abuses have become more visible and women's rights are now seen as an issue of universal consequence, not simply a minor matter of women's issues. The visibility of gender issues in organs of the United Nations has been a boon for Kuwaiti women because it allows them to connect to the global network and to report to concerned agencies domestic laws and norms that conflict with those adhered to, at least in principle, by the member nations of the international community. This includes discrimination against women through personal status law.[17]

Of all of the conventions and congresses, perhaps the most significant as an agenda setter and watchdog over women's rights is The Convention for the Elimination of All Forms of Discrimination against Women (CEDAW 1979). Also known as the women's bill of rights, it defines discrimination against women as "any distinction, exclusion or restriction made on the basis of sex which has the effect or purpose of impairing or nullifying the recognition, enjoyment or exercise by women, irrespective of their marital status, on the basis of equality of men and women, of human rights and fundamental freedoms in the political, economic, social, and cultural, civil, or any other field."[18] Kuwait signed CEDAW in 1994, indicating a willingness to pass legislation that embodies these principles and to annul legislation, laws, norms, and practices that contravene these principles.

But a provision guaranteed by international law, allows states to sign the convention "with reservations," as many Muslim countries, including Kuwait have done. (Of the sixteen states that have not ratified CEDAW ten have majority Muslim populations.[19]) Kuwait entered reservations with respect to article 7, regarding equal voting rights (rescinded in 2005); article 9, paragraph 2, concerning rights of citizenship; article 15, which grants women equality before the law; article 16, which requires states to eliminate discrimination against women with respect to family law, marriage, and family relations; and article 2, which addresses relations in the private sphere—though often invisible, the site of most egregious forms of gender discrimination, particularly violence. The reservations that Kuwait entered all concerned the alleged incompatibility of these articles with shari'a. Kuwait is not unique in this respect.

Arab resistance coalesced around CEDAW and in 1990, the Organization of Islamic States, to which all Muslim countries belong, issued a collective rejoinder to international efforts to establish women's rights in the domestic sphere as human rights. The Cairo Declaration on Human Rights in Islam established that all rights were subject to Islamic law and that when there was a contradiction between international law and shari'a law, the latter would take precedence.[20]

National sovereignty cannot be abridged and the United Nations has no way of enforcing the provisions of the UN Charter, The Universal Declaration of Human Rights, CEDAW and various other covenants on social, political, and economic rights, and other instruments issued by the UN and its specialized agencies. As is the case with all international human rights agreements, to have any import for female citizens of a particular country, the provisions must be translated into domestic law.

This is particularly problematic for women in countries such as Kuwait, in which legal jurisdiction is ambiguous or divided. In the case of personal status law, Islamic laws that govern marriage, divorce, custody, and inheritance are incongruent with article 16 of CEDAW Shiite and Sunni judges will not uphold claims based on the principles of gender equality. If unable to enforce compliance, the international community can provide inducements to comply with international standards of human rights, primarily in the form of public criticism or praise. The Kuwaiti government and press respond to both in a limited way.

The UNDP/UN Resident Coordinator's Annual Report for 2006 made headlines in several Kuwaiti newspapers for praising Kuwait's activities in support of extending political rights to women (May 16, 2005), saying that Kuwait has made more progress than most Gulf nations, that women are well integrated in the work force, and comprise two-thirds of university-level students.[21] Critical reports were taken to heart about the 1996 legislation passed by Islamists in the National Assembly re-segregating all university classes by gender, reversing a government decree that integrated them in 1990. (The movement to re-segregate is still alive, but as of 2010, had not been carried out.) It was noted in the UN report that although women's participation in the labor market has steadily increased, women are prohibited (with the exception of health care) from working between the hours of 8 P.M. and 7 A.M. (This supposedly protective law was passed unanimously by National Assembly on June 11, 2007, but is being hotly contested by women.) The report also noted that women do not enjoy complete legal equality, particularly in personal status law. Women's testimony is given less weight in court proceedings, nationality law permits only the father to transmit citizenship to wife or child, and Kuwait permits discrimination in divorce and inheritance decisions.[22]

Without disputing the importance of international human rights conventions, discourses, and norms, the state is still the central actor because it turns international norms into legislation. In the final analysis, nations provide the most significant context of citizenship. Only the Kuwaiti government can enforce its laws and punish their violations.

National Level: The Constitution, Laws, and Politics of Equal Citizenship

The Kuwaiti constitution recognizes the principle of equality regardless of "race, origin, language, and religion" but makes no specific reference to gender. National laws continue to discriminate against women. With respect to political rights, components of the legal system that pertain include article 80, "the National Assembly (*Majilis Al-Umma*) shall be composed of fifty members elected directly by universal suffrage and secret ballot in accordance with the provisions prescribed by the Electoral Law." With respect to equality, the constitution provides in article 7, "Justice, Liberty, and Equality are pillars of society." Article 29 states, "all people are equal in human dignity," and "all people are to be treated as equals before the law." Additional principles enshrined in article 6 include the commitment to democracy and sovereignty of the people. If sovereignty is understood to reside in the combined citizenry, then logically, the undifferentiated sovereign power must reside in women, as well as men.

The Electoral Law 35/1962 and its first article stipulated that "every Kuwaiti man of 21 full years of age has the right to vote, except for those who have not been Kuwaiti citizens for at least 20 years according to Article 6 of the Amiri Decree no. 15 of 1959 on Kuwaiti citizenship."[23] The text of the original "males only" version of the law was finally amended under law no. 17/2005 to read, "Every Kuwaiti of 21 full years of age has the right to vote, except for those who have not been Kuwaiti citizens for at least 20 years. Article 6 of the Amiri Decree No. 15 of 1959 on Kuwaiti citizenship states, "women must, to vote and stand in elections, abide by the rules and provisions approved by Islamic Shari'a." This troubling clause was not in the bill presented by the government that came before the National Assembly. It was an addition, reflecting a last minute compromise and is ambiguous, at best. It is clearly discriminatory in that it is only applied to women, when presumably all citizens are required to comport themselves in accordance with public order and public morals (article 49). It indicates Kuwait's divergence from the liberal democratic model, by which citizenship represents a relationship between the individual and the state, not between the individual and religious authorities doubling as elected officials. This clause is currently being used in an attempt to discipline the two female MPs who do not cover their heads. (Neither head covering nor *abbaya*, robelike dress, are required by Kuwaiti law.) Many MPs see their majority votes against women's suffrage as exercises in supposed democracy, ignoring that elected representatives exercise their legislative prerogatives within the confines of the constitution, and that article 1 of the Electoral Law and the denial of women's right to vote was in clear violation of the constitution.

Seen in the context of the multicultural accommodation debate the Kuwaiti power-sharing deal with religious authorities might be framed as multicultural sensitivity on the part of the government. But as the US Supreme Court ruled in the case of Kiryas Joel,[24] a grant of even partial authority by the state to a non-state actor, in this case, a religious community, implicates the state in any violation of individual rights by the group. Neutrality is not possible because any actions on the part of the communal authority that violate the constitutional rights of community members in their capacity as national citizens makes the state a party to oppression and seems to confer the imprimatur of the state on the religious authority. As Ayelet Shachar and Susan Moller Okin illustrated, the costs of government accommodation of patriarchal religious communities falls most heavily on its women members.[25] The state must bear the ultimate responsibility for the enforcement of individual rights of its citizens.

Kuwait must ensure that public and private entities act within the confines of the law. For this to happen the division of authority must be clear. Overlapping authorities leave the state potentially subservient to non-state actors when it comes to legislation, adjudication, and enforcement of law. The status quo in Kuwait seems likely to lend itself to instability and impasse.

Social Context

The salient features of Kuwait social life are resistance to change and desire to maintain social order and stability. Kuwait, like most of the Gulf States, is a traditional society. The waning of progressive nationalism in favor of conservative Islamic forces has allowed Islam to be used as a pretext for the denial of women's rights. Tribal and patriarchal authority is pervasive in Kuwait. Many of its families and clans, as well as its religious and cultural institutions, existed largely uninterrupted for generations. Even when oil was discovered, attracting foreign corporations and skilled technicians, Kuwaitis were able to exploit the economic opportunities without disrupting social patterns. Traditional merchant families, who had dominated the fishing and pearling industries, positioned themselves to transition into banking and construction, thus maintaining the family structures that predated the oil boom. The informal alliance that had long existed between the ruling family and the merchant (now financial and trading) class has become a more formalized political alliance. Economic and political powers are conjoined and many members of the National Assembly come from elite families.[26]

The social status of women and their access to education and professional life varies. As in so many patriarchal and traditional societies, an elite stratum of women has attained professional and political status even though such attainments are far from the norm. The attainments of elite women may act as a force consolidating class power rather than encouraging the mobilization of either lower class women or men. Upper-class women may pose less of a threat to upper class men than to men from the lower classes. Filling vacancies in government or the professions with elite women may be more desirable than promoting true social mobility.[27]

Voluntary associations or non-governmental organizations (NGOs) are legal and enjoy freedom of assembly rights, but operate under government supervision, licensing, and funding. They have social and political impact because they face no competition from formal political parties, which are banned in Kuwait. The state is careful to restrict the number and overlap of NGOs, meaning that in the case of women's advocacy, the field has been limited. The state granted official recognition to the Women's Cultural and Social Society (WCSS) and has kept others women's organizations out, perhaps fearing that associations may oppose the government. An independent civil society has been stunted by this requirement. A law passed in

1962 and amended in 1965 still issues licenses to those groups whose activities are confined to social, professional, cultural, entertainment, religious, athletic, and welfare functions.[28] Many charitable organizations that were religiously based permitted women to fund-raise but prohibited them from becoming participating members. Even committees and associations that permitted female membership kept women out of positions of leadership. In the absence of legalized political parties, many organizations have political agendas and involvement in the political arena, if only informally. Excluding women from participation in voluntary associations has effectively excluded them from access to politics.

Meanwhile, under the watchful eye of government, there were signs of trouble from the so-called guests, immigrants who had been expelled by Nasser and were gaining adherents in Kuwait. By the mid-1970s, they achieved some political power. The Muslim Brotherhood was ideological kin with the Salafi movement in Kuwait. Their interest was in establishing a pan-Islamic polity based on shari'a. Competing secular versions of Arab nationalism were dealt a crippling blow by the victory of the Israelis over the combined Arab forces in 1967, heightening the appeal of the Muslim Brotherhood. They received another boost in 1979 when Iran declared itself to be an Islamic nation. The amir perceived their agenda as a threat and undertook to invigorate nationalist and liberal counterforces as a bulwark against political innovation.

This was to evolve into a fateful pattern of playing blocs off against each other. In this case, the government's enemy's enemy was not its friend. It was in this vein that the amir and government granted citizenship, belatedly, to the tribal Bedouins to counter liberal elements. Many Kuwaitis now regret this move and see themselves as paying the price by having empowered a large and very conservative political bloc. In 1981, taking advantage of the opening, the Salafi movement, which strongly resembled the Wahabi movement in Saudi Arabia, began to agitate for a formal return to the original sources: Qur'an, hadith, and shari'a. The Salafi are more radical than the Muslim Brotherhood in that their aspirations include not just political, but extensive social reforms, which in the case of Kuwait, would require a complete retreat from its program of modernization and constitutionalism.

Now increasingly fearful that it had created a monster, the Kuwait government, in preparation for the 1985 elections, began to foster the liberals as counterweights to the Salafi, just as they had fostered the Muslim Brotherhood and Salafi as counterweights to the nationalists and liberals. But the Iraqi invasion and occupation meant that the National Assembly was not restored to operation until well after the defeat and expulsion of the Iraqis in 1991.

The Fight for Equality

Kuwaiti women have a history that differs dramatically from that of Kuwaiti men. In earlier times, many women who were wives of pearl divers and fisherman had to fend for themselves and their children for portions of each year. This has come to be part of Kuwaiti feminists' self-presentation. Though most of the activists that I interviewed did not descend from these independent working women, all of them referred to this heritage, with pride in a Kuwaiti precedent that justifies their current quest for equality.

Women were the eventual beneficiaries of modernization that followed the development of the Burgan oil fields. They were not immune from the demonstration effect of their brothers' increasing educational and professional opportunities, not to mention greater freedom of movement and encounters with foreign ideas. By 1950 newly educated sons of merchants had been exposed to the ideas of Arab intellectuals, many of whom had been educated in Europe and were proponents of *nahda* (progress). They regarded their own countries as backward and promoted a program of nationalism and Western-style education in order to progress toward modernity. Central to their program was the emancipation of women. But the call for emancipation focused on the benefits to the nation of allowing educated women to enter the professional workforce and advance Kuwait's standing among developed countries. Nationalists, not unlike later Islamists, wanted to harness women to the model of republican motherhood without according them independence, political participation, or self-determination.

Kuwaiti men had begun going abroad for their university education because Kuwait did not have a university until 1966. Soon daughters of the merchant class were following their brothers and seeking education both at home and abroad. Women began to protest Kuwait's restrictive employment policy, complaining that they had equal education and skills and should be granted equal employment opportunities.

The logic of employment and educational equality fueled demands for political access. Yet politics was not considered a suitable activity for women. The Kuwaiti understanding of women as essentially (ontologically and biologically) different from men continued to dictate narrow, gender specific roles. Family is defined as the cornerstone of the society, and the mother's role in rearing children, now made more vital because of her own educational attainments, was considered paramount and sacrosanct.

Women's Organizations

The first women's organizations came on the scene soon after Kuwaiti independence. The Cultural and Social Society, which was renamed the Women's Cultural and Social Society (wcss), functions to this day. It evolved from a primarily social club for leisured elite women into a critical actor in the fight for a range of women's rights including suffrage. While still engaged in charitable projects, of which members are duly proud, they have earned their credentials as a women's political and social advocacy group. In meeting with its members in their headquarters, it was clear that they are rightfully proud of their activities and accomplishments. They are now recruiting a new generation of young professional women.

The wcss was, in its earlier days, reluctant to deploy confrontational methods and was not convinced that the vote was attainable or even desirable. An alternative, now defunct organization took up that role. The Arab Women's Development Society (awds) was overtly political and began struggling for women's rights in the early 1970s. They saw the wcss as replicating the prevailing kin and class privileges.

The awds, drawing on a more middle-class membership, brought into sharp focus the contradiction between calls for modernization and emancipation of women and the norm of women's subordination. By the 1970s, they were promoting equal employment, equal rights in divorce and custody, nurseries for working mothers, and the like. In the mid-seventies, the wcss joined the campaign, but in collaboration with the Kuwait government. When the un declared the Decade for Women (1976–1985), the president of the wcss headed Kuwait's delegation. Drawn into the sphere of international human rights, Kuwait would have to respond to world opinion with respect to its women's rights record. But the wcss, while recognizing the need for women's rights, was not ready to push for enfranchisement on the domestic front. It was the awds that brought an equal rights bill before the National Assembly in 1973, attempting to shift the national agenda from modernization and education of women in the national interest, to promoting equal rights for women. Members even attempted to cross class boundaries by setting up lectures for Bedouin women, albeit without much success.

In 1975 the National Assembly was poised to take up two of the issues from the AWDS's proposed bill of rights, gaining suffrage and ending polygamy. Members of the Assembly expressed outrage over this challenge to shari'a. They countered by citing passages from Qur'an and *ahadith* that glorified mothers and wives, essentially denying that Kuwaiti women were in need of emancipation. Women, in their view, had already been given an honored position in Islam, one that accorded with their divinely created nature. The backlash that the activities of the AWDS called forth led to the loss of its official recognition and subsequent dissolution by the government in 1980. The vacuum it left was filled in the 1980s by Islamist women's groups, which emphasized a return to domesticity and Qur'anic values and the overt rejection of feminism as a corrupting and alien import from the West.

Now divisions among Kuwaiti women were not only classed-based, but theological. Prominent female Islamists joined their male counterparts and began their own women's campaign, supported by the imams. In the 1980s the government licensed two Islamic women's organizations, Bayader al-Salam and the Islamic Care Society. The Kuwait government was looking to offset the challenge posed by liberals and nationalists, not yet recognizing that by promoting the re-Islamization of Kuwait, they would soon face a different set of challenges.

The Islamic Care Society (ICS), which was formed after the dissolution of the AWDS, appropriated their building for their own headquarters. The founder of the society was in an unassailable position, being a member of the al-Sabah family and the wife of the crown prince and then prime minister. The objective of the society was to purify and promote Islam across society, though the membership of the ICS was predominantly upper class. The founder and chairwoman, Sheikha Latifa, could count on full support from the government and could draw on government money, as well as her own, in order to fund a religious school, charitable institutions, and Islamic centers. The agenda was distinguished from that of the Muslim Brotherhood, Salafi, and Bayader, in that ICS combined the nationalist patriotism and loyalty to the Kuwait state, with an emphasis on religious devotion. In the ICS, religion and state became mutually supportive, rather than mutually threatening.

But not all religious women could be counted on to oppose women's rights any more than non-religious women could be counted on to support them. While the ICS continued to be a mouthpiece for the government, other Islamist women were demanding their rights, albeit in the context of Islam. Prominent Shia activist Khadijah al-Mahmeed joined forces with the WCSS rather than the Sunni-dominated ICS.

Watershed: The War Helps the Women's
Rights Movement Come of Age

The invasion of Kuwait by Iraq on August 2, 1990, took the government and citizens by surprise. Kuwait was quickly overwhelmed and succumbed to defeat almost without a fight. The government, including the amir and many members of their families fled abroad, a pragmatic decision because there was no question that the Iraqis intended to eliminate symbols of Kuwaiti sovereignty. Many prominent figures and politicians who remained were executed in Kuwait or upon deportation to Iraq. Damage to the infrastructure, property, and lives was enormous. Of the estimated 200,000 Kuwaitis who did not flee the occupation, it was women who came to play the most prominent role in the resistance, becoming known as the steadfast ones.[29] They volunteered in hospitals and schools, scrubbing, cooking, and nursing, even though many of these women had not done such chores at home.

Many men were forced to go into hiding, and women took on the role of resistance, as curriers of weapons, news, medicine, and food for their neighbors and male relatives. Women formed an underground network and, realizing that they were better able to move in public in the traditional *abbaya*, even those women who had previously discarded it or had never worn it, used it to conceal their identity and as a symbol of grief and unity. While the *abbaya* did give them greater freedom of movement (some Kuwaiti men reportedly donned *abbayas* when they went on the streets), many women were still arrested or shot by Iraqi soldiers as they chanted and protested in the streets. The *abbaya* soon became a symbol of resistance. It is authentically Kuwaiti, unlike the increasingly popular *al-zayy-al Islami*, a recent fashion import associated with Muslim conservatism worldwide. Kuwaiti women donned the *abbaya* not in opposition to the West but to express their resistance to the Iraqis. The *abbaya*, the organizational and networking skills, and the determined activism were retained and redeployed in the women's fight for rights after the war.

The resistance to the occupiers was motivated by patriotism, and the nobility of their risks and sacrifices did not go unnoticed. But it did go unrewarded. While the government and men in general recognized and applauded the contribution of Kuwait women to the war effort, they expressed that the need to restore order and stability to the nation would have to take precedent. They implied that order could best be achieved by returning to the status quo ante, meaning traditional gender relations. This made the renewed demand for gender equality look like an unpatriotic, polarizing act of sabotage against the national rebuilding effort.

In May 1999 the amir once again dissolved the National Assembly. While the Assembly was not in session, he issued dozens of decrees, including one giving women both the right to vote and to run for office by 2003. This decree took everyone by surprise, even women's groups. Opponents, many of them Sunni Islamists and their Bedouin supporters, were outraged. The decree was problematic on constitutional grounds, for the constitution declares that only emergency measures can be issued by decree when the Assembly is not in session. This provided opponents with a somewhat principled political argument, but most of the opposition was couched in religious terms. A leader of the Muslim Brotherhood announced that the Qur'an does not demand obedience to political rulers who go against G-d's will,[30] raising the threat of a full-blown breach between civil and religious authority. Opponents accused the Kuwaiti government of bowing to United States pressure in an attempt to fulfill promises made to the allies about post-war democratic reforms. But there was more to the amir's concession than the desire to mollify the United States.

Political motives were behind the amir's decree. If there was a perceived need to check the growing social influence and political power of the Islamists, facing them down over gender issues seemed pivotal. As is so often the case, women were at the center of a tug of war. It was the proclaimed goal of Islamists to secure gender relations firmly under shari'a and religious control. This seemed to both the amir and his religious opponents as good a place as any for the inevitable standoff.

The amir sought to shift the balance in favor of women and liberals. Giving women the vote would expand the electorate and possibly reduce the stranglehold of conservative voting blocs. (Indeed, when Islamists finally came around to accepting the vote for women, they did so in order to become the beneficiaries of what they reckoned would be a double vote for Muslim husbands.) But while conservative men might therefore favor women's votes for this reason, it would be precisely for this reason (the feared conservative numerical advantage) that liberals would oppose it. This was the same strategic calculation behind the earlier debates over whether to enfranchise the staunchly conservative Bedouins. What probably persuaded Shi'a to support the vote for women was the desire to bolster their numbers, as they were a minority in a country where nearly 70 percent were Sunni. This means the decision would be based on considerations about the composition of the electorate rather than a more principled desire for gender justice.

Liberals were no more immune to the benefits of male privilege than their conservative opponents. As Amira El-Azhary Sonbol has noted, "even though there are clear distinctions between the liberals and conservatives in regard to political and economic issues, both have favored more patriarchal interpretations of Islamic laws dealing with what is termed the 'woman problem.' "[31] A favorable vote in the Assembly would only be achieved through the collaboration of Shi'a and liberal members. The strongest opponents were Sunnis, but they soon found themselves in the minority. Even the Muslim Brotherhood, which enjoyed wider support among Kuwaiti women than the official women's organizations or liberals, was a canny enough political actor to see the benefit of expanding its own voting power through women. Tribes and Bedouins have remained fairly steadfast in their opposition, and many complaints to this day have been raised against them for putting obstacles, such as divorce threats, in front of their female relatives' exercise of their political rights. For the Bedouins, politics is still about identity rather than interest.

After this stinging defeat and with warnings of *fitna* (sexually induced chaos) ringing in their ears, a religious woman's voice was desperately needed. This need was answered beautifully by Shi'a scholar Khadijah al-Mahmeed. She brought to bear her erudition and unassailable comportment to demonstrate that the roots of women's political participation could be found in Qur'anic sources, that historically Muslim women had been much more active in public and religious life than they now were, and that the prohibitions against a more active role for women were later overlays contradicting the original intent of Qur'an.

Women's rights activists could now deploy a religious argument in addition to the medley of arguments based on the constitution and international human rights declarations and conventions. They employed strategies reminiscent of Susan B. Anthony's including street demonstrations, lobbying efforts, petitions, lawsuits, and even attempted to enter the polling booths and register as voters. They donned *abbayas* and blue ribbons on which were printed the demand for enforcement of constitutional rights. They designed placards and posters. The wcss invited parliamentarians to speak at their headquarters and to march with them to the National Assembly.

At least eight lawsuits were filed against the Ministry of the Interior for preventing women from registering to vote, alleging the unconstitutionality of article 29, and the provision that restricted the vote to men. In May 2000 the case filed by Rola Dashti (prominent activist and chair, Kuwait Economic Society) was accepted for review by the Constitutional Court, to the jubilation of her comrades. In July Dashti's complaint was dismissed on procedural grounds. The other cases that were filed never advanced. In 2005 the Women Lawyers' Association debated in Parliament. The representative for the women, herself a highly respected lawyer, argued not only points of law, but presented verses from Qur'an to demonstrate that women's rights come from G-d and cannot be abrogated by man. She also challenged the mps to "show me any text in Qur'an or *ahadith* that prohibits women from participating in politics." Her performance in this debate was decidedly a moral victory for women. In 2005, after nearly forty years of determined effort, the right to vote and run for election was theirs. But this was certainly not the end of the struggle.

The first election in which women participated was in 2006 and the second in 2008. Results were decidedly disappointing to those who believed that attaining the vote would immediately rectify gender inequality and lead to women-friendly legislation and reforms. In being interviewed, respondents presented many insights into why women failed to be elected as mps and how strategists would have to respond in the future. Several themes emerged almost universally among the respondents:

1. The need to emphasize gender rights as part of the broader commitment to human rights and Islam. It must be demonstrated that Islam and democracy are compatible and emphasized that women had greater rights and public involvement in early Islamic history, including roles as political leaders and religious scholars and teachers.

2. The inexperience of women as voters and candidates. The wcss now runs leadership training programs. Many women simply lack confidence and expect failure and defeat. Some are intimidated not

only by men, but by educated professional women. Some believe that women's participation in politics is anathema to divine will.

3. The lack of public funding. Whereas Bahrain provides funding for campaigns, Kuwaiti women (and men) must rely on private and family funds, privileging the rich and particularly wealthy and connected men.

4. The lack of public space. Men have their *diwanyas*—established clubhouses where they meet socially. These physical spaces double as political gathering places. Women can hold somewhat equivalent meetings in their homes, but often end up canvassing door-to-door or in grocery stores. Men regularly discuss politics in the mosque, whereas women only attend mosque on rare occasions.

The political tradition of personal contacting and pleading reinforces a patron-client relationship and a factionalized and localized style of political expression, particularly among rural tribes. Women feel, with some justification, that they will receive a better and more immediate response to their problems when they go personally before a tribal or clan leader. National politics seems remote, abstract, and impersonal.

Lack of political and legal literacy means that many women have no idea of what they are entitled to under either civil or religious law. Many women feel that shari'a will give them a better deal. In fact, many of its provisions are more protective of women than civil laws. Freedom and equality create their own downside. Many fear the image they have of Western women rejected by husbands and forced to fend for themselves and their children in a harsh world.

Women are divided among themselves, undercutting each other. This was more of a problem in the past, when women's organizations were divided on strategy and goals. But class divisions are still problematic. Even though the middle class is now ascendant, the distinctions between the elite urban women and the rural traditional women are vast. The process of assimilating tribal and Bedouin cultures to democratic political culture will be extremely difficult. Many women expressed dismay that citizenship having been granted to Bedouins in order to offset the influence of Shi'a has created a huge, intractable, and supposedly backward bloc that will be an obstacle to progress and stability.

The quota controversy reflects disagreement over the costs and benefits of instituting a quota system for electing women MPs. This is a sensitive topic. Some women support its use, at least as a temporary measure, until Kuwaitis become habituated to seeing women performing in a political capacity. Some see the quota system as a strategic error, likely to create a backlash and give rise to demands for quotas for other minorities and factions. Quotas may keep women in a perpetually dependent, tutelary position, fulfilling their roles in a merely symbolic way. Most of the women interviewed preferred a policy functionally equivalent to quotas, but at the party or political bloc level. Most expressed great dismay that none of the political blocs, whether Islamist, moderate, or liberal, placed any women on their candidate lists voluntarily.

Not all women emphasized legal and political reform. Some saw the laws as adequate but under-enforced. Others saw a need for gender-friendly budgeting, economic reform (diversification and reduction of dependence on oil), privatization, sustainable development, and mid-level management opportunities as key to women's empowerment. Others would shift the exclusive focus from getting women elected to Parliament to achieving favorable legislation. The problem with this approach is that the women-friendly proposals were found in the campaign platforms of almost all of the women candidates, but did not appear central to any of the men's platforms. Counting on male MPs to promote women-friendly legislation may be futile. Issues in need of redress, which were often included in women candidates' platforms, include ending discrimination in family law, housing bonuses, the ability to pass citizenship to children, gender violence, the end to discriminatory labor laws and hiring policies, ending corruption, equalizing pay, and connecting the wage scale in the public sector to productivity.

Rethinking strategies after two big electoral defeats may prompt women to pull back, reduce their expectations, and use gradual rather than confrontational approaches. After all, American women did not succeed in getting elected to office within three years of gaining the right to vote. As one Kuwaiti professor put it "there can be no shock therapy for Arabs."

Combating religious illiteracy among women and religious prejudices among men is essential to drawing the boundary between tradition and religion. Selectively pointing out the handful of *ahadith* or Qur'anic verses that are unflattering to women, or simply ignoring Qur'an altogether in favor of customary practice, has been used to set back women's equality. Imams have issued fatwas condemning women who participate in politics and even fatwas entitling husbands to divorce wives who vote. The opposition must be addressed by increasing the religious education of women. A variety of higher schools of Islamic law now grant entrance to women and prepare them as scholars and jurists. Religious support for women's public roles must be garnered from the texts and ratified by religious authorities.

Women's political rights do not fall under personal status law or family law and, therefore, should not be subject to religious authority. Even if Islam treats men and women as different by nature, those differences should not reach into the public realm and have nothing to do with political participation. "Islamic scholars should not impose rules of family life on public life."[32] As Lulua al-Mulla, pioneer of the women's movement, told the *Kuwait Times* reporter who asked her if what she was doing was un-Islamic, "Islam has nothing to do with my political rights. [Citing] Islam is an excuse."[33] Opponents of reform are using tradition masquerading as religion. She added that the fundamentalist movement (Islamic bloc) was the biggest threat to Kuwait. "They never cared for the will or the prosperity of society."[34]

Public Opinion: For or against Women's Political Rights?

How salient were women's issues in the two elections since women gained the right to vote? Since many of the women candidates prominently included women's issues in their platforms, why did they fail to win support, even from women, who constitute more than half of the electorate? Among Kuwaiti voters, the biggest popular concern was economic, specifically the high cost of living (64 percent); the next priority was traffic jams; third was education; and then unemployment.[35]

About 34 percent of those surveyed strongly believe in women's political rights. Sixty-six percent would encourage women in their families to vote, but only 38 percent indicated that they would support a woman candidate. While expressed support for Islamists and Salafi is moderate, awareness of their political activities is high, and religious personalities were liked best among social leaders (37 percent) as compared with politicians (29 percent). Religious personalities beat out political ones for favorable recognition by 51 percent to 43 percent in 2007.

DASHED HOPES IN 2008

After repeated warnings about the lack of cooperation between government and Parliament, and citing the need to safeguard national unity, on March 17, 2008, the amir, Sheikh Sabah al-Ahmad al-Sabah, dissolved the opposition-dominated Parliament, calling for new elections on May 17. He stressed that "there is no place in the country for fanaticism or allegiance to a sect, tribe, or a social class at the cost of the nation." The 2006 election had produced a nationalist and Islamic opposition majority in the fifty-member Parliament, as well as two years of political crises and power struggles.[36]

As in the 2006 elections, for which women had about a month to prepare campaigns, women had very short notice. Despite their failure to win any seats in 2006, fifty-four women put themselves on the ballot. None succeeded. Optimism had been generated by the reduction of voting districts—where no single candidate or unofficial party could monopolize a district, but would have to compete among a more diverse constituency. None of the political blocs, even those that claimed to be staunch supporters of women's rights, put women candidates on their lists. Women probably undercut each other by competing in the same district and thereby fragmenting their share of the vote.

The amir retained a woman, Nuriyeh al-Sabih, as education minister and appointed another woman, Mughi al-Humoud, the minister of housing and administrative development. He lauded the role played by women in all fields and called for "a greater and more comprehensive role, with women working hand-in-hand with their brothers and actively bearing the responsibilities of development in all fields." He asked the new government to put the interests of the nation above all others and applauded Kuwait as a model of "liberty and democracy."[37]

Yet the appointments to the cabinet would provide grounds for the opening volley from the opposition on the first day that Parliament was seated. The first controversy was the appointment of the two women; the second was the heavy representation of the al-Sabah family (five family members and the amir's nephew as prime minister again out of a total of sixteen ministers). This was nothing unusual. The al-Sabahs have always controlled the key portfolios, particularly the so-called commanding heights (defense minister, foreign minister, and interior minister). Calls for the amir to relinquish sole power to appoint ministers are part of the opposition's agenda. The big winners in the elections to the National Assembly were the Islamists (Salafi and Muslim Brotherhood) and tribal conservatives (including the re-election of MP Fadhel Safar, who was accused the previous March of membership in the Kuwait wing of Hezbollah and of participating with other Shia activists in a rally to mourn the death of former Hezbollah military commander Imad Mughnieh in Syria).

The consolidation of power by conservatives is especially alarming for women. Already, there are attempts to roll back women's gains. Nine Islamists under Salafi MP Mohammad Hayef al-Mutairi promised to lead a walkout of the official opening of the new Parliament over the two women ministers who do not wear the hijab. The conservatives claimed that the Electoral Law had been violated. The provision they cited states that women must adhere to Islamic law with respect to "Muslim guidelines for behavior and dress." The Parliament has already approved a proposal by Islamist and tribal MPs to refer the issue of hijab violation to the legal and legislative committee. The use of tradition rather than law in their complaint demonstrates how easily the two are merged. In a second action, conservatives called for severe penalties for the hospital staff that apparently gave a mixed-sex party on the premises, again citing violation of Islamic custom and tradition. It is clearly the intention of the majority Islamist bloc to police civil society. The Committee for Studying Negative Phenomena in the Parliament appears to be modeling itself after the Commission for the Promotion of Virtue and the Prevention of Vice in Saudi Arabia. In addition to having authority over religious issues, it is attempting to expand its authority in both politics and the private sector.[38] Attempts are afoot to change the wording of the constitution that refers to shari'a as a guide for legislation to wording that would require all law to be derived from and fully congruent with shari'a, as interpreted by Islamists.

Women's legalized vote will not bear fruit for long if the transition from rights to empowerment does not occur. If democracy entails the duty of the state to respond to the public will, there is significant public support for the elimination of the secular component of state rule. If the views of the elected MPs reflect the will of the people, then democracy may produce its own demise. Yet those who would challenge democracy are still forced to adopt the rhetoric and terminology of freedom and democracy in an Orwellian transformation of meanings. For instance, Waleed al-Tabtabaei is a member of the radical Islamic Salafi Alliance that made the biggest gains in the election. He is called a champion of human rights by his colleagues and serves on the Human Rights Committee, which is intended "to cooperate with the government to improve and protect the human rights of Kuwait citizens and residents." One of his goals is "to protect the identity and traditions of Kuwait,"[39] a code phrase for imposing shari'a law. Al-Tabtabaei opposed granting political rights to women saying, "women's rights are not prohibited in Islam, but the time is not ripe to accept them in Parliament."[40]

He is now disappointed. In the 2009 election, the third since 2006, sixteen women were among 210 candidates who stood in the election. Liberals Maasouma al-Mubarak, Aseel al-Awadhi, and Rola Dashti, and independent Salwa al-Jassar won seats in the new house. All are US-educated and hold doctoral degrees in political science, economics, or education. The two mainstream Sunni groups, the Islamic Salafi Alliance and the Islamic Constitutional Movement, the political arm of the Muslim Brotherhood, were dealt a blow, winning just three seats, down from the seven they held in the previous National Assembly. Their tribal Islamist supporters were also reduced from fourteen to eight seats. Liberals and their allies added one seat for a total eight. The Shiite Muslim minority emerged big winners, almost doubling their strength from five seats to as many as nine. Five of them are Islamist Shiites, and Rola Dashti is a Liberal. "Frustration with the past two Parliaments pushed voters to seek change. And here it comes in the form of this sweeping victory for women," said al-Mubarak, who was also the country's first female cabinet minister.[41] Al-Jassar stressed, "The elections are now free, flying with two wings. Women have proven their ability to enter the Parliament and effect change in the political system." She shared the victory with the late amir, Sheikh Jaber al-Ahmad who approved the political rights of women."[42]

Rola Dashti is a veteran contender. She put up an impressive campaign in the 2006 election, the first after women received the right to vote in 2005. Dashti was not deterred by her loss and gave it another try in 2008, concentrating her campaign on economic freedom, involvement of citizens in the investment shares, and agitation for amendment of residential law to enable Kuwaitis to buy houses, rather than on the obvious women's issues. While she did not win, she came very close, and she also became a household name. In the subsequent campaign, she emphasized initiatives to overcome the economic crisis.

Despite the euphoria over the electoral success of these women, some groups expressed concern over the return of so-called troublesome MPs such as Faisal al-Muslim, Waleed Tabtabaei, Daifallah Bouramiya, Musallam al-Barrak, and Mohammed Hayef. Several of their staunchest opponents from the previous Parliament were also reelected. This is the traditional recipe for political instability and the call for new elections. Nonetheless, that women have been elected to office is now part of Kuwaiti custom and political tradition. Women in office are on their way to becoming a permanent feature of the Kuwaiti political landscape, even if the next round of elections does not replicate the national mood of dissatisfaction that may have been responsible for putting women in the current National Assembly.

Justice versus Unfairness, Tyranny, and Oppression

The promise of gender equality stands to be lost to Kuwaitis if an Islamic answer to the Islamist opposition is not convincingly enunciated. While no amount of scholarship is likely to sway the conservative Islamists, it may certainly sway the general population, who may not recognize that Islam has an emancipatory potential and is not at odds with women's political rights. Women's rights and equal citizenship must be promoted in tandem with religious literacy—knowing the texts and reclaiming them—and educate other women as well as men, who may make assumptions about what Islam permits and prohibits without consulting the texts. Reliance on imams is not advisable since, despite their scholarly achievements, they are responsible for misogynist interpretations passed down through the ages.

As Riffat Hassan writes, "G-d, who speaks through Qur'an, is characterized by justice, and can never be guilty of zulm. Hence, the Qur'an as G-d's word cannot be made the source of human injustice."[43] This is the lens through which many Muslim feminists read their sacred texts. Shari'a encompasses laws derived from the primary texts, Qur'an, *ahadith*, and other laws deduced by interpretive methods that were developed early in the history of Islamic jurisprudence. Methodology and hermeneutics vary among *fiqhs* and scholars: both *ijma*, consensus among jurists, and *ijtihad*, reasoned opinion based on rules of logic, open the way for collective reinterpretation. Not everyone agrees that the doors of *ijtihad* are still open, and there is certainly controversy as to who is authorized, what counts as credentials, under what circumstances, and with what motive reinterpretation is undertaken.

All over the Muslim world, women scholars are preparing themselves to demonstrate Islam's compatibility with gender equality. In Kuwait Khadijah al-Mahmeed's discourse on women's rights and equality creates a possibility for bridge building between liberals and traditionalists. She has opened a dialogue on politics and on Islam from a position of connected and loving criticism. Khadijah has credibility in Kuwaiti society.[44] She is dressed in *al-zayy-al-Islami*. She has a Ph.D. from a British university, is the mother of seven children, and has the full support of her husband and family. Her brothers are among her biggest boosters, and I believe, hope to see her eventually in elected office.[45]

Al-Mahmeed's research objective is to demonstrate that women's rights and the full range of political leadership roles are achievable within the confines of Muslim morals and behavior. She criticizes that opponents handpick among unfavorable *ahadith* that condemn women's political involvement and raise the specter of social chaos in which women display themselves in public and abandon their familial duties.[46]

Al-Mahmeed envisions the Islamic state as a constitutional and civil state, committed to protecting and defending human rights and social rights. She asserts that these rights should include personal freedom, intellectual and religious freedom, freedom of speech and opinion, and civil and political freedom. While Islam does not specify the precise structure of government or the administrative forms or technical arrangements of the system, it does specify its values and essence. This accords flexibility to adapt political structures to changing circumstances.

She also investigated the extent to which the public is influenced by religion. The evidence that al-Mahmeed presents suggests that the pious look to religious authorities as they form opinions. For others, the distinction between tradition and religion is blurred. Prevailing tradition has a large influence on the public view of women's political rights, even among those who are not very religious. Al-Mahmeed examined the opinions of Kuwaitis who had no special training in shari'a and found that:

1. Social customs and traditions are influential in determining attitudes toward women's political rights.
2. Respondents are influenced by the schools of Islamic thought to which they subscribe.
3. The degree of loyalty to school influences convictions (a slight majority of Kuwaitis are not committed to a specific school and do not follow any Islamic juristic judgment with regard to women's political rights). Sixty-two percent of Kuwaitis think that custom and tradition are the strongest factors. Forty-two percent think the Kuwaiti constitution is vague on women's political rights. Fifty-three percent support women's assumption of political posts. Forty percent support right of women to vote. Forty-three percent would

prevent women in their custody from voting; 33.8 percent would encourage women in their custody to vote.[47]

4. Women and men hold similar opinions, with women being slightly more supportive of women's rights.

5. Kuwaitis (men and women) from the tribal areas tend to be more opposed to political rights for women. Al-Mahmeed's findings are congruent with those of Dashti, above, suggesting that Islam may serve as an obstacle to, or as a promoter of, greater gender equality. But getting the public and the religious authorities to subscribe to a woman-friendly reading of Islam and shari'a will be no easy task.

Kuwaiti women activists have made powerful use of the narratives of the international human rights discourse, especially the CEDAW to expose the discrepancy between the promise and the performance of their government. In 2007 the National Assembly's Women's Affairs Committee called a conference on the status of women and will no doubt continue to point out the distinction between Kuwait's stated aspirations and its reality. In 2008 and 2009 the WCSS, along with Freedom House and UNIFEM, organized fora on women's rights and civil status.[48] Women have been using their citizenship to take aim at the discrepancies between their constitutional rights and actual practice. They understand that political reforms for women have only been successful when women have carved out a public space in which to debate and act. This presupposes the existence of a civil society that is capable of resisting the smothering power of religious authorities. Political activism has already begun to bear fruit, drawing on legal challenges, the deployment of citizenship as a lever of emancipation, and the influence of international human rights institutions and international and local NGOs. But it is also understood that no reforms are sustainable if they cannot be shown to be congruent with religious law and tradition.

Conclusion

In the final analysis, nations are the backdrop and context of citizenship. Kuwait is a nation with a regime that is composed of diverse and competing elements: monarchy, democracy, and at least two strands of Islam. As democratic citizens, women are treated as formal, equal, rights-bearing individuals whereas according to tradition and custom, they are treated in their ascriptive familial role. By the monarchy, women are treated in their kinship and tribal roles. Modern, liberal democracies promote women's advancement and grant women equality, but traditional regimes, especially monarchies such as that of Kuwait, may also promote women's advancement. Viewing women both as citizens and in their ascriptive, maternal roles may actually improve their political and social status. Eileen McDonagh asserts that "Traditional monarchies to this day retain significant power for defining nationality and for enhancing political stability, as is evident in contemporary discussions of what are considered the more forward-looking monarchies in the Middle East."[49] I am skeptical that Kuwait will fit this model. No doubt the amir is a supporter of women's rights but in a mixed democracy/ theocracy/monarchy in which democratic methods ratify but don't establish the agenda, a woman-friendly monarch may be undermined by an oppositional Parliament backed by religious authorities. Ironically, while the status of women may be the best measure of a democracy, democracy may also result in the undoing of Kuwaiti women's fragile gains. The newly elected women members of the National Assembly seem to be well aware of the need to institutionalize their political presence. National Assembly member Maasouma al-Mubarak recently reminded Kuwaitis of the patriotism and political readiness of Kuwait's women and praised the formation of a committee devoted to women's affairs. In her speech, "The Role of Women: Expectations and Challenges," al-Mubarak said that, "One of the first decisions we made after being elected into the Committee was to suggest an amendment to the bylaws of the Parliament to include this committee among the roster of permanent parliamentary committees, thus cementing its importance to the nation."[50]

Women have begun to scrutinize family laws with an eye to challenging their general characterization of women as being dependent on men. The committee is currently studying two proposals for social and civil women's rights and several proposals to amend discriminatory articles in several laws. These include the Housing Assistance Law (no. 47 of 1993) so that single women may have the same access as men to housing and housing subsidies and loans, the Social Security Law (no. 22 of 1987), and other laws that treat women as dependents of men or restrict their access to public programs, freedom to travel, working hours (Labor Law no. 38 of 1964), retirement age, custody rights, and the security of families, particularly those of Kuwaiti wives married to non-Kuwaiti husbands. The committee also succeeded in putting women's issues on the priority list of the Parliament, which is comprised of twenty-three priorities for the upcoming session starting on October 27, 2009.

But al-Mubarak understands that until women are fully represented in local, national, and international decision-making bodies, their issues will not be priorities, the necessary resources will not be allocated, and fragile gains could easily be reversed. Institutionalizing women's leadership takes more than voting rights. It relies on public opinion and community support for women in governance.[51]

How mobilized is public opinion behind women's full political participation in accordance with their constitutional rights? Will sectarian forces use the issue to fuel their competitive tensions? In a disturbing development, MP Maasouma al-Mubarak received a threatening letter that also included threatens to her fellow female MPs, Rola Dashti and Aseel al-Awadhi. In addition to the email, she handed over to the police an envelope that she had received at her National Assembly office containing two doctored photographs of her, one depicting her with a beard and another with Stars of David on her hands. In a separate letter, she received a death threat along with accusations that, along with fellow parliamentarians Rola Dashti and Aseel al-Awadhi, she had received financial support from the American Embassy during the parliamentary elections.

Kuwaitis are, by and large, far too politically sophisticated to take these accusations seriously. Nonetheless, if a rise in sectarianism, political strife, or plots of terrorism can be attributed to the presence of women in political life, voters could conclude that electing women MPs is not worth the risk. The backlash against women by the religious MPs with the backing of popular religious authorities will make women's political gains even more precarious.

4 *Israel*

DIVIDED JURISDICTION

Israeli women enjoy the same rights of citizenship as men. Gender equality, a norm of Israeli civil society, is imbedded in popular culture and history and accepted by the majority of the population. So why would Israeli women still claim to experience disabilities based on sex, when their position seems enviable? This chapter explores the relationship between civil law and family law in Israel and reflects on the implications of this bifurcated legal system for women's equal citizenship and for democracy and the unitary state. Having discussed the structural legal context of women's lives in Israel and the history of Israeli feminism, we will turn to the efforts of Orthodox women who seek reforms within the parameters of halakha. Their two most significant initiatives rely on raising the halakhic literacy of women and pushing for solutions to the problem of the *agunah* (woman chained to a dead marriage). The *agunah* dramatizes the legal disabilities faced by Jewish women, Orthodox or not, under Jewish law. It also illustrates the dilemma faced by the state when there is a stark contrast between religious law and a woman's rights as an Israeli citizen.

When we apply the age-old rabbinical injunction about obedience to the law of the land, to which set of laws are we referring? Even in ancient Israel, the question of political authority, namely the role of kings, priests, scholars, and prophets was never resolved. Currently the law of the land is fractured into two spheres, civil and religious. According to Israeli law the civil government has ultimate authority when the two spheres conflict, but the state has shown reluctance to impose its will on, and thereby alienate, the religious authority. Israel, for practical purposes, represents a non-unitary state that tolerates overlapping jurisdiction and sub-national sovereigns acting in a quasi-governmental capacity.

With respect to gender equality, the irony of the Israeli legal system is palpable and dramatic: it is among the most advanced with respect to secular laws and women-friendly public policies and programs. Israeli women are visible in all areas of public life. But their equality in the public realm contrasts with their inequality under religious law, and in Israel, religious law is not restricted to the private sphere. Religious law is the basis of family law. The separation of religion and state is not a feature of Israeli political culture. "The Israeli legal system is marked by a deep dichotomy between traditionalist preservation of patriarchy in matters related to religion, on the one hand, and progressive and even radical legislative and judicial policy on matters of gender equality not related to religious norms, on the other."[1]

This reflects an ambiguity at the very core of Israel's identity. Its Declaration of Establishment defines Israel as a "Jewish" and "democratic" state. As a part of the Ottoman Empire and then as British Mandatory State from 1918–1948, Israel inherited the Ottoman legacy of a divided legal or millet system, which continues to complicate the status of its citizens. Israel is a democracy even though the odds may have been stacked against it. While Jewish voters in the United States outrank almost all other groups on scales of democratic values, immigrants to Israel overwhelmingly hearken from countries that lack democratic regimes or liberal values. Despite this, a vibrant democracy thrives. Israel is an anomaly among nations that Jews inhabit. Jews are not outsiders, the other, or even a minority. Yet being a Jew in a Jewish country raises its own complications.

Is Israel a Jewish state or a state of Jews? Will Israel be a democracy? Can it be a democracy without sacrificing its Jewish nature? Can it be a Jewish state without sacrificing women's equality? Will these issues be resolved in a formal and principled way or in the current ad hoc, ongoing, political bargaining among multiple political parties, many of which regard women's equality as peripheral to their immediate and more urgent interests (as has also been the case in twentieth-century Kuwait and in nineteenth- and early twentieth-century America).

If Israel is a Jewish state, what is the relationship between civil law and halakha? And if halakha provides guidance for civil law, which interpretation of halakha is official? Will Orthodoxy maintain its monopoly or will Israel recognize pluralistic forms of Judaism? Should traditions (*minhagim*) and cultural practices associated with halakha be treated with the same reverence as halakha itself? What if these cultural practices are patriarchal and incongruent with democracy?

Israel fits in many ways the concept of an imagined community.[2] Although its founding ideals are ancient, its political resurrection is not shrouded in a remote past. The founding of Israel as a modern state involved contributions from a variety of idealists and visionaries—often with conflicting ideals. Secular Zionists anticipated, quite wrongly (as did many sociologists and politicians worldwide of that generation), that religion would fade away in the face of science and Enlightenment principles and eventually resolve the power struggle in favor of secular civil government. In fact the opposite has happened. Religion has remained a powerful force worldwide, and recent times have seen the renewed vitality of religious forces laying claim to political voice. In Israel, this is reflected not only in the composition and platforms of political parties, but in the demographic makeup of the country, due to the higher birthrates of Haredi (ultra Orthodox) Jews as compared to less observant or non-observant citizens.

A political compromise between socialists and Orthodox Jewish men, in order to achieve sufficient support for statehood, gave religious courts jurisdiction over matters of family or personal status law. This arrangement has been maintained for sixty years. The status quo reflects the general consensus among Jews, religious and secular, that Israel must remain a Jewish and democratic state, though the costs of this arrangement may be born disproportionately by women.[3] This creates a tension in society in which a large portion of the population embraces egalitarian principles, yet daily encounter a religious framework that excludes or subordinates women.

To this day, the self-definition is contested, yet most Israelis are proud of their democracy, though with respect to many issues and policies, it is apparent that religion and democracy are at cross-purposes. When religious principles are at odds with the principle of equality that animates democracy, ad hoc compromises usually defuse the tension until the next thorny issue arises. Occasionally, the fundamental conflict is explicitly broached: Former Israeli chief rabbi Lau (currently the chief rabbi of Tel Aviv) warned, "You want to introduce pluralism, liberalism, reforms? There are enough countries who claim to exercise this," he pointed out. "There are 192 democratic states—but only one Jewish state."[4]

Berel Wein notes, "The Basic Laws of the State of Israel declare that Israel is to be Jewish and democratic. Like all high-minded phrases, this one lacks practical definition. What does Jewish really mean? Who defines what is Jewish? What does democratic mean? How do we rule when the two concepts clash? What type of Judaism and what type of democracy is envisioned in this statement?"[5]

But even when the question seems to demand resolution, Israelis rely on the status quo that has held for sixty years. This live and let live compromise often leaves Israelis on both sides dissatisfied with government policies that appear to allow "Jewish" to trump "democratic" or "democratic" to trump "Jewish." The religious often complain that a combination of "democratic," aligned with market forces and the profit motive, disadvantages the Jewish element of the state. Secular Israelis complain when lawsuits are brought by religious Jews that represent religious coercion of non-Jews and non-observant Jews. Every democracy exercises coercion of some of its members by a majority of its members, and according to religious citizens, "G-d apparently prefers 'Jewish' to 'democratic' when the two clash."[6]

The compromise that continues in Israeli political life is not likely to come from the religious side. The Haredi Orthodox population has shown itself to be politically sophisticated, well organized, tactically shrewd, and highly engaged in political life. They are represented by a coalition of religious parties and are willing to step outside the traditional avenues of electoral politics or legal challenges by mounting street demonstrations that can become quite violent. The state is reluctant to use force, and when it does, scenes of pitched street battles do not reflect well on its public image. Supporters of the Israeli Haredi community abroad attempt to use their influence, even as non-citizens, in favor of Haredi demands. The demographics favor the Haredi community, and this will be reflected increasingly in election and policy outcomes on a variety of fronts, from public transportation to Sabbath closings.[7]

Typically, the government will attempt the sort of compromise illustrated by a bill proposing that public transportation run in Jerusalem on Shabbat, while avoiding religious neighborhoods. Another recent controversy has to do with mixed seating of men and women on public transportation. The Haredi community has demanded that the Ministry of Transportation accommodate their demands by forcing women to sit at the back of the bus or even provide separate conveyances.[8] There have been several instances of women suffering verbal and physical abuse for having refused to give up seats at the front of the bus. "The same forces that have insisted on back-of-the-bus seating for women on some public bus lines are those that now control the Jewish religious apparatus of the state. Is it any wonder, then, that so few of us turn to the officially-appointed and publicly-salaried rabbis of our neighborhoods, cities, and regions for any sort of assistance or guidance, even in the realms in which they supposedly have a monopoly? How many even know who those rabbis are?"[9] Many Israelis are anxious about the power of the Orthodox rabbinate over the state, but while Israelis, including feminists, may be critical of the rabbinate, they are not by and large, in favor of anything like the American establishment clause.

"Non-Orthodox Jews with a commitment to tradition, whether part of existing denominations or members of the many grassroots ad hoc communities that have sprung up around the country, do not seek a 'separation of synagogue and state' . . . Like most Jewish Israelis, we do not find it odd or objectionable that the State of Israel would provide support for expressions of Jewish religious life of all sorts: institutions of Torah study, synagogues, *mikvaot* (ritual baths), publications and others. All we expect as citizens and taxpayers is that all expressions of Jewish religious life be eligible for state support."[10] The reforms sought by many Israelis have to do with greater pluralism in Jewish life and a clarification of the powers and roles of religious authorities and the state. It is the government's responsibility to create "balances between the needs of the nation's various populations."[11] Political constituents and their concerns will be met in Israel as in any other democracy through tactical compromises and careful balancing of interests.

A host of other national and local issues in the cross-hairs of the secular-religious divide include military exemptions for the Orthodox, the generous family stipends that benefit large religious families, issues of kashrut as state policy, and immigration and citizenship status, especially involving the highly-charged definition of who is a Jew? Contentious issues such as the division of Jerusalem, the return of the Golan Heights, the dismantling of settlements, do not always divide Israelis along religious and secular lines, but religious allegiances often play a significant role in determining citizens' stances.

The overlap of state and religion is evident in the party system and religious party alliances.[12] The Israeli government approved the transfer of authority over religious services from the prime minister's office to a new ministry to be called the Religious Services Ministry, headed by a member of the religious right party, Shas. "Prime Minister Ehud Olmert was adamant that the decision did not constitute the re-establishment of the Religious Affairs Ministry, closed some four years ago" (the various responsibilities of this ministry were then parceled out among several offices, with the responsibility for rabbinical courts and for non-Jewish religious courts having been transferred to the Justice Ministry). Senior officials in his office dismissed as fabrications reports that the move was taken to keep

Shas in the coalition after the release of the Winograd Committee Report (the report that criticized Israeli military for its handling of operations during the Second Lebanon War).

Meretz MK's said that the establishment of the ministry would endanger the separation of church and state. MK Ran Cohen added that the ministry was Olmert's bribe to the religious parties. This dynamic is pertinent to women because their rights may become bargaining chips.

While women are abundantly represented in the legal field, elected political office poses a challenge, despite the precedent set by Golda Meir. The Kadima party's front-runner to replace Olmert was Tzipi Livni. She did not fare well with the Haredi community because they are not supporters of the Kadima platform. But Haredi newspapers digitally erased photographs of Livni on grounds that they could not show the face of a woman, making her politically invisible to many voters.

The Haredi community is not the only obstacle to women's equality in the political or business realm. Security credentials, specifically high-ranking military experience, seems to be a prerequisite. Despite Livni's playing up her role in the Mossad during the 1980s, these credentials are insignificant compared to the military experience of her male rivals. Rina Bar Tal, chair and president of Israel Women's Network, said, "The fact that she is a woman, and as such was not a general in the army, is a real issue for her chances of winning the Kadima primaries." Hebrew University political scientist Naomi Chazan, veteran Israeli feminist and former Knesset member, voiced, "People here say political ability, but what they mean is military experience."[13] Golda Meir's election took place against a very different set of background conditions. Israel was coming off a sense of invincibility after the Six-Day War, not the Second Lebanon War, and did not face the threat of Hamas, Hezbollah, and Iran, which heightened the credibility of the military and military solutions to foreign policy threats. The militarization of society creates a political and social atmosphere that favors traditionally masculine virtues and practically makes these virtues a prerequisite for elective leadership. The army has social as well as military significance in Israel. It is the primary network of old boys with respect to career and politics and a major source of recruitment for all sectors of society, public and private. Military service is also a signifier of the truest form of citizenship, going back to the ancient Greeks. Combat positions hold the most prestige, and rank is less important than showing that you did not serve as a *jobnick*, a non-combat position. Israeli women are obligated to serve in the military, but are far less likely to have combat roles. The diminished prestige attached to Livni's service in the Mossad (Israeli Intelligence Agency) was highlighted by her political opponents during her campaign. Livni's opponents in Likud offered a new slogan, "She cannot handle this," taking advantage of end of the Hamas cease-fire, renewed and intensified rocket attacks against Israeli's, to foster uncertainty of Livni's ability as a woman to respond with sufficient force if warranted.[14] Both Kadima and Likud charged the other with emphasizing the gender of the candidate, suggesting that no party wants to be depicted as anti-woman, which may indeed be an advance for women.

Another problematic issue is the case of the Women of the Wall (wow), an issue that has presented a twenty-year headache to the government. The movement, which is controversial, even among Orthodox feminists, myself included, demands greater religious equality in a very public setting. In principle the government supports equality for women in the public realm, but the Women of the Wall have insisted on state enforcement of their putative right to conduct prayers with the Torah out loud at the Kotel (Western Wall). The prayer areas are gender-segregated, and while the Women of the Wall are quite content to conduct their prayer groups on the women's side of the partition, their voices carry to the men's side, as does the knowledge of their activities. The ensuing ruckus, sometimes rising to violence, requires state intervention to restore peace, while avoiding resolution of the question in behalf of the women or the Haredi community. This raises yet again the question of state sovereignty and legitimacy. The state serves as arbiter, but on whose behalf? Avoidance is the state's remaining option when all of the required compromises would have to come from the state in deference to the Haredi community. This strategy would showcase the weakness of the state and give rise to further demands from the Haredi. Supporters of the Women of the Wall note the irony that "only in Israel, and at the site most holy to Jews . . . are Jewish women prohibited from praying aloud in a group with a Torah."[15]

The High Court was finally forced to render a decision as to the legality of wow's actions, in the face of the ongoing collision between civil law and religious sentiment. The court ultimately rendered a series of three decisions. The first, in 1994, turned the issue over to the Knesset, which gave wow an alternative site in an Arab neighborhood of Jerusalem. wow returned to court, and a unanimous three-judge decision ruled in favor of the women. The state immediately appealed the decision and, in a nine-judge five-to-four decision in 2002, the court ordered the government to build a prayer site for the women at Robinson's Arch, an archeological and tourist site far from the Kotel. It would appear to outsiders that wow has been defeated, at least for the present. What members find most painful is that the tie breaking vote was cast by the president of the Supreme Court, Aharon Barak, considered a liberal humanitarian with a reputation for defending Palestinians in Israeli courts, but "who refused to grant justice to women in this era."[16] On November 18, 2009, the next chapter in the dispute was written when Nofrat Frenkel wrapped herself in a *talit* (traditional man's prayer shawl) and attempted to pray with a Torah on the women's side of the Kotel, rather than the compromise site set aside by the High Court. The rabbi of the Western Wall called it an act of "provocation" and "mutiny," adding, "even if it is allowed according to Jewish law, the Kotel should remain out of disputes."[17] But the rabbi's outrage was not the end of the story. Frenkel was arrested by the Israeli police for violating a law on wearing appropriate dress at the holy site. Accompanied by forty women protestors to the police station, Frenkel was soon released in what promises to become a monthly ritual.[18]

These controversies illustrate the dilemma of the state with respect to enforcing women's equal rights under civil law in a setting of hostility to such enforcement by much of the population. Women activists will enter a highly charged political arena in which gender equality is highly contested and often harnessed to less than principled bargaining between secular and religious parties.

Israeli citizens are highly mobilized, politically aware, and engaged. Israel has a vibrant multi-party system with proportional rather than winner-takes all representation. This requires any winning party to garner support in the Knesset of fragmentary groups, each clamoring to have its special demands met as a condition of entering into the coalition. All parties, especially the Haredi, have been beneficiaries of this system. MK Yossi Beilin said, "Israel is the only democracy in the entire world where the rules that govern marriage are based on religious code. . . . this will increase the power of political parties that are trying to force laws upon the secular population."[19] The situation of Israeli women must be understood against this backdrop of unresolved tension at the very heart of Israeli society. They must enter a fractious political sphere to advance their claims and keep their demands from being framed in terms of national allegiance or loyalty issues, as has often been the case. Resisting the argument that women's rights are an example of particular rather than communal goods requires that women's rights be understood, as they are by the United Nations, as a category of human rights.

While the balance between religion and democracy is unresolved, it leaves open the question whether Israel is a unitary state. Gender equality provides only one of several vivid illustrations of this concern. A unitary sovereign government cannot brook all challenges from competing quasi-governmental sources. Its grant of partial sovereignty to the religious authorities may have set the stage for precisely this situation. Israel has made it clear that it will not, for instance, permit its authority over the military to be fragmented. The state has not tolerated periodic attempts by rabbis to nullify the government's monopoly over its police powers by persuading soldiers to ignore their commanders' orders to clear Jewish occupants from contested communities. Should the civil authorities regard rabbinical attempts to nullify gender equality laws as analogous? Can it permit its legal system to be fragmented by competing sovereigns?

If one considers these questions under the rubric of multicultural accommodation, Israel and other pluralistic societies might be expected to do just that. Faced with diverse sub-communities, of which religion constitutes one category, Israel might explicitly resolve the thorny issue of multiculturalism by granting autonomy to sub-national nomic (moral-religious) communities, continuing the legacy of the Ottomans. In this case, the various religious communities would be the recipients of a grant of state power to legislate and adjudicate according to their own nomos. Israel might be applauded as a showcase for pluralism, minority rights, and cultural integrity, especially since the United Nations has designated cultural rights as a category of human rights.

With a few exceptions most liberal democracies treat religious subgroups as if they were voluntary associations, which they resemble, but only in part. In the United States (but not in Israel or Kuwait) religion is voluntary in that one has the option of practicing a variety of religions as well as practicing no religion. But in Israel Judaism, in its Orthodox variant, approaches having a monopoly of authority, and for most purposes, is treated as the official version of Judaism. Secular and non-observant Jews have no official standing with respect to important status determinations, such as whether one is Jewish or not, or if one can obtain a divorce. The religious court is composed of Orthodox rabbis (Sephardi rabbis seem to be more woman friendly in many cases than Askenazi rabbis), who exercise a state recognized monopoly of authority over the interpretation and application of family or personal status law. There is more recognized pluralism with respect to the Christian family courts (which operate according to distinct denominations) than there is with respect to Judaism and its diverse practices and interpretations.

Unlike other liberal democracies, Israel does not provide an exit option, to adopt Hirschman's language.[20] Israeli feminists may not opt out of their religious membership, only religious practice. Nor would many choose to given that opportunity. Many observant Israeli women have recognized that they must seek another of Hirschman's options—a voice. Activists run the gamut of religious commitment and observance. Does Orthodox Judaism constitute a culture? Treating them as coextensive would be problematic. The Orthodox and secular Jews cross cultural lines and political fault lines. If religion in general is treated as a culture and overrides other cultural differences, can Orthodoxy be conceptualized as a subculture in the context of multicultural theory? If so, the Israeli state, established before the development of multiculturalism as theory or law, would embody an extreme form of multicultural accommodation. As Ayelet Shachar has noted, this would have a distinctive impact on women.[21] The delegation to separate communities of control over its members, especially women, would result in citizenship in Israel being mediated by religious communities. This would construct the citizenship of Israelis, particularly women, in strange and damaging ways. The state would be asked to abandon women citizens to the rule of non-state or sub-state authorities.

The liberal state can justify this stance on two grounds: (1) by assimilating religious and cultural subgroups to the model of voluntary associations, in which case the state is only responsible for insuring the availability to members of the exit option; (2) by granting partial sovereignty to subgroups in the name of the principles of toleration, respect for diversity, and a strong reading of the principle of freedom of association and free exercise. Neither position puts the internal behavior of subgroups completely beyond state scrutiny, but it would permit the state to turn a blind eye to violations of individual members' civil rights or even criminal harms against vulnerable members by the group. Israel behaves as if individual membership in Orthodox communities is voluntary, while the reality that an Israeli citizen can only obtain a divorce as a Jew, Muslim, Druze, or Christian, implicates the state at every turn. There is simply no civil divorce in Israel. With respect to family law, Israeli citizens must function as willing or unwilling members of their respective religious communities. This makes it difficult for the state to punish behaviors that are in keeping with the internal rules of the communities that it has recognized. This has been problematic in cases where men (Orthodox or secular) have maliciously withheld gets or extorted huge concessions from their wives as a condition of granting a divorce. While the state has authorized the rabbinical courts to punish recalcitrant husbands, even with prison terms, and has allowed state courts since 1992 to intervene after the Beit Din (religious court) has issued a settlement in order to force a more equitable adjustment, these measures are piecemeal and ad hoc. The structure of authority remains intact. Women rely on luck, hoping to find a sympathetic Beit Din. Web sites in the United States and Israel often rate and rank Batei Din (plural of Beit Din) according to their sympathy or harshness toward women plaintiffs. This leaves outcomes to chance and hard bargaining. The religious courts even have the power to retroactively negate a divorce if they judge that the husband gave the get under any kind of coercion.

The case of Israel demonstrates the unfortunate aspects of multicultural accommodation for women and for the state itself. The bifurcation of civil and religious legal authority is likely to lead to the subversion of the state's legal system by the religious system. This permits the state to fail to defend the civil rights of citizens in ways that would never be acceptable in the face of rights violations by non-religious associations. This demonstrates the fallacy behind the claim that religious communities can be thought of as voluntary associations. (In Europe, Canada, and the United States, it is a combination of multiculturalism, freedom of association, and the free exercise clause that promote grants of semi-sovereignty to religious communities, but often with the proviso that these groups adhere to liberal norms.)

In Shachar's view, which I share, the state is not exonerated by its claim of multicultural sensitivity. Nor may it be exonerated on grounds that it treats religion as a private matter. States are the creators and maintainers of the private realm and have a fiduciary obligation to protect the rights of all citizens, regardless of gender. In Israel, there is no equivalent of the US establishment clause. The line between religion and state is not only permeable, but the two spheres are nearly merged. Israel cannot neglect the private realm, because religion and conscience are political and have political consequences.

The religious community often relies on what they call halakhic prohibition, yet, in many cases, the prohibition is not halakhically specified. Either there is disagreement among authoritative sources or the halakhic prohibition cited is really cultural or traditional, and arose in a specific and no longer relevant social context. For instance, the commonly offered concern for a woman's modesty or for the dignity of a community as a reason to exclude women from public life has long been a basis of practice that has no explicit foundation in halakha. But, while the government has shown a willingness to draw a line in the sand and square off against religious authorities over some issues related to gender equality, religious women are not merely passive observers and have demonstrated that they are perhaps the best agents of change from within.

Reclaiming the sacred texts is one of the reforms that heads the agenda of observant feminists. Attempts to reread religious texts and codes in a more gender-equitable light are often condemned as a betrayal of the faith, family, and even G-d. Religious authorities have been especially sensitive to challenges raised by women, as women tend to be the custodians of culture and religion. Observant Israeli women have adopted many strategies, which are non-adversarial, introducing new roles and rituals that are not in any way offensive. They exploit areas and issues over which there are already existing conflicts and multiple textual interpretations among religious authorities. They gently encourage a dialogue involving religious and democratic/humanistic trends. They focus on widely shared premises and concerns.

Feminists could pursue a course of action that included placing family law under civil jurisdiction or attempt to work within the religious communities for greater gender equality. Israeli feminists are divided on theories and tactics, but Orthodox ones are inclined to favor internal reforms or state interventions of a limited nature that don't put religious authority under the aegis of the state. A more gender responsive and sympathetic Beit Din system would be the best result according to this approach. Increasing mastery of the texts may reveal that the contest is not really between irreconcilable principles of civil versus religious law. If gender equality is congruent, even mandated by halakha properly interpreted, then the issues that cascade from the apparent contradiction between state and religious authority, democracy and Judaism would be resolvable. Accordingly, the most significant revolution has been in women's education about their religious and civil rights.

What are the goals of Israeli feminism? Feminism in Israel, as elsewhere, is a movement that seeks to improve the religious, legal, social, and economic status of women both within Israeli secular society and religious society. There is more consensus among diverse categories of women with respect to public issues, much less consensus with respect to gender inclusive and innovative religious roles, with Orthodox women insisting on conforming to halakha and less observant women willing to step outside these boundaries. Two principles seem to mark a consensus among women:

1. The Israeli state should uphold and support gender equality using courts, legislation, and enforcement, though the Orthodox and secular women's organizations may differ on whether to privilege liberal and democratic norms over halakha when norms conflict.

2. Reform cannot be imposed on religious authorities but must come from within religious circles. The burden is on feminists to demonstrate that Judaism is compatible with gender equality. Both principles may require policy compromises, but the aim is that women not be regarded as the sacrificial lambs. The most successful, unifying, and concrete issues that have the ability to cross class, cultural, and religious lines are problems of domestic abuse and problems of obtaining divorce for *agunot*, both of which will be examined below.

Constitutional Status of Women: The Formal Context of Women's Lives

The Israeli legal system is a combination of English common law, British mandate regulations, and Jewish, Christian, Druze, and Muslim personal status or family law. In matters pertaining to personal status law, the system of shared or overlapping jurisdictions has allowed for civil and criminal legislation to intervene in the application of religious law to a limited degree; this is uncommon in the case of Jewish law and even rarer with respect to non-Jewish religious courts. The Israeli state law and Supreme Court have final jurisdiction since the Basic Law on the judicature regulates the creation of the Beit Din. A great deal of autonomy is granted to religious groups. Rabbinical courts have formal jurisdiction over family law, and while they are subject to supervision by the state Ministry of Religion and the High Court of Justice, it cannot be assumed that the civil courts will intervene on behalf of women claimants when family matters are under review.

In this setting, notes Pinhas Shifman, the family status of women from the perspective of the Israeli legal system is marked by dualism: religious (halakhic law, which is pervasively read as supporting male prerogative) covers matters of marriage and divorce, while secular civil law is based on gender-equality and covers matters of child support, division of marital property, and custody.[22] According to Shifman the rabbinical court system has not kept pace with civil society's increasing recognition of social norms of equality in marriage. Jewish law views women as repositories of ethnic ascription. Not so with men. According to Jewish law, membership in the community of Jews descends from the mother, not the father. Since the Jewish woman passes her Jewishness to her children, she is central in her role as mother and responsible for the survival of the community. Therefore, women are simultaneously citizens and symbols.

Leaving aside family matters, will civil authorities defend women's guaranteed civil rights?[23] While Israel has no constitution, it has a functional equivalent in its Declaration of Establishment (1948), the basic Laws of Knesset (Parliament), the Israeli Citizenship Law, and other foundational documents and court rulings that have constitutional significance.[24] The 1948 Declaration of Independence grants equal rights to citizens, regardless of gender, race, or religion. Israel has failed to fulfill this promise with respect to women. Israel's Declaration of Independence was one of the earliest state constitutive documents to guarantee social and political equality. In 1951 the Knesset passed the Women's Equal Rights Law, which, although not granting authority to courts to nullify legislation, stood as an interpretive tool for the Supreme Court to introduce a range of rights.

Religious authorities have persistently attempted to thwart the statutory imposition of women's rights, but not always successfully. In 1992 the Knesset partially circumvented religious opposition by instituting a constitutional bill of rights—the Basic Law. The text of the Basic Law: Human Dignity and Freedom states in article 1: "the purpose of this Basic Law is to protect human dignity and liberty in order to anchor in a Basic Law the values of the State of Israel as a Jewish and democratic state."[25] The Basic Law protects six basic rights:

1. Right to life, bodily integrity, and human dignity.
2. The right to property.
3. The right to protection of life, body, and dignity.
4. The right to individual liberty.
5. The right to leave and enter Israel.
6. The right to privacy.

But do these rights apply to the private sphere? Do they include full gender equality? The terms dignity and equality are polysemic and difficult to translate into a standard for formulating public policy. Are policies fostering social accommodation for maternity leaves, participation in the labor force, participation in the military, and affirmative action in the public sector congruent with the dignity and equality of women? Some policies, such as maternity leaves, are based on the differences between men and women and are congruent with difference feminism but not with the liberal variant of feminism in which equality demands identical treatment.[26]

As the school of critical legal theory points out, a nation's laws are an important indicator of a society's commitments, philosophy, and social concerns. Israel has an impressive record of passing positive laws and policies. But this obscures the gap between law and enforcement and the multiple repositories of power in society in addition to positive law and legislative authority. This is due to the overlapping structure of the judicial branch. The judiciary is comprised of the Supreme Court, district courts, and magistrate courts. The Supreme Court is the highest court of appeal. The lower courts serve as courts of first instance with separate family chambers that have jurisdiction over personal status cases that are under shared jurisdiction of religious and civil courts under the Basic Law.

Religious courts have jurisdiction in matters of personal status (marriage, divorce, maintenance, guardianship, adoption) vested in judicial institutions of the respective religious communities: Jewish Rabbinical Courts, Muslim (shari'a) courts, Druze religious courts, and ecclesiastical courts of the ten recognized Christian communities. The Muslim courts apply the Ottoman Law of Family Rights of 1917 and British Mandate Ordinance of 1919 of the Hanafi *fiqh* to the majority of the Muslim population, yet, particularly in rural areas, the Shafi'a *fiqh* applies. In addition to Muslim Palestinians, there are also Christian Palestinians. Ironically, the minority courts have nearly exclusive dominion over matters concerning personal status and family law. While religious law inhibits gender equality in the private sphere, extensive protections for equality exist in the public realm. In the private sphere, Israeli courts do not interfere with the statutory license and prohibition of marriage and divorce by the religious courts. Yet the Supreme Court has applied the principle of gender equality in a number of cases, namely property ownership and domicile rights. In 1994, the High Court of Justice imposed on rabbinical courts the obligation to abide by principles of equality in the division of matrimonial property, irrespective of religious law. Legislative initiatives reflect the official and ideal conception of citizen equality, ranging from non-discrimination and removal of obstacles, to affirmative discrimination in order to accommodate women's specific needs in the workplace. From 1990s, the Israeli government transformed the principle of social and economic equality into a progressive and powerful one.

As for accommodating women's professional needs, labor Zionism did so from the start by providing maternity leaves, child allowances, protection from job dismissal, affordable day care, and women's military service. The notion of full equality, however, began to be deconstructed in the 1970s and 1980s when feminists noticed that presence does not equal power. A round of feminist legislation was initiated, and in 1987 series of laws were adopted regarding equal retirement age, equal employment opportunity, equal pay, the prohibiting of sexual harassment, and an amendment to the Defense Law to secure the right to serve in any capacity in the military. The 2000 amendment to the Women's Equal Rights Law consolidated equality of opportunity and affirmative action. Violence against women laws were instituted, including those against rape and marital rape. Abortion is permitted under certain circumstances: age (under sixteen and over forty), pregnancy resulting from a prohibited relationship such as incest or adultery, or a pregnancy considered detrimental to the physical or mental health of the mother. In the 1970s, religious parties successfully lobbied to repeal socio-economic circumstance as a permitted reason for abortion, but otherwise, the civil law is more or less congruent with halakha, which has no blanket objection to abortion.

The Israeli state is answerable to its citizens for the formulation and enforcement of domestic laws, and as in Kuwait and most states, it is also answerable to its international treaty obligations to international human rights. Israel is formally required to abide by the UN documents and provisions that it has signed, and Israeli feminists, like their Kuwait counterparts, monitor the state's compliance with gender-related laws. The 1948 Universal Declaration of Human Rights, adopted by the United Nations General Assembly, has become the international standard against which the human rights performance of all countries is measured. The 1950 European Convention for the Protection of Human Rights and Fundamental Freedoms was adopted to enhance and reinforce the 1948 declaration through the creation of the European Court of Human Rights. Both article 12 and protocol 7 of article 5 declare that men and women shall enjoy equal rights in marriage. In 1966 the United Nations General Assembly adopted the International Covenant on Political and Social Rights, also calling for equal rights of men and women in marriage, regardless of religion.

The Convention on the Elimination of all Forms of Discrimination against Women (CEDAW), commonly referred to as the women's bill of rights, is a comprehensive document adopted by the UN General Assembly in 1979. It combines provisions of many documents pertaining to women's political, economic, social, and cultural rights. CEDAW provides mechanisms for reporting and monitoring, identifying obstacles, and at least symbolically holding countries responsible for their policies.[27] Israel ratified CEDAW in 1980 and signed in 1991 but with the legal reservations to two CEDAW provisions: the inadmissibility of appointing women as judges on the religious court (Beit Din) and article 16 regarding gender equality in family law, "to the extent that the laws on personal status which are binding on the various religious communities in Israel do not conform with the provisions of that article."[28] By May 2001 CEDAW had been ratified, albeit with reservations by 168 states including Israel and many Muslim states. There continues to be a gap between commitment and enforcement, and all provisions of international accords are fundamentally meaningless unless they are followed up by domestic legislation in the member countries.

Feminists often call on the 1993 Conference on Human Rights in Vienna, which proclaimed that "women's rights are human rights," making member state failure to legislate and enforce gender equality a blot against their human rights record.[29] The 1995 UN Conference on Women's Rights in Beijing reiterated that women are widely subjected to human rights violations, often under the aegis of religious law. The resulting platform for action recognized that religion might present an obstacle to full equality for women and called on governments to review laws, customs, and traditions to ensure full implementation of women's rights. But where religion exercises political authority, the fulfillment of this goal remains unlikely.[30]

Israel is sensitive to international perceptions of its human rights record and responded to the UN's expressed concerns, stating that "Israel . . . is committed to a gender-blind society . . . and . . . to tailoring our legal apparatus towards these important ends."[31] In 1998 Israel established the Authority for the Advancement of the Status of Women in the prime minister's office, and this hailed a new era of increased use of legislative and executive power to push this agenda forward. Israel also created a parliamentary committee for the advancement of women and an inter-ministerial committee. In 2002 the state established the Council for the Advancement of Women in Science and Technology, composed of public, private, and academic institutions, and all of Israel's colleges and universities have followed suit by instituting advisors to university presidents.

Israel has sought to address the problem of violence against women, backing a host of feminist legislative initiatives, authored in cooperation between NGOs and the government. The government fosters workshops to educate women about their rights, and has prosecuted several high-profile harassment cases, imposed stalking laws, and generally, taken the concept of women's dignity and liberty seriously.[32] There are fifteen government-run shelters, including two for Arab women, and fifty centers for preventive training and programs for violent men.

Special attention is given to the problem of sexual abuse of children, which has been particularly problematic to enforce within the Haredi communities, which typically close ranks against any form of state intervention. "Religion is one way that sexual abuse is often rationalized and effectuated by intimate access to women and girls and sometimes to men and boys as well."[33] Israeli activists such as Sharon Shenhav (one of Israel's delegates to the UN Commission on the Status of Women in 1994, 1997, 1998, and to Beijing in 1995, and director of the Women's Rights Project) have focused attention on marriage and divorce laws in Israel, which represent one glaring area of injustice.[34] As with other Israeli feminist activists, she attempts to use relevant human rights instruments to compel Israeli government officials to take action in resolving the plight of *agunot*. Israel justifiably represents its record on gender rights, which predates United Nations initiatives, as something of which it can be proud.

Because violations of Israeli women's rights pale in comparison to the situation of women in most other nations, and because Israel has been the ongoing favorite target of UN condemnations organized by Muslim countries (countries that have a far worse record with respect to women's rights), Israeli women are not always inclined to air their grievances in public. Israel is more likely to focus on its achievements. Israel ranks highly in measures of UN member countries. For instance, Israel's sexual harassment law, which was enacted in the mid-1990s, must be considered one of the most "detailed, concrete spelling out in the world in a statute of what sexual harassment law might cover."[35] Even with respect to the issue of marriage equality and divorce rights, "there is more activity on it now in the Knesset then there has ever been. . . . It is being debated in connection with Israel's Basic Laws which function as an unwritten constitution."[36] Yet complacency is not warranted, as feminists began pointing out in the 1970s. The Israeli feminist movement, at about the same time as its North American and European counterparts, began to recognize the salience of class and ethnicity. Sephardi women were highly critical of the dominant Ashkenazi leadership and agenda, forming their own spin- off organizations. Meanwhile, the left wing of the feminist movement sought to build bridges to Palestinian feminists, with some modest though temporary successes, which were subsequently eclipsed by increasing political tensions.

The status of women in Israeli public life has undeniably advanced. Israel has had its first woman chief of the Supreme Court, former attorney general, Justice Dorit Beinisch. The appointment was viewed as unremarkable and generated little press attention, which speaks to the general public status of women in Israel. Daphna Hacker, civil rights lawyer for women at Tel Aviv University says, "women are simply commonplace in the Israeli legal system. . . . 'Israel has the highest percentage of judges who are women compared to any other country,'" and more than half of Israeli law students are women.[37] As Sharon Shenhav noted, "She [Beinisch] is a perfect role model for young women. 'She is a mother and has been all of her career. Her rise to the top of the law system is characteristic of what women can be in the Israeli society. Women in Israel don't compromise. Israel is a model society for combining family and career. When women see other women in positions of power, it proves to them they can do it.'"[38]

Are these success stories signifiers of women's status? Has Israel achieved high marks in gender law and policy, or are these achievements merely spin-offs of the high level of socio-economic and educational attainment of Israeli women? Is the success of Israeli women a product of a welfare state that distributes wealth widely and progressively? Certainly indirect measures can have a significant impact on women's well being. Israel's manifest progress on most parameters such as health, education, access to medical care, life expectancy, and the standard of living as measured by UNDP (UN Development Program) in its annual HDR (Human Development Report) using the HDI (Human Development Index) place it among the top ranking nations of the developed world.[39] Israel's generally high level of development is an example for other countries.

The two biggest obstacles to full gender equality in Israel are the state's lack of will to enforce existing law and the bifurcated structure of the judicial system, which requires the state to share authority with the very community that is most resistant to gender equality. An important factor in the state's reluctance to enforce law with sufficient stringency is the distaste that government officials feel when directly confronting religious authorities. A third obstacle, internalized by many Israeli women, is the constant awareness of the fragility of the very existence of the Jewish state. The constant need to be on war footing makes complaints about women's inequality seem, even to women, a subsidiary issue and even a act of disloyalty. The apologetic tone of many feminists is evident. "However, as the Intifada of 2000 continued to rage against Israel, as did the United Nations, Muslim terrorists, and Western academics everywhere, I did not have the heart to join the jackal chorus against the Jewish state. . . . But such silence is not possible forever. Is Israel head and shoulders above Egypt, Jordan, and Saudi Arabia in terms of women's rights? Absolutely. But our struggle also proves that justice for Jewish women is quite imperfect in the only Western-style democracy in the Middle East."[40]

Beyond Formal Law: Cultural Obstacles

Orthodox feminists feel that Orthodox religious authorities deserve their reputation as patriarchal and even misogynistic. Orthodox feminists hold that there is no halahkic excuse for some of the anti-woman behavior on the part of religious courts. In Israel Orthodox feminism has concentrated on two spheres, religious education and legal issues. But unlike American counterparts, Israeli Orthodox feminists are more oriented toward the private sphere and are less focused on public synagogue participation. This is consonant with centuries of intense private prayer by women, alone or in groups, as initially modeled by Hannah when she prayed for a baby (as described in 1 Samuel). Historically the learning of Talmud and even Torah was controversial in some Orthodox communities, but Orthodox women are now engaged in rigorous studies with the approval of many Orthodox rabbis. Institutions of higher learning are flourishing, and women are gaining credibility and expertise in Jewish law, which has massive advantages for women in the legal sphere and in terms of personal satisfaction (Torah study has always been regarded as a chief form of rendering respect to G-d, tantamount to prayer).

Naming and challenging patriarchy has been complicated, not just by religion. As in any community, cultural and traditional attitudes toward gender roles are persistent, and while intertwined with religion, have a life of their own. Israel, for all of its modernity, contains its own entrenched traditional beliefs with respect to economic and political life. Conservative attitudes reinforce and are reinforced by religious beliefs. It is not always easy to discern where religion ends and culture begins. Israeli Orthodox feminists may challenge culture but have no intention of challenging religion. Their assumption is that in challenging misogyny they are challenging the overlay of culture, which can be peeled back without damaging the underlying halakha.

Israeli women, ironically, have been victims of their own success by succumbing to a myth of cultural gender equality that has rendered their continuing problems nearly invisible. Israelis have their pioneer and kibbutz epic myth. Early gender equality was driven by ideology and practical necessity, calling forth the labor and military service of women. The legendary participation of women in the founding of the state, as soldiers and farmers, was seen by some, especially the religious communities, as a temporary expedient. Religious men and women are, by and large, exempt from military service, creating a culture gap between them and other Israelis. Many Orthodox men do serve in military and even combat roles, but Orthodox women are far more likely to be married or to claim a religious exemption.

The psychology of masculinity and femininity is an oddly constructed composite in Israel. There are two stereotypes that are at odds with each other when it comes to gender roles. On the one hand, the stereotypical, almost feminized submissive shtetl Jew is paired with the aggressively protective and dominant figure of his Jewish wife, who is depicted in popular stereotypes as overbearing and controlling. In reality, she often was a breadwinner and economic manager, especially if her husband was a scholar—the most prestigious and lowest-paying profession in shtetl life. Zionist ideology replaced the shtetl Jew with his diametric opposite—a strong, physically active, fierce male, armed with a hoe and a gun. Gone were the thick glasses, urban pallor, and deferential attitude. The ideal Zionist woman was like her American pioneer woman counterpart: strong, capable of making the desert bloom, and defending the country's borders while not overpowering her husband. This ideal collided with Israel's need to ensure the production of its future workforce.[41]

Outside of the kibbutz, Orthodox gender roles continued, based on tradition and Jewish law. The virtues of the ideal religious Jewish woman are those of wife and mother. A central virtue among the Orthodox is that of *tzniut*, modesty, which is best fulfilled by women in their private homes. *Tzniut* applies to the behavior, speech, and dress of both men and women, but women bear the greater responsibility for not exhibiting themselves publicly in a way that might draw male attention. This is not to be confused with the ideal of the Victorian era that depicted women as the angel in the home, temperamentally unsuited to the down and dirty world of politics. The Orthodox argument never rested on claims about women's lack of intellect or reason.

The concept of women's real natural state being in the home is constructed from the phrase, "The king's daughter is all glorious within."[42] Rashi used this to denote that the most praiseworthy life for a women is to be sequestered beyond the view of unrelated males, caring for her husband and children and avoiding the risks of public life such as attracting desire and gossip, all of which supposedly could culminate in adultery.

Feminism and Its Development in Israeli Theory and Organization: A Little History

Israeli feminism experienced its own learning curve, full of dead ends, false starts, and successes. It evolved from exclusion to inclusion, from political to social welfare concerns, and from a focus on exclusively public issues to private ones, including religious life. The first hurdle was women's suffrage. Deborah Weissman illustrates the early debates between religious and secular authorities over enfranchising women.[43] As in the United States, citizenship was not held to imply the right to vote. The most important voices were those of the two most prominent Israeli rabbis, Rabbi Kook and Rabbi Uziel. Politics, religion, precedence, and practicality were all elements of the debate. The ultimate resolution in favor of women's voting rights involved rethinking of the traditional Jewish notion of public dignity to demonstrate that the dignity of the public was not jeopardized by women's entrance into politics; indeed, excluding them was at odds with the dignity of women.

During the *yishuv* period, when Palestine was under the British mandate, the issue of women's right to vote had already arisen in the context of elections for *yishuv* institutions. The discussions about women's rights were tracking developments in Europe and America. The secular Zionist parties advocated full election rights for women, in keeping with their doctrines of equality, including gender equality. The Haredi (non-Zionists) did not participate in elections. That left only the religious Zionists with an acute concern over the halakhic issues that might be raised by extending the vote to women. Two significant authorities applied their opposing interpretations of halakha to the right to vote. Rabbi Avraham Yitzhak Ha Kohen Kook, the widely respected first Ashkenazi chief rabbi of Palestine, who in many respects was quite supportive of women, took the view that the Torah and the scholarly writings through the ages would have prohibited voting by women as a modern innovation not in keeping with halakha.

Yet Rabbi Kook held that women were fully capable of understanding and developing acute political opinions that should be shared with the men in their family. His position was based on the sanctity of the family. This corresponded roughly with the family unity position that was being used as an argument against women's rights in the United States.[44] "The family is far more profoundly sacred to us than it is in the entire modern world. And this is the foundation of the happiness and dignity of Jewish women."[45] Note the association of dignity with the fulfillment of a woman's role in the home. "We thus discover that other peoples must speak in terms of women's rights because their basic condition is degraded. . . . The rights of Jewish women are based upon the refined content of 'spiritual worth.' "[46] Rabbi Kook concluded that the rough and tumble nature of political life was not suitable for women's innately refined character and would have a corrupting influence. This was a common position in that era and is echoed in contemporary Muslim societies, in which political participation is regarded as a modern and foreign import. This claim is then related to the argument proceeding from women's innate nature, which makes them supposedly too good to enter political life.

The third element of Rabbi Kook's argument fixed on the preservation of modesty, a central Jewish virtue. Assimilated to these claims is the cautionary note that women are entrusted with communal preservation. How can a woman feel anything but elevated, responsible for producing the next generation and transmitting to it the ancient legacy of a people? What similar honor and satisfaction could a man claim?[47] Other rabbis and scholars, both inside and outside of the *yishuv*, did not share Rabbi Kook's views, and, in 1926, he modified his position, agreeing to suffrage for women as long as men and women used separate polling booths. (This is also a common compromise in the Muslim world.)

Rabbi Ben-Zion Meir Hai Uziel, chief Sephardi rabbi of Palestine and later of Israel, took a view based on halakha that was at odds with Rabbi Kook. On the subject of women voting he wrote, "We have found no clear basis to forbid it, and to deny women this personal right would be untenable."[48] He went on to argue that under a democratic government, where women are responsible for accepting the authority of the state and its laws, we cannot ask any group of people to obey their officials if they did not have a hand in electing them. One of the central justifications of the superiority of democracy was that citizens were obedient to the laws that they themselves had authorized.

As to the claim by some sages that women are frivolous, he responded that we would then have to exclude the many frivolous men from voting. Pertaining to the modesty and dignity argument, he asked, "What promiscuity can there be in each individual going into a booth and casting a ballot?"[49] Rabbi Uziel rejected the proposed parallel between public prayer and public political life. The traditional rationale for excluding women from public prayer was that her participation would diminish the dignity of the community. The same rationale was being applied by some of his peers to politics. Rabbi Uziel responded that if a woman were to be elected, it would be a representation of the popular will, therefore proof that the community did not feel humiliated. In Kuwait, feminists made a similar argument that women's political leadership in an elected rather than appointed position is permitted. Qur'anic injunctions against women as political leaders relate specifically to monarchies. This may not prove that elected leadership is permissible, but it does give credence to the possibility.

Basing his argument on traditional sources and practical thinking, Uziel managed to persuade many members of religious Zionist and the Haredi parties to accept women's suffrage. There may have been nothing particularly principled about their acquiescence; it may have reflected self-interest and practicality, for they would otherwise find themselves outnumbered by the combined votes of secular men and women. A similar line of reasoning won over the traditional Muslim men in Kuwait in the 1990s.

During the *yishuv* period the issue of women's suffrage was already resolved. During that period the dominant Zionist Socialist Labor Movement was supportive of women's equality, and not just of political rights, but of full social, economic, and military equality. This made a separate women's movement look disruptive, self-centered, and unnecessary. Therefore the many women's organizations did not separate off to create distinct organizations, nor did they articulate specific women-oriented demands. The religious women's organization attached itself to the National Religious Party. The national labor unions had a women's division, as did Herut, Likud, and the Communist Party. The largest women's organization is Na'amat, which associates with the Labor Party. Only WIZO (Women's International Zionist Organization) was independent and remained so, never affiliating with a political party or wing. These organizations furthered a feminist agenda on the one hand, by encouraging women's participation in politics and economics. On the other, they did not challenge traditional gender roles or division of labor.

The founding ideology of Israel was a mix of Zionism and socialism. The kibbutz represented the nucleus of a communist utopia, the model for the future predominantly agrarian society of workers and equals. Women's Equal Rights Law (1951) emerged from the idea that "a man and a woman shall have equal status with regard to any legal action."[50] To this extent, at least in the context of kibbutz life, the agenda of liberal feminism (equal-rights feminism) was furthered. Yet the liberal feminist model did not become anachronistic as a tool of analysis and change, particularly outside of the kibbutzim, which have always represented a small portion of Israeli population. The equal rights agenda is still pertinent to women's daily lives because of the unique legal position of the family in Israeli law. Exposing the interface between gender and law is ongoing.

Because of the socialist bent of Israel's secular founders, feminists did not have to fight for social welfare programs. Israelis, while often grumbling about their high tax burden, have never been hostile to government provision of comprehensive services. The next stage in feminism that emerged in the United States and Europe did not require the same kind of consensus building in Israel. The 1949 Compulsory Education Law, the 1964 Equal Pay Law, and similar laws and programs exemplified the first stage of Israeli feminists' history from 1949 until the early 1970s. When 1975 was designated by the United Nations as the International Year for Women, an Israeli commission on the status of women was appointed. But the ideal of equality, while actualized to an impressive extent, had also achieved the status of a national myth—an indelible feature of popular culture. This fostered complacency on the part of many Israelis.

Even though the Foundational Bill does not use the word equality the use of the word dignity is taken as implying equality. Orit Kamir observes that liberal concepts of freedom and equality may not capture the ethos of women in Israeli society, and the concept of dignity, used by Jewish law and

Israeli law, may be more appropriate. It is closer to the Aristotelian notion and to the concept of equal human worth and, in the Israeli context, is derived from Judaism. "From this perspective, human dignity may be better suited to address culturally based sensitivities than equality. . . . The rhetoric of equality risks privileging human features and preferences which are unique to the members of powerful, ruling classes, but presented by them as universal 'common denominators' . . . Through the prism of human dignity, it may be possible to respect and defend culture-specific dignity as well as fundamental human common denominators."[51]

"Equality as sameness," as underpins the liberal model, is not useful to Israeli feminists, especially Orthodox and essentialist feminists who accept the idea of gender differences as more deeply imbedded (whether by divine intent or biology) than is accounted for by socialization models. The notion of equality that would apply would not be equality as sameness but equality that borrows from Aristotle's notion of equality as consisting in "treating likes alike."[52] This perspective calls for recognizing rather than dismissing difference when it is a requirement of justice. That would rule out discriminatory treatment but would not rule out setting up categories of similarly situated individuals to receive some benefit that pertains to their special situation.

This theoretical turn provided an opening for Orthodox women to share a common cause with secular Israeli feminists. For instance, Haredi women have traditionally regarded self-sacrifice as proof of dignity and strength required to enable husbands and sons to engage in Torah study. Modern Orthodox women who focus on boosting women's Torah and Talmud scholarship or who strive for greater inclusion in the public prayers and rituals, community responsibility, and leadership, often see their quest as an aspect of their human dignity that has been denied, not in terms of imitation of men. It also permits the acceptance of difference as promoted by feminist essentialists or culturalists, taking into account that women may require special protections during pregnancy and child rearing years, known in Israel as social rights.

"These include rights pertaining to the security of body, issues of sexuality, and protection from violence." The Prevention of Sexual Harassment Law and the Authority for the Advancement of Women Law are part of comprehensive package signaling the fourth stage of evolution, in which law was consciously used to promote social change and the creation of an institutional framework for governmental agency. Affirmative action for women is explicitly framed in Israeli law as a 1993 amendment to section 18A of the 1975 Government Corporations Law.

By representing an unequivocal declaration of public policy against gender discrimination and for women's equality, legislation such as the Women's Equal Rights Law supplies powerful expression of the desired social norm. "The amended Women's Equal Rights Law can indeed be described as 'constructing an overall social framework based on the principle of equality.' "[53] Public norms have been injected into the hybrid and private institutions of the private sphere as well. The 1988 Equal Employment Opportunities Law prohibits all forms of discrimination in the workplace. Despite all these advances, the jurisdiction of religion over family law continued to be exempt from judicial review by the Supreme Court, significantly weakening the effect of women's equal citizenship status.

There are still many Orthodox women who either do not know or care about these issues or are opposed to the feminist agenda. Yet the recent upsurge in feminist activism among women who describe themselves as Orthodox is dramatic. What precipitated the change? Was it the egalitarian developments in the other branches of Judaism or the attainments of women in public, professional, and academic realms? In Israel, the more radical American Modern Orthodox immigrants (*olim*), who have settled largely in Jerusalem and several outlying communities, have wielded considerable influence. They characteristically include open-minded women with a high level of education, who voice their increasing discomfort over women's dichotomized roles within Judaism. While American influence is clearly felt in Israel, Israeli influence is likewise felt in the American Jewish community. The hundreds of American girls who spend their gap years in Israeli in various study programs are accustomed to equality, and the first higher Torah learning programs were for English speakers. But the foreign girls were quickly joined and outnumbered by natives. The American and European girls returned home with renewed enthusiasm, higher education, and confidence.

Despite the cross-pollination between Israeli and US Orthodox feminists, there are still palpable differences. "Whereas in Israel the opening of the higher reaches of Torah learning to women preceded Orthodox feminism, in the United States the reverse is true. Both because of the centrality of the synagogue in Orthodox life in the United States, and because of the language barrier which limits access to higher Torah learning, American

Orthodox feminists focused upon women's *tefillah* (prayer groups) and upon changing synagogue ritual to be more inclusive of women. Sharing neither idiom nor scholarship with the rabbinic community, some Orthodox feminist leaders couched their concerns in confrontational terms. In return, some rabbinic leaders displayed virtual paranoia about Orthodox feminism," believing that the hidden agenda of feminists was really rabbinical ordination.[54]

In the United States, conflict within the Orthodox movement over defining women's roles led to the development of right and left wings. But, because of the separation of religion and state none of the individual or organizational actors had the power to impose its will. While the stakes may be high, individual loyalty to any position is purely voluntary, and each congregation acts as a mini-democracy, deciding the extent to which it will adopt or resist innovation concerning women's roles. Even if communal criticism is toothless, Modern Orthodoxy in the United States displays a certain defensiveness in the face of more traditional Orthodox groups that accuse Modern Orthodoxy of having strayed off course.

"In their opposition to reconfiguring religious leadership within Orthodoxy to include women, some American rabbis may be fighting the last war. Concerned lest the Orthodox feminists overturn *Halakhah* and ultimately sway Modern Orthodoxy from its Halakhic posture, these rabbis have missed noticing that the younger, intensively Torah-schooled modern Orthodox generation of women is neither feminist nor does it identify with the thrust to change synagogue ritual, but rather with a desire to make for itself a place within the world of traditional Talmudic and Halakhic scholarship."[55]

Israeli Modern Orthodoxy does not suffer from this inferiority complex, even in the face of their politically powerful Haredi critics. In Israel a multitude of communities and synagogues make up the substantial segment of voters that constitute the national religious circles. Possibilities for alliances abound. There is no fear of a schism among Israeli Orthodox over the issue of feminism as there is in the United States. But this may simply demonstrate that Israeli political life is rife with more pressing issues.

Orthodox Israeli scholar and educator Rabbanit Henkin noted that first generation Israeli feminists understood that education was the big agenda item, whereas fighting for issues such as women's *minyanim* (prayer groups) was fakery. Henkin was instrumental in founding the highly respected women's educational program, Nishmat, which had to fight for recognition among long-established male institutions. Henkin still believes that women's education met with more resistance in the United States than in Israel.

Yoetzet Halakha (*Family Law Consultants*)

In keeping with the general strategy employed by Israeli feminists, Nishmat did not lay claim to a contested area already occupied by men or engage in adversarial behavior. In training women in an area of family purity laws, an area of crucial importance, not only to Orthodox women but to the maintenance of the entire Jewish family system, she provided a service that Orthodox male authority respected and had been unsuccessful in providing. She identified and filled a vacuum. Her hotline and web site on *taharat ha mishpacha* (laws of family purity) responded to a real need with expert, confidential advice provided by women. The number of calls and website hits testified to this unfulfilled need. Women were clearly more comfortable talking to other women about intimate details of family life. This reduced the risk of halakhic violations that arose because women with questions were not seeking advice. The rigorous training program for women as experts on halakha of family law, as well as women's reproductive health, gained the respect of Orthodox rabbinical authorities. Women from Haredi families soon began to enroll, with the approval of their families, for training as *yoetzet halakhah*.

Does this new role challenge rabbinic hegemony or reinforce it? Rabbanit Henkin reassured the suspicious rabbinate that her students were not would be rabbis. By seeking out areas of expertise without challenging rabbinic authority, these new respected professionals may be setting a precedent for expanded roles in the future. Critics may say that these women have accepted crumbs. Tactically, seeking out openings in the power structure that already exist is typical of the less confrontational Israeli feminist style. The goal of the program was to provide a service to women and families while creating a niche for a highly educated group of women who have succeeded in winning respect for their intensive training and comprehensive knowledge of the laws.

With several graduating classes in the field, this can be judged a discreet but momentous feminist initiative. Rabbanit Henkin sees as her goal to serve halakhic purposes rather than a search for empowerment, status, or authority. She recognizes that she has created a new role rather than usurping one from rabbis. She has no ulterior goal, such as turning her graduates into rabbis. She sees them as consultants rather than decisors. She understands that the reason she met with minimal opposition was because her program was not labeled a feminist endeavor.[56] Nishmat marks the beginnings of the "reallocation of prestige" especially in Israeli national religious circles.[57] Yet at fairly recent conference on gynecology and halakha there were no women speakers.

According to Henkin, this generation of Israeli Orthodox women is learned and, therefore, radicalism and militancy has declined. Her program, which has been operating for more than eighteen years, has graduated more than one hundred and fifty women since its first class in 2000 and produced the first women to study Talmud on a level that made them experts in the area of family purity laws. Rabbis were initially opposed, but the *yoetzet* program has now gained nearly unanimous support across the Orthodox community. Women enter the program from even the most conservative Orthodox sects. They receive upwards of 50,000 calls a year and have apparently met with approval because they have helped more women to observe halakha.

Rabbanit Henkin is gratified to see the rabbinate responding appropriately to her graduates, but she does not mince words when it comes to her assessment of Orthodox religious authorities.[58] The problem is men, not the law. She calls the Beit Din horrific, and the Haredi *dayanim* (judges) she notes, are occasionally given to nepotism and a bad work ethic. The judges often reflexively take the husbands' part, even with regard to the problem of abused women. Henkin points out that *pikuah nefesh* (the Jewish principle that saving a life is paramount) should override all other considerations. With respect to the problem of the *agunah*, the Beit Din's rejection of solutions such as prenuptial agreements is a cultural and sociological problem, not a halakhic one.

Toanot Halakhah (*Court Advocates*)

A second issue-oriented initiative, undertaken in 1988 by Nurit Freed, established the *toanot halakhah* program, which educates court advocates that represent the wife's interests in divorce cases coming before the male-dominated Beit Din. This program served as a forerunner of many women's advocacy groups. As with the *Yoatzet*, despite pronounced opposition from various camps, the court pleaders have won widespread support among the Orthodox. The Monica Dennis Goldberg School for Women Advocates is part of Midreshet Lindenbaum, an institution of higher learning with various programs for women. The advocates program prepares women as court advocates on a par with men who have been studying in yeshiva for years. The first step, in 1990, was to appeal to the Israeli Supreme Court for the legal right for women to practice in the religious courts. Candidates must already hold a degree in law, psychology, or social work, and study Jewish law in great depth relating to personal status law (family law) testimony, civil damages, and the like. The program graduates about twenty students a year. Three women advocates have been chosen to sit on the newly formed Council of Rabbinical Court Advocates, along with three men. Women lawyers and *toanot* can appear before Beit Din representing both men and women.

The *toanot* contributed the widespread acceptance of pre-nuptial agreements, intended to preempt the problem of the *agunah* by requiring both bride and groom to affirm that in the event that the marriage dissolves, neither would create obstacles to a full halakhic divorce. But the *dayanim* (judges) do not like prenuptials, and when they accept them, they require that they be written with or by *dayanim*. In the United States, the Rabbinical Council of America and advocacy groups such as JOFA provide a downloadable template on their websites. Conservative rabbis maintain their opposition is principled and religious, but there is certainly an element of power involved. They see the widespread adoption of prenuptial agreements as preempting the Beit Din. Such was certainly part of the negative response by some Orthodox rabbis to the New York State get (writ of divorce) law. As with the *yoetzet* that the rabbinate feared might be a cover for edging women into the role of rabbi, the fear with the *toanot* was that they really harbored the goal of becoming *dayanim*. But most Haredi approve of the role, and the program has been accepting applicants from Bnei Brak, the Belz Chassidim, and even Dvorah Brisk, the daughter of a judge on the Beersheva Beit Din.

Having *toanot*, or women court advocates, is helpful once a woman comes before the Beit Din, but the most important problem is still that of the *agunah* and the *mesorevet* get (woman in limbo waiting for her husband to issue a get). There are various calculations producing conflicting estimates about the number of women waiting for divorces based on those who want a get (thousands) versus those who are still formally waiting or have been denied after coming before the Beit Din (hundreds). But progress toward the resolution of this problem is being made. Public opinion tends to side with the *agunot* in Israel, Europe, Britain, and North America, and in Israel, the *toanot* have played a role. In addition to advocating in the courtroom, activists and *toanot* provide information to women about the Beitai Din, by region or by the personality of the judges, telling which are reputedly most sympathetic to women. For instance, it is widely held that Sephardi chief rabbi Amar is more sensitive while Ashkenazi chief rabbi Metzger is less so. The Beit Din only meets every six months, and lawyers are notorious for dragging out proceedings, so there is a need to carry on negotiations between the husband and wife before the judges and potentially, for years on end, to go back and forth between civil and religious family courts. The *toanot* can provide continuity and support through this byzantine process.

The *toanot halakha, yoetzet halakha,* and the *madricha ruchanit* (spiritual counselor) are all new titles and roles that reflect the new recognition of women by Orthodoxy, yet is it a substantive change or merely the creation of new roles that men do not want? The shift in women's status is palpable and has permeated even the Orthodox community. Some activities, such as dancing with the Torah in women-only groups on Simchat Torah, women's prayer groups, women saying kaddish (the prayer recited three times a day for eleven months, typically by a son or close male relative of a deceased person), and even women leading parts of the Sabbath service may provoke rebuke, but they no longer provoke surprise. Others, such as Chabad, supplement women's traditional roles with more learning, women's Sabbaths, Rosh Chodesh, bat mitzvah celebrations, annual women's conferences, and the like. Underpinning the revolution in women's roles is the growth of institutions of advanced learning for Orthodox women. The Talmud is no longer beyond reach. The sincerity of women scholars is no longer called into question. *Bubbes* (grandmothers) now boast about their learned granddaughters. *Minhag* (custom and community standards) has always played a role in deciding what practices are acceptable. Clearly there is an ongoing shift in community standards. The shared goal of many Orthodox men and women feminists is the creation of a spiritual community of equal men and women before G-d.

Good Citizens: Hadas Women's Hesder Program

Orthodox Jewish women are serving in the IDF (Israel defense forces) in greater numbers than ever. They take their citizenship, with its attendant rights and responsibilities, very seriously. Approximately one-third of modern Orthodox women decide to serve in the army. Most forego army service and the challenge of living in its secular environs in favor of national service, where they work in hospitals, schools, and museums. For those who decide to serve, the army can be a difficult place to navigate. Many come from all-girl high schools, and the army is their first experience in an environment that is both secular and coed. "Rachel Karen, who teaches at the female religious seminary Midreshet Ein Ha'Natsiv in northern Israel, says about 80 percent of her students enlist in the army. They study in a program that combines Torah studies with army service, based on the *hesder* model used for Orthodox young men."[59] Since 2002 in collaboration with Ohr Torah Stone of Midreshet Lindenbaum, there is a new *hadas* track, the Intelligence Corps. Some 40 percent of religious recruits meet the rigorous standards. This program creates a bridge between the religious and the less observant and shatters stereotypes not just about women, but about the religious, who are sometimes considered shirkers.

Accommodating the religious needs of Orthodox women in the military is a goal of the Israeli military.[60] Tens of thousands of religiously observant female soldiers serve in the army, but until recently, they did not have a woman to serve their special spiritual and practical matters. The Rabbinate Corps, under the supervision of the IDF's chief rabbi, Avi Ronsky, created the position for a female officer. "'There are many subjects'—such as sexual harassment, issues of modesty and prohibitions against co-ed touching—'for which it is very difficult for young women to talk to a rabbi and which it is much easier for them to speak about with another woman' . . . The main function of the Rabbinate Corps is to ensure that the army adheres to the tenets of Jewish law. The unit ensures that food on IDF bases is kosher, that observant soldiers are able to pray and that non-essential exercises are not held on Shabbat."[61] They provide Jewish education and oversee Jewish burials. "Some of the members of the Rabbinate Corps were taken aback by the presence of a woman in the department. But they soon found a way to work well together, she says, and rabbis in the corps now regularly refer cases to her—especially ones they believe might be better handled by a woman." Chana Pasternak, the executive director of Kolech, who helped lobby for the creation of the post, says, "Jewish women serving in the army finally have somebody they can turn to on religious and spiritual matters."

Top of the To Do List

The divorce issue is the rallying point for Jewish women internationally. The tragedy of the *agunah* is perhaps the clearest illustration of the political nature of the Beit Din and its keen interest in preserving its power against any challenge. The position of the Beit Din in Israel creates injustices for Israeli women, and has an impact on the ability of Beitai Din worldwide to provide relief for what is recognized to be an injustice by invalidating foreign courts' gets. This issue is more significant than the actual number of women who are affected by it might indicate. Nor does its salience have to do exclusively with its dramatization of the asymmetrical impact of halakha on women. The most compelling injustice is that halakha is represented by the Beit Din as granting men unilateral and absolute power to withhold a divorce, when, in fact, there are a variety of means at the disposal of the Beit Din for ending a dead marriage, even in the face of a husband's recalcitrance. What is lacking is the will, not the way. In 1953 rabbinical courts jurisdiction gained power over marriage and divorce law, governed by religious law.[62] Parties to the divorce are governed by their own personal religious authority. Civil courts govern other aspects relevant to the divorce, such as custody, support, and division of marital property.

The *agunah* issue highlights the failure of the religious authorities to protect women and marks the point where the jurisdiction of state and religious authorities converge. Though the religious court has exclusive jurisdiction over the issuance of the divorce decree, it shares jurisdiction over ancillary matters such as property distribution and child custody with the civil court. This provides an opening for civil courts to exercise power, as they are the default court in these matters.[63] However, the ability of the civil court to do so in areas of concurrent jurisdiction may depend on which spouse initiates the action by attaching these ancillary issues to his or her divorce suit and making a dash for the court that is most likely to best serve his or her interests. Women are likely to see themselves as able to secure a better deal from the civil court while husbands have every incentive to steer the divorce suit to the Beit Din.

According to Halperin-Kaddari, this is a case of the blatant failure of the state to take firm control over family law.[64] It is also the case that best illustrates the unwillingness of civil law to challenge the religious authorities with sufficient vigor. She warns that the balance of power is shifting further toward religion. The conflict as she understands it is mostly about personal and institutional power rather than religion and ideology. Secular institutions such as the Supreme Court, for instance, are losing power since Ehud Barak retired. When the secular legal structure confronts religion, it isn't usually on behalf of women. The situation will worsen for women unless the civil system narrows the jurisdiction of the religious court by putting all matters involving children, property, and support under the civil courts.

Most provisions of religious and civil laws apply equally to men and women, yet a man can remarry without a get with no consequences for offspring of the new union. The woman who has not received a get is prohibited from marrying unless she leaves Israel and marries elsewhere according to a civil ceremony. In that case, her marriage will be considered an adulterous relationship according to the religious authorities, and her offspring will have the status of *mamzer* and cannot marry any member of the community with the exception of those who share his or her status. Theoretically both parties' free will is required for a marriage to be dissolved, but the man can circumvent the lack of a freely given get, while a woman cannot. Traditionally a man can get the signatures of one hundred rabbis to nullify his marriage and even commit legal bigamy by remarrying without a get from his first wife. But receiving the get is an absolute requirement for the wife if she wishes to remarry. The rabbinical court requires evidence that the get was given by the man in an uncoerced manner. Therefore the man has unilateral power to hold his wife in a married state. This opens the door to bitter, drawn-out battles, wherein a vengeful husband has the ultimate bargaining chip, allowing him to extract concessions from the wife (child custody, martial property, and support) or otherwise hold her hostage.

The rabbinical courts have a variety of precedents and venerable sages to draw upon to obligate the recalcitrant man, but are loathe to do so. There are, and have always been, alternative readings of law. Maimonides, the medieval Jewish philosopher, asked judges to put themselves in the woman's position, exhorting them to recognize that a woman should not be bound to a man against her will, as she is not a captive. And there are historical and contemporary scholars, rabbis, and halakhic authorities who have found grounds for annulling marriages when men refuse their wives gets or, more recently, in Israel, Europe, and the United States, the recognition, even requirement that an agreement to dissolve the marriage at the behest of either partner, be inserted as an addendum to the traditional *kettubah* (marriage contract). But the selective reading of sources to exclude those, such as Maimonides, who felt strongly enough about the injustice to advocate violence against men who willfully withhold the get tend to be treated dismissively, as do practical solutions such as prenuptial agreements, which are widely used outside of Israel.

Susan Weiss, one of Israel's most notable legal authorities and advocates for *agunot*, understands that change must come from both sides: greater civil oversight and enforcement and greater receptivity by the religious courts to halakhically acceptable solutions. "By law, the personal status of married women in Israel is determined by the (almost) unfettered discretion of their husbands (and not by the State)."[65] Israeli law thus sanctions gender inequality. Marriage and Divorce Law 5713, 1953, gives rabbinical courts exclusive jurisdiction. Weiss notes, "Of course, Israeli law frowns upon bigamy in principle, nonetheless, article 179 of the Penal Law 5737, 1977, recognizes such rabbinical court orders as legitimate exceptions to the bigamy law. The sense of justice would seem to operate to free a man from an unwanted marriage, but does not extend to freeing a woman in the same circumstances."[66] The state can and should impose civil and criminal penalties. In 1995 the rabbinical courts Enforcement of Divorce Decrees law was passed, allowing the use of indirect measures and negative incentives: freezing the bank account of the recalcitrant man, revoking his professional and driver's licenses, and even imprisonment, but with mixed results. The application of these measures may make the man miserable, but ultimately, cannot compel him to give the get. Many women still wait for years in limbo.

Additional injustices proceed from this asymmetry, according to Weiss. The law, for instance, condones the blackmail of women, as many husbands seem to have a price that they are willing to accept in exchange for giving the get. Though a get is considered null and void if a man is subjected to any form of coercion, this requirement does not apply to women, who are routinely subjected to coercion in order to secure their divorce—child custody rights, family property, division of assets, and even an outright monetary bribe. The rabbinical courts may or may not approve of such practices, but it reinforces them every time it counsels a woman to make a payoff as the only way that she can hope to secure her get. Men may be encouraged raise the amount in response to this practice, increasing the payoff to the extent that the market will bear. Neither the civil nor the rabbinical courts are likely to interfere with these forms of extortion, as the idea of a marriage contract and a divorce contract can be likened to transactions in the marketplace, where contracts are in principle considered to advance self-interest, and agreements reached after negotiations are assumed to be free-willed.

While the rabbinical courts oversee marriage and divorce, the civil courts govern the distribution of marital property. "According to the Spouses (Property Relations) Law 5733, 1974, women are theoretically entitled to half the value of all property accrued during the course of the marriage."[67] But article 5 of the law stipulates that is applicable only after the "dissolution of the marriage." If a man refuses indefinitely to grant his wife a get, then the marriage may never be officially dissolved. This means that Israeli civil law makes the woman dependent on her husband's good will to dissolve the marriage, no less so than does religious law. A woman who has moved out of the family home may have to live and support her children indefinitely without recourse to support from the husband. The husband has every incentive to obstruct a divorce, and a woman may be faced with real disincentives to even begin divorce proceedings when she knows that her husband may hold her hostage for reasons of material self-interest or even mere spite. Former chief justice Meir Shamgar called this "a property arrangement with outrageous and absurd consequences, which grants one of the parties license to cynically manipulate and abuse the judicial process."[68]

The Property Relations Law was amended in 2009 to deal with problems when the get is used by the husband to bargain for money. It was proposed that the division of marital assets could occur after a period of time, even without the issuance of a get. While supported by various women's advocacy groups and by the Israel Bar Association, the proposal was opposed by ultra-Orthodox political parties. This was predictable, as the religious parties typically oppose anything that reduces the power of the religious courts. But ironically, the religious parties claimed that the proposed amendment to distribute marital property equitably would have the actual effect of encouraging husbands to wage custody battles, challenging the courts' traditional predisposition to favor the mother as custodial parent. This prediction was not persuasive. The primary change, when the proposed amendments were brought to a vote, was the addition to paragraph 5a of the law. It states, "The rights to equitable distribution will be vested in either spouse even before the dissolution of the marriage if a petition for dissolution is filed and certain conditions are met." The conditions are then elaborated. Of significance to the *agunah* is the condition that the court can make the distribution of assets contingent on the spouse depositing a written consent to give or receive a get. According to legal scholar Edwin Freedman, the recent amendment to the law "is the most significant legislative change in Israeli marital law in the past thirty-five years."[69]

For Weiss, if the rabbinical courts will not find a humane and halakhic solution to the *agunah* phenomenon, then the state must make use of its authority to rectify injustices, even if it means encroaching on the power of rabbis and lawyers who are involved in blackmail, breach of ethics, professional misconduct, or even criminal behavior. Husbands who obstruct should be made liable for damages to their wives for the suffering their behavior has caused.[70]

The civil courts will have to become proactive in treating the withholding of a get as a wrongful act by making it a cause of action for damages. Tort law turns individual harm into collective harm. Even when lawyers are unsuccessful in litigating a case, the state is more likely to later address the issue. The publicity generated by the cases demystifies the raw power relations and reveals the patriarchal will of religious courts. Susan Weiss speaks for many feminists in proposing very concrete policies that, in her view, would redress the injustices currently reinforced by civil and religious courts:

1. Eliminate CEDAW exemptions 7 and 12, which exempt discrimination based on cultural and religious sensibilities.
2. Establish and enforce civil equal rights law and eliminate the personal status law and millet system inherited from Turks. There will be an ensuing power struggle over who will define the law, so the state should set the set terms of the debate.
3. Recognize the pluralism of Jewish identity and practice and break the monopoly of the ultra Orthodox.
4. Engage in civil challenges to rabbinical authority.
5. Adopt proposals such as Haviva Ner David's to promote prenuptials, a pragmatic way to dissolve marriage amicably.
6. Recognize that the Torah is a living blueprint.
7. Make religious courts conform to modern life. Find and reinterpret halakhic solutions or at least clarify halakha and free it of ambiguity.

8. Neutralize the unilateral power of husband. Give power to the rabbinical court to declare marriage over or *void ab initio* with or without the husband's consent.

9. Introduce a civil marriage and civil divorce option for non-observant Jews. This would stem the tide of couples going abroad for civil ceremonies. "Israelis who have chosen to seal their bond solely with civil ties have until now been forced to do so outside of the country. The foreign marriage certificates are recognized by the Interior Ministry, allowing the couple to register as married without a religious wedding."[71]

10. Recognize that "rabbinic obstinacy [on the issue of civil marriage] will create what they claim they want to prevent: *mamzerim*, the fragmentation of the Jewish community . . . the breakdown of the Jewish family and an attenuation of Jewish identity."[72] The rabbinate "can take modernity by the horns. . . . Or they can shun modernity, fortify their fortress of holiness and leave Jewish women in the dust."[73]

11. Create financial incentives to give the get.

12. Civil courts can make it clear that you cannot harm women while hiding behind G-d's laws.

Another Israeli activist group, ICAR (International Coalition of Agunah Rights), represents a coalition of twenty-seven organizations working for solutions to the divorce issue. They hold an annual march from the rabbinical court to the Knesset on International Agunot Day, timed to coincide with Ta'anit Esther (fast of Esther on 13 Adar-Bet).[74] Director Sharon Shenhav, who has been practicing law in Israel for almost three decades, contends, as do many Orthodox feminists, that there have always been halakhic remedies, but rabbis have not been willing to apply them.[75] ICAR sent letters to all *dayanim*, including chief rabbi Shlomo Amar and chief rabbi Yona Metzger, posing the following questions:

1. Why don't you use halakhic solutions to free battered women from their abusive husbands who refuse to give them a get?

2. Why do you assist men who make exorbitant demands as a condition of freeing their wives with a get? Why do you advise women to waive property, child support, or pay huge monetary bribes in order to obtain a get?

3. For more than a decade, the Beit Din has had the legal authority to impose civil sanctions such as the cancellation of driver's licenses

and passports and even incarceration on recalcitrant husbands, but this power has only rarely been used. Why?

While rabbis have claimed that their hands have been tied by halakha, the last few decades have produced dozens of scholarly articles by rabbis and academics demonstrating that historically rabbis have supplied halakhic remedies going all the way back to King David. Creative solutions such as prenuptial agreements are contentious, and some rabbis see them as anti-halakhic. But others see them as fully legal in the Jewish context. What has emerged from these debates is that there have always been remedies available to resolve the current problem of *agunot*.

Facing the Backlash

Israeli feminists contend that halakha is not the real problem but rather the lack of rabbinic will to apply it. Feminists cite a rabbinic backlash directed at the Supreme Court and the government because of the revaluing of women's socio-legal rights. Dozens of hostile articles have been published in the last decade seeking to discredit the *agunah* movement, and worst of all is the phenomenon that feminists call retroactive get invalidation. The Beit Din, under its own initiative, may invalidate a get, usually on grounds that the husband was coerced, even when the husband has not requested that they do so. From a halakhic perspective, this has the potential to create a real crisis because it mamzerizes (denies the baby's legal status) when they result from the woman's subsequent marriage, though she is under the impression that her get, and therefore, her subsequent marriage are valid. This robs the children that issue from her subsequent marriage of legitimate status under halakha because they are now treated as children of a forbidden alliance.

Ironically, creating a generation of children without legal status is precisely the concern expressed by the rabbinate about improperly dissolved Jewish marriages, though the rabbinate, itself, is now compounding the problem. This is clearly part of a pattern of obstruction that is itself, part of the general backlash. But rabbi Shlomo Aviner asserts the argument that "It's unnecessary and dangerous to change standards which have been in place throughout our 2,000 year tradition."[76] He is opposed to women's Talmud learning, for instance, because "Women's brains are different from men's. . . . Talmud is a technical discipline which requires male logic."[77]

Perhaps the most palpable symbolic backlash was a gesture that dashed emerging optimism that the rabbinate was actually waking up to the injustice of the *agunah* issue.[78] The groundwork had been laid for what promised to be a path-breaking collaboration. In November 2006 a cadre of Orthodox rabbinic judges were scheduled to come to Israel to join their counterparts to discuss the problem of *agunot*. Feminist activists were dismayed that no woman has been asked to participate, yet hopeful that positive policies would emerge.[79] The International Council of Jewish Women (ICJW) and a variety of international Jewish groups spent two years planning the conference in which rabbis and advocates from all streams of Jewish life were to participate. At the last minute and with no explanation, it was abruptly cancelled by Israel's chief rabbi, Shlomo Amar. It is presumed that he was responding to intense pressure from the Haredi community. Many leading Orthodox rabbis and *dayanim* are calling for an alternative meeting in the United States, with or without their Israeli counterparts, under increased "pressure from community leaders" to "do something" about this "painful" problem.

Hopeful Signs and Success Stories: Appointment of Dayanim

IJWR 2007 reported "a virtual revolution" in the way *dayanim* are chosen in Israel.[80] The story began in 2002 when activists objected to the appointment of a particular *dayan* to the Rabbinical Court of Appeals (Bet Din Hagadol), who was widely known for humiliating women before his bench and for dismissing their demands. He was appointed despite protests, demonstrations, and petitions to the Israeli Supreme Court. ICAR then changed its strategy and lobbied to appoint women to the ten-member Commission to Appoint Dayanim, before the Israeli bar elected its two members to the statutory commission in December 2002. Sharon Shenhav, an international women's rights lawyer and expert on marriage and divorce in Jewish law and member of the Israeli delegation to the United Nations Commission on Status of Women, was elected to the commission.[81]

In March 2007, when the established legal procedures were violated in the appointment of fifteen *dayanim*, four separate groups, including women's organizations, the Israeli Bar Association, and Orthodox rabbis filed four separate Supreme Court petitions demanding the cancellation of the appointments. The minister of justice spoke about the need for the "*dayanim* to be sensitive to the problems faced by women seeking a religious divorce and he exhorted them to find and apply halakhic solutions in order to free *agunot*."[82] The Ministry of Justice cancelled the appointments and drafted guidelines for interviewing, evaluating, and appointing new *dayanim*.

Triumphant feminists responded that "for the first time in its over fifty years of operation, the Commission to Appoint Religious Court Judges has failed to operate as a tool of Israel's Orthodox establishment. A unique combination of factors has led to a stalemate in the last three years that has prevented the Haredi faction from controlling the appointments. Women's organizations and the media have had a major impact. That two women are serving on the formerly all-male commission has succeeded in bringing women's voices to the negotiations. The increased public interest in the commission's functioning combined with the new demands for transparency and proper procedures has successfully ended the well-established 'secret deals' that prevailed in the past."[83]

Conclusion

Women may achieve full civic citizenship in the nations to which they belong. But women's roles are not limited to those of the citizen. Nor are they, in Kuwait and Israel, based only on a fictive contract as in the liberal model of community membership. Women's status as mothers lodges them in all sectors of life, public and private. They are, therefore, guided not only by civil law but by religion and custom. As difference feminists have emphasized, the liberal model of feminism neglects the essentialist perspective. It is the perspective that seeks policy that is explicitly gendered in a friendly way to ensure the well being of families. It is essential that governments move beyond treating family status and civil status as dichotomous and mutually exclusive. In her cross-cultural analysis of women's contemporary office-holding patterns, Eileen McDonagh asserts that women's political citizenship is enhanced by government policies that affirm both individual equality and women's family status. She seeks to demonstrate that women's political inclusion is strengthened not by either a sameness principle (asserting women's equality to men as individuals) or a difference principle (asserting women's group difference from men) but rather by a combination of both.[84]

McDonagh's conclusions are suggestive in the Israeli case where the parallel universes of religious law and civil law seem to track the parallel universes of status-based law and contract-based law. Israeli women straddle these legal worlds. Understanding this may provide an opening for creative new ways of thinking. The theoretical impasse at which Israeli feminists find themselves is clearly intolerable, as is the reality of their situation. If the religious authorities remain unwilling to find a halakhic and compassionate way to resolve the concerns that Orthodox women raise, they will leave no alternative but for the state to design the program of reform. Feminists in Israel are actively deploying their status as full civic citizens to press the state into advancing their agenda of greater equality for women in the parallel system of religious law. Orthodox women are not demanding that halakha be overturned. Nor do they favor the liberal solution of gender-neutral equality. They are not looking to be generic citizens for whom equality implies sameness. They feel that halakha and civil law already provide the remedies that they seek and are confident that the only obstacle to the application of these remedies is rabbinic rather than halakhic.

5 The United States

FEMINISM MEETS MULTICULTURALISM

Din ha Malchutah Din
(the law of the land is the law).

The Jewish diasporic legal principle is:
"there can only be one law of the land."
    ❧ Rabbi Jonathan Sacks, chief rabbi of the United
      Hebrew Congregation of the Commonwealth[1]

"There can only be one law of the land"
    ❧ Abdullahi An-Na'im, Muslim scholar and
      law professor at Emory University[2]

Jews characterize the United States as a "country of kindness."[3] Prominent American Muslim scholar and activist Muqtedar Khan calls the United States "*dar-ul-amman* (a house of peace [order])" The United States receives appreciation not so much because it provides religious choice but because it protects the right of the devout to associate and constitute themselves as communities in its midst.

What is distinctive about the United States and other democracies when it comes to the relationship between civil citizens and religious law? Consider, for instance, that when an Istanbul University student, Leyla Sahin, sued her university in 1998, arguing that the ban against wearing her hijab on campus violated her religious rights, she lost in Turkish courts, which enforce a policy of strict secularism and gender equality in public institutions. In 2004 the European Court of Human Rights handed down an extraordinary unanimous decision backing the Turkish court's ruling on grounds that Turkey has a legitimate right to promote a secular, pluralist, civil society. Ironically, after the ruling, Ms. Sahin took up residence in Vienna, where she can wear her hijab without interference.[4]

Karl Marx noted ruefully in his essay *On the Jewish Question* that in polities such as the United States, where great pains had been taken to separate religion and politics, religion actually seemed to thrive all the more for it.[5] Minority religions such as Islam and Judaism benefit from the prohibition against religious establishment or even favoritism on the part of the state. Legal theorist, Kathleen Sullivan, contends that the neutrality of the state makes minorities the greatest beneficiaries of the contract (First Amendment establishment clause) that put an end to the war between religions that would have ended with the majority religion as the clear frontrunner, in a position to squelch other contenders.

This chapter considers the implications of the American treatment of religious groups from the perspective of: (1) Religious subgroups that attempt use current principles of multicultural toleration and the free exercise clause to shore up their chances of survival in a liberal society. (2) Devout women who are caught between their loyalty to their religious communities and their desire for greater gender equality within their communities. They may encounter the state's policy of toleration as an obstacle to their attempts at reform from within. (3) The state's competing obligations to respect cultural diversity and religious freedom on the one hand and liberal norms and laws, such as gender equality, on the other. Our American commitment to competing norms of toleration, free exercise, anti-establishment, and gender equality create challenges and opportunities for religious feminists, for minority cultures, and for the state that hosts them.

In the United States both Islam and Judaism are minority religions within a system that views conscience and belief as a private matter and regards religious groups as analogous to voluntary associations composed of autonomous individuals. Some accommodations for religious practice are justified under the free exercise clause, but are always assessed as to whether they run afoul of public order, child welfare, criminal law, and the establishment clause. The default presumption, however, is that where no coercion of members or violations of criminal law are present, religion is a private affair. With respect to practices that are not congruent with public norms, such as gender equality, the court also assesses the centrality of the tenet or practice to the religion in question. For instance, the Catholic Church is allowed to determine who is eligible for the priesthood, and its exclusion of women from this role has not called forth any action on the part of the state in defense of gender equality. But there is no immunity from criminal prosecution for domestic abuse and the like.

Devout Jewish and Muslim women may find themselves in a bind.

When the state, in the name of free exercise, grants exemptions to religious groups from otherwise generally applicable laws, the benefit to the group may impose a burden on its female members. While a woman may take advantage of the option to leave the group, in countries such as the United States, this imposes a high cost. Why should a woman accept a choice between putting up with injustice or giving up her religious affiliation? This is particularly painful when those who hold religious authority may have strayed from divine intent when they strayed from gender justice. It is all the more painful for women who have, along with male members of minority groups, experienced discrimination at the hands of the wider society. This experience is likely to militate in favor of greater solidarity and insularity on the part of members of the community in question, including women.

Religious leaders must accept that in the United States, religious affiliation is purely voluntary. Religious courts have no power to force a recalcitrant individual to appear before its judges or abide by their rulings. Yet, both Muslim and religious Jewish women have qualms about taking religiously based harms into public courts. Habits of submission and loyalty to the beleaguered minority group often trump a woman's complaints about her personal experience of injustice. While minority groups may go to court to protect their collective civil rights, for a woman to take a complaint before an outsider, particularly a civil authority, may be treated as an act of betrayal.

Both Islam and Judaism have comprehensive and ancient systems of law pertaining to marriage, divorce, custody, family property, and inheritance that impact women profoundly. This is also the category of law with which civil courts have the most difficulty. Not only will civil courts have to navigate the minefield of the establishment clause prohibitions, but their general strategy, which is to attempt to draw analogies between Islamic, Jewish, and us civil codes, often yields no results. Nor are American courts eager to adjudicate cases involving religious practices. To do so would risk becoming overtly entangled with religious questions, constituting a violation of the Lemon test of the establishment clause.[6]

If civil courts were to avert their attention from the internal practices of religious groups, women could be exposed to a double injustice. In addition to her inequitable treatment under religious law, she experiences the erosion of her full complement of rights as a citizen of the United States. For the United States, which until recently has struggled with vestiges of inequality since passing the Fourteenth Amendment, the Twenty-first Amendment, and the Civil Rights Act, the idea of unequal citizenship is anathema. Gender equality is a liberal norm backed by a democratic consensus, so it would seem that the enforcement of laws pertaining to gender equality would be given high priority.

But here is where two norms of nearly equal importance can collide: the state is also committed to accommodating cultural and religious diversity, resulting in what Shachar has termed the "paradox of multicultural accommodation."[7] She is referring to a situation experienced by Israeli and American women, Muslim and Jewish, in which grants of partial sovereignty to religious groups further entrenches, with the unwitting imprimatur of the state, the patriarchal power hierarchy of the status quo ante, all but silencing the voices of vulnerable members of the group who are invisible to state officials. In the United States this creates a tension between liberal democratic norms and the group-differentiated politics of recognition, multiculturalism, or identity.[8] This tension has also created a backlash directed at the academic purveyors of this principle and the public officials who have adopted it. Popular opinion in many European countries, Australia, Canada, and the United States, has come to associate multiculturalism with mass immigration, particularly of Muslims, and governmental hospitality to non-liberal ways of life as undermining the unitary legal system, democracy, and even national security. The fear that the academic and official promotion of multicultural accommodation comes at the expense of gender equality has put the issue of women's rights at center stage in these debates. The quandary for postmodern academic feminists is the incompatibility between their support for women's rights regardless of country or culture and their condemnation of liberalism's claim that it stands for universally applicable norms. How can one treat all morality and cultures as local, particular, equally valid, and incommensurable without turning a blind eye to the oppressive practices of some of these cultures at home and abroad?

Further complicating multicultural accommodation is the ambiguity when it comes to theorizing the nature of groups as democratic actors. Are religious groups simply a variant of the conventional interest group or voluntary association, or do they constitute a less benign presence in American political life? If religious groups are understood under the rubric of multiculturalism and toleration, how can a liberal democracy still remain true to its principles? What do we make of groups that are not structured according to democratic rules and do not see their membership as an aggregate of voluntarily affiliated, autonomous individuals connected by horizontal rather than hierarchical and patriarchal relationships? Can non-liberal groups serve democratic purposes? To many critics of indiscriminate multicultural toleration, such groups are at cross-purposes with liberal democracy and antithetical to women's equality and the American way of life.

From the Perspective of the Group

Preserving communal integrity, survival, and identity in an inviting and hospitable society presents contemporary minorities with perhaps the greatest challenges of any time in history. Today's Jews, Christians, and Muslims are still grappling with the issue of personal autonomy versus institutionalized religious authority. No religion has remained immune to the conflict between rationalism, secularism, empiricism, and postmodernism, on the one hand, and submission to traditional authority, on the other. The behavior of government toward religious groups inadvertently plays a role in encouraging or discouraging internal reforms, particularly related to gender. Society presents a myriad of possible lifestyles featuring fewer restrictions and duties than the religious life of Jews and Muslims.

The United States "is a country of Christians, but not a Christian country,"[9] yet while Christian religious precepts are not legally established, they are so intertwined with the culture that they appear to be facially neutral at least from the perspective of the majority. Ironically, the very comfort of life in the United States, with its notable diversity, tolerance, and endless menu of lifestyle choices, creates alarm among many religious parents. Desire for their children to succeed professionally and academically is often matched by fear that their children will assimilate and intermarry. Freedom of religion is protected, but so is freedom of non-religion. Protestant parents may be able to rely on passive osmosis of religious symbols and norms embedded in the culture, but minority parents must be proactive if they are to succeed in transmitting their religion to the next generation. Cultural drift, assimilation, and cross-pollination affect minorities more than majorities, especially among the generations born in the host country. Minority communities must build resistance to the majority without generating hostility in their children toward the wider community. Toleration of minorities by majorities may seem principled and admirable because it reflects a choice. But minorities, whether they want to or not, have no choice but to acknowledge the pervasive majority culture, even while devising ways to preserve and transmit their own to the future generation.

The commitment to individualism that is shared by Protestantism, liberalism, and capitalism is not shared with the more communal religions such as Islam and Orthodox Judaism. Americans typically see religion as a choice reflecting a Protestant notion of individual conscience and moral autonomy. As a sociological principle, this was articulated by Robert Bellah[10] following the lead of Will Heberg.[11] According to the Pew US Religious Landscape Survey (2008)[12] some 25 percent of Americans change religions at some point. While 90 percent of Americans identify themselves as religious, they describe religion in more personal, subjective, amorphous terms. The idea of religion as a choice in a bustling marketplace of lifestyles, in which each competes for a market share, is so pervasive that it can blind us to the communal and totalistic way that Orthodox Jews and Muslims envision their religious commitments as a priori obligations rather than voluntary choices.

As Michael Sandel noted, many religious people do not regard their religion or the obligations that it imposes on the believer as a matter of choice.[13] For them, faith is tied up in family and community, and unlike Kantian notions that humans can only be obligated by a freely undertaken contract, religious people regard themselves as having been claimed even prior to birth. G-d chose them rather than the other way around. In the case of Jews, they may adopt a contractual language, but it is a contract that dates to Mount Sinai and is as incumbent on this generation as it was upon the first generation that accepted the covenant at Sinai. This conception does not reject the idea of free will and self-determination, rather it views freedom as the choice to take on "the yoke of heaven."[14] Christians often cite the Biblical verse in which G-d instructs Moses to tell Pharaoh to "let my people go," but they rarely cite the second part of the command, "that they may serve Me."[15] The Jewish and Muslim understanding of freedom is more akin to Isaiah Berlin's notion of positive freedom or self-mastery and the fulfillment of duties as opposed to the liberal notion of freedom from restraint.[16]

The post-Enlightenment binary notion of religion and reason obscures more than it reveals. No religious Jew, Muslim, or Christian, regards his or her faith as antithetical to reason. Like Aristotle and contemporary civic republicans or communitarians, they are likely to believe that religious thinking is the background condition that makes reasoning possible. Attachment to religious duty does not preclude moral autonomy or free choice. To be religious in the modern age is a choice. It is not simply a flight from reason or freedom.[17] Religious people might be seen in terms used by Foucault, as injecting a rival voice into the "monologue of reason."[18]

Another communitarian dimension of Islam and Judaism is that they are structured according to patterns of kin and family descent, transmitted from one generation to the next. Jonathan Boyarin uses the terms diaspora and genealogy as alternatives to the American liberal organizing principles of individualism and territoriality.[19] Both groups are shaped by a sense of being in diaspora, in both temporal and geographical distance from their Mecca and their Jerusalem. Both groups experience life as minorities. Both groups contain a large immigrant population, many of whom came from non-liberal and non-democratic countries. Orthodox Jews and Muslims more closely resemble nomic communities than interest groups or associations. They have sacred texts and codes of law that operate in some respects as alternative constitutions, and they are more likely as citizens to find themselves occasionally caught between two sets of law. While American law is infused with Judeo-Christian morality, there are areas of law, particularly family and personal status law, in which the religious and civil codes conflict.

With respect to citizen skills, both groups' first generation of immigrants may be unfamiliar with democracy, having come from communities where they lived under the legacy of the Ottoman millet system in the Middle East and North Africa, or corporate systems in Eastern Europe and pre–World War I Russia. These regimes may have permitted a degree of communal isolation that afforded communal authorities near religious autonomy. Both Muslims and Jewish immigrants have experienced generational differences in approaches to the wider culture, with American-born generations more likely to feel fully at home in the United States. The generational differences are also reflected in political style and participation. Immigrants from both communities may refract American politics through the lens of their previous experiences, as a process of personal contacting and patron-client relationships. American-born generations of Jews and Muslims, however, have become masters of American political and associational life as participating democratic citizens.

Jews in America

We begin with a bit of background that suggests that the political history of Jews in Diaspora or Muslims from the Middle East was not particularly supportive of liberal democratic political culture. Ghetto and *kehillah* (Jewish community) in Europe, and particularly Russia, were simultaneously oppressive and protective. The insularity came with a degree of autonomy and self-governance and habits of self-help and life for the *edah* (political and legal community) according to the Torah and local religious authorities. This history of semi-autonomous communal life left a mark on the contemporary Jewish life of emigrants.

Jews and Judaism fared best in places where they were granted partial self-government, even when this came as a result of ghettoization. Ottoman-style millet systems in the extensive area that came under Turkish rule in both Europe and Arab regions dealt with religious and ethnic diversity by permitting the establishment by each group of its own religious court system and other forms of limited self-rule. Catherine of Russia, while cordoning Jews off in the pale of settlement, permitted Jews a good deal of autonomy. Although Jews were subject peoples and suffered burdensome discriminatory policies in these states, Jewish law and authority guided daily life. Russian authority even subcontracted political authority to the *kehillah* and offered to back up Jewish rulings with state power. Thus, the czar's policy of isolating the Jews was more beneficial to the preservation of Jewish communal life than Napoleon's policy of granting Jews rights as individual citizens on the condition of assimilation. After the nineteenth century, the majority of Jewish immigrants came from Russia and Eastern Europe, and the habit of entreating authorities is occasionally still evident in the political practices of some Orthodox communities. The same political habits accompanied later Jewish immigrants from Muslim areas. Special pleading and personal contacting of government officials on behalf of the group is still an important political legacy of life under the czars and the Ottomans. This culture of defensive isolation and reliance on an appointed representative or *shtadlan* is not antithetical to democratic politics, but neither is it particularly conducive to democracy.

Judaism confronted the Enlightenment and political emancipation movement in Europe in a variety of ways. Moses Mendelssohn, the torchbearer of the *haskallah* movement, counseled German Jews to devote themselves to being solid citizens of the land in which they resided, but to remain steadfast in the religions of their fathers in the privacy of their homes.

Napoleon also emphasized that French Jews, if they were to be citizens, must not distinguish themselves from other citizens in the public realm. As Tonniere said, "for Jews as citizens, everything; for Jews as Jews, nothing."

Unlike many Jewish immigrants in the late nineteenth and early twentieth century who came to the United States in part to slip the bonds of Jewish observance, many of the Orthodox, especially the Chassidim, were late comers to the American scene, arriving as a shattered remnant from Eastern Europe and Russia after World War II. Their hope was to reconstitute, as nearly as possible, the lost communities of pre–World War II Europe. They are especially appreciative of the principle in the First Amendment that protects the free exercise of religion and free association. The American Jewish community constitutes about 1.7 percent of the population of the United States. It is highly concentrated in several states and in urban settings. The majority of affiliated Jews identify with either Reform Judaism, which arose in Western Europe as an attempt to reconcile Judaism with the demands of secular society, or with Conservative Judaism, which arose in the United States in response to perceived assimilationist excesses of Reform Judaism. There are several smaller denominations, such as Reconstructionism, which also have their origins in the United States.

Orthodox Jews currently constitute less than 10 percent of the American Jewish population, but have the lowest rates of intermarriage and the highest birth rates. Among Jews, the Orthodox include several variants. Some refer to the ultra Orthodox or Haredi, which usually refers to Chassidim, black hat, Yeshivish, or Litvish Orthodox. Then there is a spectrum of Jews characterized as modern Orthodox or *dati* (observant). Both men and women in this community tend to be strongly supportive of the state of Israel, have secular as well as religious educations and professions, and tend to be active politically. Historically, observant Jews were political outsiders but followed the dictum that translates "the law of the land is the law."[20] Law-abidingness constitutes a minimalist definition of citizenship and does not provide clear guidance in the event that civil law contradicts or violates Torah law. For Jews living in the United States, conflicts between Jewish and civil law have rarely arisen, and with respect to Sabbath observance, ritual slaughter, blue laws, and circumcision, conflicts have historically been resolved in favor of Jewish law. In several cases, such as the one involving Satmar Chassidic school children, the denial of benefits and services such as school buses that were available to other communities was based on a rejection of the Satmar demand that the state accommodate its request for only male school bus drivers. This demand was judged by the Supreme Court as contravening both the union contract and gender equality, as well as violating the establishment clause.[21] But these cases did not interfere with the free exercise rights of the Orthodox. Orthodox enclaves are left more or less to themselves unless they overtly violate civil or criminal law. They choose the extent to which they integrate into society.

Since the first twenty-three Jews arrived on American shores from Brazil in 1654, they have formed literally hundreds of self-help burial societies and free loan associations based on town of origin in the homeland. This legacy of Jewish communal life has translated positively into democratic political habits. Yet Orthodox and less observant Jewish groups have developed rather different political values. Reform and Conservative Jews are the staunchest supporters of the Democratic Party and come out at the top of surveys testing liberal values. This led Seymour Martin Lipset to quip that "Jews earn like Episcopalians but vote like Puerto Ricans."[22] They are also more individualistic in their orientation and strongly committed to civil liberties. They are also among the strongest proponents of the separation of church and state and have lobbied against state funding for religious schools, school prayer, and public religious displays.

Differences in religious concerns and political styles between Orthodox Jews and non-Orthodox Jews do not affect either group's respect for the rules of American political life. They engage with equal frequency in voting, lobbying efforts, and submitting amicus briefs before the courts. However, Orthodox Jews are less likely to see the establishment clause as erecting an impermeable wall between religion and the state. They worry that the establishment clause is often interpreted as banning what the free exercise clause permits. Orthodox Jews have broken ranks with Reform and Conservative Jews on issues such as the public display of menorahs or the right to install an *eruv* (threadlike boundary around a Jewish neighborhood that transforms public into private property), permitting Jews to carry objects outdoors. Orthodox tend to favor state funding for parochial schools, the voucher plan, and school prayer. While the public schools served immigrant non-Orthodox Jews as a conduit into the middle classes, Orthodox Jews most often send their children to private schools. Non-Orthodox Jews outnumber Orthodox Jews in the United States, but organizations such as the Orthodox Union, Agudath Israel, United Torah Judaism, National Council of Synagogue Youth (NCSY), Chabad Lubavitch, Aish HaTorah, and dozens of others are active on many fronts and are regarded as models of political efficacy. Among Muslims, many political lobbying groups, such as MPAC, were consciously modeled on the America-Israel Public Affairs Committee (AIPAC).

Muslims in America

The American Muslim community is a microcosm of American diversity. A noticeable presence of Muslims in North America is a fairly recent development, whereas an indigenous Islam has been practiced by African-American Muslims, mostly going back to the early decades of the twentieth century. The size of the Muslim community, just as that of the Jews in the United States is difficult to calculate with precision because religious affiliation is not requested on the US census form. The Pew forum has undertaken the most authoritative survey, which it published in 2008. The Muslim population is variously numbered between six and eight million,[23] and is fairly evenly divided among Sunni and Shi'a, with a growing number of Muslims who identify with Sufis. They represent a multitude of national and ethnic backgrounds including immigrants from Africa, South, and Southeast Asia, Bosnia, and the Middle East, not to mention second- and third-generation American Muslims and the significant portion of native born African American Muslims associated with the Nation of Islam, founded in Detroit in 1930. There are now several splinter groups, such as the one under the leadership of Louis Farrakhan. Islam is one of the fastest growing American religions due to an increasing influx of converts, over 50 percent of whom are women.

About a thousand mosques are mostly in major metropolitan centers such as Philadelphia, New York, Los Angeles, Dearborn, Michigan, and the northern Virginia and Washington, DC, vicinity. Large cities and campuses may have several mosques, catering to different denominations, but in most areas, the community is not large enough to support separate congregations. Fusing and mingling for religious and social purposes is the norm.[24] This tension is attributed to the newly arrived immigrants from strife-torn areas, who have transported their disputes to America; "If you have nine Muslims in one [association], they have to get along.... If you have 90, there's enough to break into splinter groups."[25] Many Muslims have signed on to the New Muslim Code of Honor, aimed at countering hostilities and divisions, moving in the direction of so-called big tent Islam.[26]

Like American Protestants, Muslims seems to be evolving into a more non-denominational community, attempting to overcome sectarian friction. "We don't want to be defined by the classification of history and the Middle East. The Qur'an is our authority," says Salim al-Marayati, executive director of MPAC.[27] If intermarriage is a gauge, "matrimonial meet-ups" at Muslim conventions cross sectarian lines and feature speed dating (supervised, of course, by the mothers). A new generation of Muslims born to mixed Sunni and Shia parentage have dubbed themselves "Sushis" with pride.[28] A 2006 *USA Today* survey found that among Muslim registered voters, 12 percent identified themselves as Shiite, 36 percent as Sunni, and 40 percent identified themselves as "just a Muslim."[29] (Worldwide figures are vastly different, with about 85 percent identifying as Sunni and 15 percent as Shi'a.)

The American Muslim community is young, with a majority under the age of forty. Young, American-born Muslims tend to share many values and behaviors of their non-Muslim peers, while managing to adhere to their religion. By contrast, younger British Muslims may be more radicalized and alienated than their immigrant parents. On the whole, American Muslims, even post-9/11, are more satisfied with their socio-economic status and feel less hostility from their non-Muslim neighbors.[30] "Compared with the tension that exists in Muslim communities across Europe, America's Muslims are a more contented lot."[31] A recent Pew forum study found that most American Muslims say that "their communities are excellent or good places"[32] to live; 71 percent say they can succeed in the US if they work. Both income and college graduation levels match the national norms. Sixty-three percent of American Muslims report no conflict between religious devotion and living in modern society. Although 53 percent of US Muslims think that life is more difficult since the terrorist attacks of 2001, most think that this is the fault of the government, not their neighbors. Seventy-three percent said they had never experienced discrimination while living in America. The younger generations have attained high socio-economic and educational levels—above the national average. In short, life is good.[33] Like Jews of their socio-economic and educational status, they vote heavily for Democrats.

Contrast this with England where it was recently reported that radicalism and support for a shari'a-based state in England is strong in British universities. Thirty percent of students support the introduction of shari'a law into Britain and the creation of a worldwide caliphate. Muslims are far less tolerant toward diversity, especially gays, it is claimed. "A large number of students think it is ok to kill in the name of religion" and "Significant numbers appear to hold beliefs that contravene democratic values."[34] (These British results have been criticized as biased by some British and Muslim groups.) Is the higher comfort level of American Muslims due to their greater integration both among Sunnis and Shi'a and exposure to American culture? Whatever the cause, it is likely to be complex. Trends in contemporary American Islam suggest to some analysts that Islam may currently be going through its own reformation as did Christianity centuries ago and Judaism in the last three hundred years. It is commonly claimed that Islam missed its chance and that Islam battled modernity and modernity lost. On the contrary, it can be claimed that Islam had own particular versions of the Enlightenment in the form of a golden age of rationalism, interpretive flexibility, and scientific discovery. In many countries, this progressive, rationalist tradition is alive, but many historians hold that this era came and went before the end of the Middle Ages and that the confrontation with modernity after that time, be it in the form of secular nationalism or colonialism, ended with victory for traditional hardliners and Islamists and defeat for modernity (other than in the realms of technology and weaponry). Many theorists contend that globally, traditional political Islam is on the upsurge, triumphing over secularism. Islam is much more variegated and open to reform than many Western analysts perceive. This is not limited to the United States. Yet this makes it easier to appreciate the advantages of American life for dissidents. The luxury of operating under the rule of law in the United States, which is protective of individual expression and dissent, combined with the lack of a centralized hegemonic religious authority structure, has been a boon to Muslims and Jews bent on rethinking and reclaiming their religions.

The challenges and opportunities faced by Muslims in the West are intimately connected to the difference between minority status in a liberal democracy and majority status in a shari'a-based country. Islamic law has long recognized that Muslims living as minorities may require some flexibility with respect to interpretation and adherence. There are differences over the status of *fiqh-al-aqalliyat* (more lenient jurisprudence for Muslims when they live as minorities in non-Muslim society), *maqasid-al-shari'a* (the objectives of Islamic law), the desirability of *madhab al-taysir* (the way of seeking latitude in religious rulings), and whether to emphasize *rikhsa* (legal dispensation) or *azima* (the strictest legal ruling). In a highly fragmented setting, it's nearly impossible to achieve consensus on legal issues.

Without a single religious authority, the number of online imams is grow-ing, or as one Muslim analyst quipped, "Imam meets Sheikh Google."[35]

Sincere appreciation for America's lack of interference in religious life is often expressed.[36] For instance, an Indonesian man who lives with his family in Newton Centre, Massachusetts, entered a blog on Islam.lib.com, commenting on the virtues of American life from the perspective of a minority and a newcomer. He was delighted with the respect given by the local library and his children's school to the Muslim holidays. "All sects and schools of thought enjoyed their freedom, because the state is neutral toward religion and supports religious tolerance. . . . The minority needs secularism which benefits them in all aspects. . . . Comparing both systems, it is clear that the secular system is superior, and it cannot be perceived except by minorities." The writer concludes that in terms of religious protection, freedom of religious practice, and security, the secular state performs better than the Islamic state.[37] And while Islamists (followers of political Islam) are critical of Western culture, even they benefit from operating in a liberal, pluralistic, and tolerant environment. They often flee their home countries in the Middle East, where they are more likely to be restricted in their activities than in the Western democracies.

The Muslim Political Action Committee recently criticized Samuel Huntington's "clash of civilizations" thesis.[38] "America, in spite of its faults, its limitations, and even its sins and sinners, is easily the best place to live on earth. If you do not believe me, then ask the millions of Muslims desperate to leave their countries, their families, their societies to come to America. The thing that is most precious about America is not its capitalist nature or its wealth, it is the First Amendment. The ideal of freedom of religion and thought in America . . . allows Muslims to practice Islam. . . . There can be no faith without freedom. . . . We, and by we I mean all Americans . . . must not allow, a few rotten apples, to impose their thought-less understanding of Islam on others, subvert free societies, distort Islamic teachings and undermine the hope for a harmonious relationship between America and its Muslims."[39]

For women, the American context offers greater opportunities for pub-lic roles, leadership, and careers. "Therefore, a new kind of American Islam is being created in which women can be at once devout and publicly active."[40] Organizations such as *Karamah*, which is composed of Muslim women lawyers who defend women's rights, both as citizens and as Mus-lims, represent the activist and the devout nature of Islamic feminism.

The View from the State: Pluribus Is Fine
but Is It Good for the Unum?

Having laid out the bare contours of Muslim and Jewish experiences in US society, we may ask how these groups are viewed from the perspective of the state in theory and in practice. Are groups the scaffolding that supports democracy? This section raises what Martha Minow has called the subgroup question[41] and investigates the controversial notion of "group rights," both the strong and weak versions, from the perspective of supporters and critics.

If we can safely conclude that Jewish and Muslim groups in the United States see themselves as beneficiaries of American law and norms, how are they perceived by US democratic theory and law? Is their acceptance and enthusiasm reciprocated? To the extent that groups in American society and politics behave as liberal associations, they can expect to be treated with benign indifference as one among a multitude of players. Yet our liberal commitment to tolerance as a society is most seriously tested by groups that appear not to share our liberal values, even when they are fully committed to our democratic process.[42] Though they are not all benign, the overwhelming majority of American Jews and Muslims do not pose a threat to our constitution. Yet they, along with several non-mainstream religions, do come under occasional criticism by political and legal theorists on other grounds. Non-liberal religious groups test the limits of tolerance, especially when they do not share liberal norms such as gender equality. That they are politically engaged and savvy raises more suspicions about motives than means. The question is often formulated as whether these groups serve democratic purposes from the state's perspective, rather than how they serve the purposes of their own members.[43]

Early concerns expressed in the Federalist Papers (in particular, number 10) regarded factions as potentially destructive of social unity. But it was also understood that factions would arise inevitably in a free society. "Publius" concluded that factions could only be eliminated by repressive means and that the loss of freedom was too high a price to pay for achieving this unity of purpose. Pluralism is a part of the national project. While the framers did not put aside all of their qualms about partitions of the whole, they elegantly theorized these competing groups as safeguards of democracy. As long as no interest of faction could achieve a monopoly of power, they could pose no threat to the polity. Moreover, the multiplication of factions meant the fragmentation and wide dispersal of power among countervailing factions, keeping each other at bay and collectively, keeping the government at bay. This would open a space for individual freedom in both the public and private realm. That said, formal power in the polity would be limited to the exercise of individual votes. This case for the multiplication of competitive loci of power became the backbone of interest group theory in the mid-twentieth century. It was augmented by Clifford Geertz's concept of cross-cutting cleavages, which would theoretically prevent permanently entrenched adversarial politics, because individuals would have multiple memberships and overlapping loyalties with respect to some interests even if they were opposed on others.[44]

Our many grassroots associations led Alexis de Tocqueville in the early nineteenth century to base his optimism for our democratic future on our habit of voluntarily forming associations. In contemporary times, that our associations form spontaneously from below is used to showcase the independent, self-help, can-do spirit of Americans, which Robert Putnam[45] calls "social capital." Associations of like-minded people, even when the shared interest that animates the group has nothing to do with politics, serve as incubators of democratic habits of toleration, equality, compassion, and mutual respect. These groups check the destructive power of excessive self-interested individualism and contribute positively to sustaining our democratic institutions, and they check the ability of the government to aggrandize power at the expense of its citizens. Democratic theorists (Lipset, Almond, and Verba) and foreign policy analysts, notably Jeanne Kirkpatrick, have also used the existence or absence of a thick network of private associations as a predictor of the success of democratic regimes. These views make associations the heroes of democratic life and resistance to state-sponsored oppression.

But contemporary liberal theorists are divided on whether all associations benefit democracy. Some hold that the internal structure and behaviors of groups must conform to democratic rules and liberal norms for the group to be a true building block of democracy. William Galston[46] characterizes the divide as between those who prioritize "diversity" over autonomy as the chief virtue of liberalism. Theorists who favor autonomy are commonly called maximalist or perfectionist liberals, because they see a link between certain liberal personality traits, such as critical thinking and individualism as requirements of political deliberation, and, therefore, as requirements of democratic citizenship. By linking liberal personality traits with democratic political competence and linking both with the state's right and obligation to educate citizens who are capable of keeping our democratic system afloat from generation to generation, these liberal perfectionists have constructed an argument for a rather muscular government. If rational political deliberation can only be exercised by liberal citizens, and the state has a legitimate interest in self-perpetuation, it therefore has a legitimate interest in the production of competent, committed, liberal citizens. The state, when confronted by recalcitrant (non-liberal religious) parents, can legitimately countermand parental authority. Attempts by the state or US government to do so has resulted in many bitter legal controversies in the context of public education between religious parents and state authority and even given rise to the term culture wars.[47]

By contrast, diversity liberals contend that toleration of difference is liberal society's chief virtue and that short of stock piling arms and endangering the welfare of children, almost any group can be tolerated. In terms of the requirements of citizenship, they would lower the bar. Law-abiding behavior constitutes adequate citizenship.

In keeping with the diversity model of toleration, Ronald Dworkin[48] made a case for minimizing state interference in order to maximize individual freedom. The instantiation of individual freedom requires, ideally, that the government be "neutral with respect to individuals' choices about the good," with the proviso that one person's good does not trample the rights of others. The workable ideal of liberty takes a form close to John Stuart Mill's harm principle, in which rights are trumps, and it is only permissible for government to interfere with individual exercises of freedom when they cause harm to others.[49]

Perhaps the most fully articulated attempt to reconcile diverse visions of the good life under liberalism was that of John Rawls.[50] He distinguished between a "political conception of justice," in which a short list of core values and democratic procedures are respected by all citizens in the name of social cooperation. As long as citizens respect the limits imposed by the political conception, they are free to hold whatever "comprehensive view of the good" they choose.[51] His view was that all religious groups could find enough latitude within the procedural rules and the handful of imperative operative norms.

Should Communities of Faith Be Treated as Interest Groups and Voluntary Associations?

In a liberal democracy, just as in any regime, a religious citizen, by definition, is bound by different and perhaps competing legal codes. Therefore, religious groups pose a special problem that bowling leagues do not. For all of the injunctions to render unto Caesar, Augustine saw Christians as dual citizens with one foot in the eternal city of G-d and one foot in the temporal city of man. John Locke's *Epistle on Toleration* (1689) set out the two separate domains of the civil magistrate and the church, but then drew the toleration line to exclude Catholics and atheists.[52] James Madison, in his "Memorial and Remonstrance," however, sided with the individual conscience, holding that a citizen's first duty is to his Creator when a conflict arises between civil and religious law. Rousseau countered with a model that allegedly solved the dual loyalty problem by merging patriotism and faith: state and G-d in a civil religion. Critics of civil religion, or any close alliance between religion and state, hold that religious citizens play their most positive role when they act toward the state as connected critics.[53] Yet these perspectives focus on individuals acting as individuals, not as members of sub-national groups based on shared communal norms.

Islam and Orthodox Judaism can be characterized as nomoi or paedaia (self-legislating communities) by Robert Cover or by John Rawls' "comprehensive conceptions."[54] They are religions that set the daily rhythms of their adherents' lives, from the daily (lunar) calendar to dietary laws, and the schedule of daily prayer. Boundary markers such as language and dress may apply to both men and women. Judaism and Islam cannot be assimilated to the model of voluntary associations or interest groups. While members are free to leave their religious community, the costs of exit are likely to exact a much higher psychic toll than dropping out of one's bowling league. The bonds of community are intertwined with bonds of religion, ancestors, family, tradition, and importantly, with individual identity. This is important to the understanding of why religious feminists, who share these bonds, do not simply abandon their faith communities.

The United States must formulate its stance toward these communities considering that the right to one's own culture is formerly enshrined as a doctrine by the UN, UNESCO, and Council of Europe. This redefines cultural identities as rights and makes states' violations of these rights legally actionable at the international, or European Union, level. This international accord on rights has played out in several Western countries, with governments taking the initiative to extend certain rights and privileges to indigenous ethnic minorities and to immigrant communities in their midst. The intention is that these accommodations would facilitate social integration rather than perpetuate social divisions, but the results so far are mixed. Multicultural accommodation, whether in the form of grants of differentiated rights or resources or creating the appearance of sensitivity toward cultural and religious differences is on the global political agenda and has legitimized communal demands against many governments.

Evaluating Group-Based Politics Models: Should Groups Be Repositories of Rights?

The centrifugal forces created by competing group demands against the rest of society may be unhealthy for national unity, even if not for democracy. However, the rights of groups may not only foster the survival of minority groups in larger society, but may provide minority individuals with a real vehicle for interest representation.

The politics of difference[55] theory holds that group-based politics magnify the votes of disadvantaged minorities that could otherwise never hope to muster an electoral majority as individuals. In the United States, history leads us to be properly wary of all legal classifications. The Fourteenth Amendment intended to end the practice of treating people according to ascriptive characteristics such as race, and later gender and class. But by the 1960s, it was becoming evident that the promise of the Fourteenth Amendment, one rule for all citizens, was not producing equality of opportunity and certainly not equality of outcome. The removal of overt discriminatory practices was a step forward, but the right to have rights was not fostering desired gains by minorities and women. The 1960s brought a wave of group identity, group assertion, and demands for group recognition in society and in politics. It was increasingly resolved that "under contemporary conditions of cultural heterogeneity, 'classical' or 'difference blind' liberal principles fail to deliver on either liberty or equality."[56] Iris Marion Young[57] proposed an alternative, "the politics of difference." She rejected the ideal of the featureless, generic, universal citizen. While group characteristics had been the basis for discrimination, they could now be used positively as the basis for differentiated rights. Her concept of the politics of difference dovetailed neatly with newly coined "modified principle of group rights."[58]

But while Young characterized women as an oppressed group, deserving of special treatment, she did not consider that women, particularly women who had experienced discrimination as members of racial, ethnic and religious minorities, were more likely to throw their loyalty to their group than to women of other races or classes. Gender is indeed salient, but women have multiple group affiliations to juggle. Young's theory of group-differentiated rights would do no more to advance the position of women within minority groups than standard multiculturalism, focused as it is on inter-group rather than intra-group power differentials. The same can be said of most versions of communitarian theory, despite their recognition of identity as an intrinsic human right in light of the psychic benefit of group life to the individual member. Rarely do they acknowledge the differential impact of group life on women and men. If culture provides a world of meaning and identity, and serves as a springboard for individual choice, then the question how women are acculturated is of real importance.

Group-differentiated, preferential policies can create new, invidious relationships between the state and its citizens. According to Shachar, identity groups become mediators between the state and the individual. Delegating rights to an identity group might strengthen its power against other identity groups or the majority, but at the cost of giving the identity group a near carte blanche to oppress the citizen-insider.[59] The group is substituted for the rights-bearing individual in this permissive approach, and women become the minority within the minority, suffering at the hands of the group what the group used to suffer at the hands of the larger society. The American view is that the private realm is sacrosanct, in which the state is loathe to intervene; this may appear to free the state from the obligation to exercise strict scrutiny over the internal workings of faith groups.[60]

Perfectionist liberalism and civic republicanism are more suspicious of sub-national groups. They are concerned that while some groups foster civic engagement and democratic citizenship, others encourage their members to throw all of their loyalty to the group. In the capacity of citizen, it is considered acceptable by classical liberal theory for one to seek to advance individual self-interest or alternatively, to nobly cast aside self-interest on behalf of the common good. But the idea of advancing the interests of the group per se is regarded with suspicion by many theorists. Critics think cult when they think nomic group. The mistake may be their tendency to conflate liberal principles and values with democratic ones. Orthodox Jews and Muslims demonstrate high rates of political participation leading to an additional discomfort among the critics of group loyalty, having to do with the very success of these groups in the political sphere.

A Society of Societies: Permeable Sovereignty

On the opposite end of the spectrum of those who advance a liberal and unitary legal system are those theorists, often associated with critical legal theory, who champion groups as contenders for partial or sub-national sovereignty. They share with difference politics an emphasis on the political salience of groups, but not in the instrumental sense of aggregating individual preferences of group members for the purpose of creating for them a greater voice. They are more concerned about the autonomy of groups, not as political actors, but as independent entities in competition with the state for near independent sovereignty over their members. The advocates of overlapping authority share some antipathy for the state's interference in private lives of citizens, and particularly, seeming attempts to establish a "moral commons." They challenge the right of the state to monopolize the right to set laws and interpret them. This is an overt challenge to the ideal of the unitary state that would transcend group differences.

Nomic groups, a term used by Robert Cover (a *nomos* is a meaningful, law-bound order), sees the ideal society as a composite of differentiated moral and legal worlds composed of fairly autonomous, self-legislating communities. Torah, Qur'an, or other sacred texts would operate as the narratives and bases of padaeic or world-creating communities within a larger world-maintaining or imperial nation. These little world-creating communities would contest the state's claim of an exclusive right to make or interpret law and remain free to not conform to any externally mandated conceptions of justice.[61] Society would become a mosaic of loosely affiliated mini-states.

The danger here is the same as in all strong multicultural theories. Group autonomy requires the state to abandon safeguards against rights abuses carried out by some members against others. Some theorists are satisfied with the proviso that members maintain the right to leave the group while others regard that as insufficient protection for at-risk individuals. Robert Cover, Abner Greene, Jonathan Boyarin, Nomi Stolzenberg, and, to a degree, Martha Minow, are more comfortable with groups engaged in boundary-preserving strategies.[62] New York state was sympathetic, but the US Supreme Court was not when[63] it ruled in the Kiryas Joel case that the New York law granting the

Satmar community a school district that tracked the lines of their village violated the establishment clause. Opponents of the New York legislation condemned the alleged establishment clause violations and the Satmar's reputation for gender inequality, hierarchical distribution of power, and lack of liberal values.

Lupu asserted a high probability of constitution flouting by the Satmars, specifically citing the power differential between men and women. Eisgruber held that the rationale of the framers in protecting dissent was to fuel an on-going public discussion and collective critical assessment of social norms. The First Amendment was not intended to shelter groups from the pervasive culture in order to live according to their own lights, but to serve wider democratic purposes by publicly modeling their alternative values.[64] While the liberalism of Lupu and Eisgruber supports a perfectionist and affirmative commitment to liberal norms and culture; postmodern theories of liberalism occupy the other end of the spectrum, allegedly revealing the cultural imperialism involved in asserting that any liberal principles are overarching, universal yardsticks against which to measure the value or goodness of other cultures.

For different reasons, Yasemin Soysal is skeptical of the sincerity of Islamists or radical Muslim citizens of Western democracies.[65] Treating them as candidates for group rights would be risky for host democracies. She notes the appropriation, for instance, of the language of women's rights by Islamists. She considers their expression of concern for women's rights to be disingenuous, as these concerns are commonly voiced only in the context of vying with the state for the protection of Muslim women.[66]

Postmodernism, Essentialism, and Relativism

Postmodernism is a cluster of academic critiques of the Enlightenment notion of universal reason on grounds that it is a meta-narrative that privileges Western culture and regards other cultures as inferior. Postmodernism attempts to rectify this bias by treating all narratives and cultures as qualitatively equal and incommensurable. Western conceit is based not on cultural superiority but on its power. The political component of postmodernism is its emphasis on the history of Western colonialism and imperialism. But the biggest danger to women is the postmodernist critique of natural rights and human rights as a mere Western construct when, in fact, the claim that women's rights are human rights has become the worldwide battle cry of the fight for gender equality.

Postmodern relativists could put us in the position of ignoring or even defending cultures that oppress their members. Would we want to abandon blacks to racist regimes or women to misogynistic regimes? This is how the extreme version of toleration shades into nihilism. To abandon women to the unchallenged power of Islamists regimes would be to fall into the trap of what Edward Said termed *orientalism*, in which Muslim cultures are simultaneously vilified and excused on grounds of their otherness.[67] Islamic fundamentalism accentuates the preoccupation with women's moral conduct.[68] Moreover, the logic of postmodernism does not respect political boundaries. If we cannot impose our culture abroad, we may have no more right to do so on non-liberal groups at home.

Brian Barry, recognizing that valorizing group rights and identity politics while asserting the particularity, moral equivalence, and incommensurability of cultures creates a real danger for women, who would find their unequal treatment justified by outsiders and their attempt to reform their culture from within, subverted. The policy of state recognition is profoundly conservative in its impact. Barry thinks the state has a right and duty to assert that "we don't do that here" in response to practices that constitute rights violations under us law. The essentialist critique of multiculturalism[69] worries that group identities can become straightjackets, solidifying boundaries and ossifying otherwise fluid, complex identities. Leaders of cultural or religious groups may hope to capitalize on their recognition by the government as the authentic vehicle for representing members' interests. This may further entrench their control over the definition of group norms and commitments and also amplify their ability to squelch dissent from within. As vehicles for political representation, the leadership of cultural groups may draw the government into complicity in this dynamic.

Liberal Feminist Critiques of Multiculturalism

In order for women to benefit from policies of multicultural accommodation, the potential for coercion and rights violations within groups must be addressed. Otherwise, women may experience life in America as a minority within a minority.[70] It may appear to outsiders that religious women are invisible in communal religious life. Some academics and policymakers refuse to let religious women speak for themselves, and they may read oppression into every gender distinction. Religious women may be dismissed by well-meaning secular feminists, who can only see religious women as victims or dupes, just as surely as equally well-meaning secular advocates for multicultural accommodation may fail to address patriarchal relations within the group.

Susan Moller Okin is a faithful representative of the position that regards most cultures and religions as patriarchal and their women members as deluded when they express loyalty to their religious community. She set up the debate between liberal theorists and diversity theorists in her article, "Is Multiculturalism Bad for Women?"[71] She asserted that "most cultures are suffused with practices and ideologies concerning gender," in that they are particularly concerned with personal law, which applies to and burdens women disproportionately and isolates women behind closed doors, where they may be subject to violence and rights deprivation. Also, she noted, "most cultures have as one of their principal aims the control of women by men."[72] Women's continued membership in their religious group and any expressions on their part of satisfaction with their lives are to be heavily discounted.

Critics of Okin dispute her claims and attribute them to xenophobia and Western liberal bias. She has been accused of failing to acknowledge nonliberal conceptions of the good and failing to take women seriously as co-owners and co-creators of their communal lives. Not all gender-based distinctions or roles are signs of oppression or denial of human dignity. Okin's blind spot may be as profound as that of the overenthusiastic and undiscriminating advocates of multiculturalism. Many women do not take advantage of the option to leave their group not because they are ignorant, but because they do not choose to. The exit option creates a false binary of choice and ignores the likelihood of reform from the inside. For Okin to have claimed that Orthodox Jewish and Muslim women "may be much better off if the culture into which they were born were . . . to become extinct" misses this point.[73]

Religions have mixed track records and while women have been oppressed in the name of G-d, oppression has been challenged in the name of G-d, as well. American citizens, under the Fourteenth Amendment and other legal protections, enjoy equal rights, regardless of gender. But having a right is not the same as being able to exercise it. And it has often been religious citizens who have pointed out the disparity between our ideals and our reality. Increasingly, religious women are fully cognizant of their civil rights and push for these rights within their religion. This is not a simple case of demanding religious rights commensurate with their civil rights; rather it is prompted by a recognition that their equal rights are given by G-d, and to the extent that there rights have been abrogated, it is attributable to an act of human injustice. The notion of human rights has its origin in religious doctrine, ratified by reason and nature.

"Progressive religious woman" therefore, is not an oxymoron in either Orthodox Judaism or Islam. While Jewish women have, for two centuries, had the option of dropping out altogether or switching to reform and conservative Jewish movements, progressive in this study has been used to describe both Jewish and Muslim women who refuse to abandon their religious affiliation and seek to reform their religion within the confines of halakha and shari'a. The rejection of patriarchy should not be read as a rejection of religion. They are suspicious of liberal feminists who argue that religious groups are irredeemably hostile to gender equality and would want the state to vigorously police the context of choice. They also reject the contention that they are powerless victims of false consciousness or that the background conditions of inequality render them incapable of autonomous action or thought.

Traditional authority, whether Jewish or Muslim, has operated in a changed world since the 1970s. The success of feminism cannot be ignored, and attempts to insulate religion from feminist debates has given way to attempts to actively engage with feminism, either to reject it or to appropriate it in an appropriately Jewish or Muslim way. This reflects an acknowledgment of the increasing prevalence of women in the public and professional world and the increasing educational attainment of Orthodox and Muslim women in their religion and laws, which creates a sharp contrast between contemporary and traditional female roles. Jewish women place an extraordinary value on higher education and have traditionally been the best-educated female cohort in the United States.[74] American Muslims are also more highly educated than the American norm.

But even in contemporary times, when women are experiencing greater equality in their public and professional lives, as mothers, being instrumental to the process of cultural and religious transmission, it is no wonder that they have been singled out as standard bearers and repositories of faith by their religious community. Dress and behavior have become highly charged and politicized and, in the case of Islamists, treated as a measure of the survival of the religion, national resistance movements, and male preoccupation with self-respect and honor. For minority groups such as Muslims and Orthodox Jews, dress is a marker of the boundaries of the community and a statement about identity as much as faith. There are a variety of reasons for donning traditional dress, not all of them explained by male oppression.

Religious women understand that the state can be a champion of women's rights or, alternatively, can unwittingly support the status quo exercise of male power. They recognize that "Multiculturalism presents a problem . . . when state accommodation policies intended to mitigate the power differentials between groups end up reinforcing power hierarchies within them."[75] They may feel that the state has a fiduciary obligation to protect the rights of all citizens, regardless of gender. The problem is how to protect a woman's rights without forcing her to choose between the enjoyment of equality and her faith. Muslim and Jewish feminists may not want to put their religious communities beyond the scrutiny of the state. The state may be their only shield from rights violations and may provide affirmation for a women's reform agenda from within. Devout women are the most likely force for change and being able to deploy their citizenship rights as leverage may be essential to their success. The state is an important actor, because it decides which groups are candidates for the delegation of exemptions from generally applicable laws. The state also has a hand, intentionally or not, in solidifying the power structure within the group simply because the group is often responsible for selecting which members speak for them to government. This problem has been partially remedied by some government agencies that demand that groups select representatives among women, the elderly, and other traditionally vulnerable group members.

Devout Feminists as Citizens:
Getting beyond Theory and Stereotypes

When minority religious communities feel that they have suffered the discriminatory impact of otherwise neutral laws, their first stop is often the judiciary. Minorities are more likely to suffer free exercise rights violations because their practices are often unfamiliar to the majority and because they are numerically incapable of achieving legislative power. While unwilling to risk establishment clause violations, the court is more comfortable taking on violations of civil rights and anti-discrimination laws by religious communities. Muslim and Jewish women have come to courts and several state legislatures to redress laws or traditions within their community that presumptively violate American laws regarding gender discrimination. While minority communities may come to court asking for exemptions and accommodations, women within those same communities may come to court asking for enforcement of their citizenship rights against their religious communities. The judicial system in India, for instance, has faced challenges in the name of equal citizenship from Christian, Hindu, and Muslim women who had experienced gender discrimination at the hands of their respective religious courts.

India is not alone in attempting to balance competing legal authorities, one religious and the other secular. No state can easily function without a uniform civil code and a process of legislating and adjudicating it. Recent controversies sparked in England and Canada pitted religious minorities against those who contend that a state must have a unitary legal system, with the judicial branch exercising a monopoly over the right to interpret, apply, and uphold the law.

Under the Ontario Arbitration Act of 1991, which allows family disputes to be voluntarily arbitrated by religious courts, and the Canadian Charter of Rights and Freedoms, which attempts to balance individual rights and freedoms against multiculturalism, Canada's approximately four million Muslims would, as of 2004, be able choose to have family law disputes resolved through shari'a-based family mediation services in lieu of using the civil courts. This sparked a debate across society that was not always civil. Feelings ran high and covered a spectrum of considerations, both positive and negative. Among opponents, some feared that Canada was on its way to a theocracy in which Islamic law would be imposed on Canadians; others argued that this was a violation of the unitary civil code that should apply to all Canadians. They attacked the act as yielding to multiculturalism and undermining a shared secular culture. Some described the measure as the first volley in a battle by Muslims to gain a separate political identity in Canada. Adding their outrage, feminists, both Muslim and non-Muslim, dubbed the act a betrayal of Muslim women.

Supporters, particularly in the Muslim community, saw the inclusion of Muslim courts under the act as the fulfillment of the religious rights of Canadian Muslims.[76] As Jewish Canadians had long enjoyed the state's recognition of voluntary, non-binding arbitration in the Beit Din Jewish courts, B'nai Brith of Canada filed a report supporting the introduction of Muslim family courts as long as participation in Muslim family law courts was voluntary and the rights of the vulnerable members were protected vigilantly by the Canadian and provincial Ontario government.[77] But there was no abatement in the public and international protest in the media and in the streets. In 2004 Ontario's former attorney general and former minister for women's issues, Marion Boyd, was asked by the current attorney general to revisit the act and to review its impact on "vulnerable people, including women." Homa Arjomand, coordinator of the International Campaign Against Shari'a Court in Canada, expressed her concerns in her meeting with Marion Boyd. She said that the Ontario Arbitration Act of 1991 had made it possible for the "Islamic movement to make another attempt to attack both secularism and the women's movement for equality." She argued that the consequence of allowing imams to arbitrate family disputes would be direct violations of women's social, political, and civil rights. Arjomand predicted that women would be pressured into using shari'a courts instead of civil courts, and that their participation would be anything but voluntary. She called on Canada to uphold the separation of church and state, concluding that "Our campaign will not . . . allow a shallow concept of 'religious freedom' to translate into bondage for thousands of women in Canada."[78] The verdict of Boyd's report was released in December 2004 after consultations with more than two hundred people and dozens of submissions from various associations. In it she reasserted Ontario's commitment to the act in the name of religious freedom, but attempted to reassure critics that protections for women's rights would be policed by the state.[79]

In the lead up to the assessment of the Ontario Arbitration Act of 1991, the Canadian Council of Muslim Women, as part of their Shari'a/Muslim Law Project, solicited a report by legal scholar, Pascale Fournier, on the "reception of Muslim Family Law in Western Liberal States"[80] to provide some guidance on the dilemma facing Canadians. Fournier reviewed the responsiveness to Muslim communities' requests for accommodation of Islamic law, particularly family codes, by Germany, France, and Britain. In all three states, individual religious freedom, sensitivity to multiculturalism, and a concern for women's equal rights are all explicit concerns. France's neo-republican commitment to a unitary culture of secularism and core values of liberty and equality, derived from the French Revolution of 1789, continue to color its response to the growing Muslim community in France. The state permits no special exemptions or representation of national minorities, even in light of a diverse society. Yet this has not stopped the Muslims of France from seeking a public policy of recognition of its numerous social organizations. In May 2003 the French Council of the Muslim Religion officially presented Muslim concerns to the French government. France expects religious associations to govern themselves according to the policy of *laicite* (secularism) in the public realm, to the point of having entered a reservation with the secretary general of the United Nations concerning article 27 of the International Covenant on Civil and Political Rights, rejecting any obligation to foster special cultural rights. Still, France is party to a number of bilateral and international private law agreements that obligate France to apply the laws of a foreign individual's country of citizenship, especially regarding family law, if it does not violate French public order. Only 25 percent of Muslims living in France have obtained French citizenship. Accordingly, French courts are not infrequently called upon to rule on cases involving Muslim family law, including polygynous marriages, divorce, and the distribution of the wife's *mahr,* best translated as a gift dower rather than a dowry, as it is usually understood (it is not a bride price).

For instance, with respect to a polygynous marriage conducted in a country of origin that permits this practice, the marriage is considered to have legal validity in France under some circumstances. Under provisions of international private law rules, French courts have enforced the institution of *mahr.* With respect to *talaq,* divorce by triple renunciation, France rejects this institution as contrary to French public order. (France's emphasis on public order may be protective of Muslim women citizens in some respects, but the recent attempts to legislate a ban and a fine on the wearing of the burqa may create more problems than it solves.)

Germany's historical conception of nationhood was developed in opposition to France's notion of citizenship based on shared civic principles. The version of national belonging based on common descent and ethnicity precluded full inclusion of immigrants as citizens until 1999. A significant minority of Muslims, mostly of Turkish origin, had become a visible presence in German society. The German constitution of 1949 permits religious communities to petition for status as public law corporations, and several religious groups, including Jews, have availed themselves of this right. Muslims have sought the same official recognition, beginning in 1977, even referring to article 4 of the constitution that stipulates freedom of religion, but have had their application repeatedly rejected. Muslim organizations are considered private associations without legal standing. As in France, Germany must, under some circumstances, respect the family laws of an immigrant resident's country of citizenship rather than domestic German law. This applies to the more than two million non-citizens from Muslim countries. As with France, Germany must rely on a definition of public order when deciding if and how to apply shari'a law to marital disputes, especially when German constitutional and civil rights are at issue. As with France, Germany has respected the validity of polygynous marriages of Muslims conducted in their countries of origin, whereas marriages of women under the German legal minimum age are held contrary to public order. While the German courts are willing to accept the Islamic institution of the *mahr,* they reject divorce by *talaq* as contrary to public order.

The principle of public order, therefore, allows both Germany and France to set limits to multicultural accommodation. Britain has relied more specifically on its legal commitment and cultural norm of women's equal rights. Britain is also an immigrant destination, with Muslims now forming the largest minority religion. Although the British government has a special relationship with the Church of England, and no formal separation of church and state, Britain's legal and political culture favors a secular and universal system of family law. Beginning in the 1970s, the Union of Muslim Organizations of the UK began to seek formal recognition of a separate system of Muslim family law that would automatically apply to all British Muslims, operating side by side with civil law. This campaign continued through 1996, but was rejected by the government because religious legal authorities could not be trusted to uphold the rights of women. The shari'a courts have instead operated unofficially in mediating family law issues. Many Muslim women are opposed to official recognition of shari'a law by Britain, but see a legitimate role for informal mediation among willing parties in family disputes. This is precisely the role of the Jewish religious courts in Britain. France, Germany, Britain, and other European governments, as well as Canada and the United States, are in an ongoing process of negotiation and discussion with minority religious communities. The hallmark of each of these countries is the delicate balance they are seeking that would respect cultural diversity and religious freedom without undermining a strong and, in some cases, prior commitment to gender equality.

Ayelet Shachar sees disputes such as those arising in Ontario, Britain, Turkey, and Europe as a trend. In her assessment of the Ontario and related disputes, she provides a nuanced account that she hopes will bridge two sets of dichotomous categorizations. The first is between public and private law and the second is between women as faithful members of their religious communities and women as equal bearers of the rights of citizenship. The recent controversies provide her with an opportunity to rethink dilemmas experienced by religious women, particularly Muslims and Orthodox Jews, who, in the context of family law disputes, experience a test of allegiance to sometimes overlapping and competing identities, commitments, legal affiliations, and authorities. Shachar argues that women would be better served if the strict line between public and private law and status were replaced by the recognition that individual citizens inhabit multiple legal spaces. This recognition could lead to a richer understanding of citizenship, affording citizens the opportunity to exercise a commitment to both the secular and religious portions of their complex identities. Shachar refers approvingly to the proposal of the Archbishop of Canterbury (February 7, 2008) that was greeted with such antipathy by much of the British public. He suggested that the British legal system would not suffer harm if it opened an area of coexistence with religious law.[81]

While Schahar also maintains that citizens should not be forced to choose between their rights of citizenship and their group membership, she is sensitive to the special dilemma faced by women when non-state norms compete with state norms. The privatization of justice, in particular family law, creates a potential for harm as well as good. Much of the literature on multiculturalism and state accommodation of diversity, acknowledges Shachar, seems to lose sight of these dangers. In the case of Ontario's envisioned arbitration act, religious tribunals would be integrated into preexisting legal infrastructure, rather than replacing it, somewhat diminishing reasons for concern. Consenting parties would be permitted to use the state or public legal system, but would also have voluntary access to a potentially less adversarial semiprivate arena of dispute resolution. Aware of the pressures that women might face to conform to group norms, Shachar sees these semiprivatized institutions with proper safeguards in place, as offering new, relatively unexplored terrain, straddling public and private spheres, in which women might be afforded greater opportunity to express their multiple identities and connections.[82]

The United States

The United States has its own experience with the complex interface between religious and secular law, especially in the realm of intimate family relations. As with other religious communities, three concerns occupy the intersection between laws of G-d and the laws of the land. The public and private divide is not absolute, particularly with respect to criminal violations of family members' rights. The state takes a keen interest in child welfare and abusive actions toward women and does not hesitate to intervene in this otherwise most sacrosanct of realms. Muslims rarely draw legal or media attention to themselves. More often it is groups like the Westboro Church, breakaway Mormon sects, Branch Davidians, white supremacist churches, and survivalists that are accused of crimes against members or neighbors.

But according to legal expert Cass Sunstein, religious groups and civil associations receive asymmetrical treatment by the courts, amounting to legal permission for religious groups to violate gender discrimination laws. He sees no barrier to the courts' pursuit of religious institutions' violations of gender quality, which in his view, should not be trumped automatically by free exercise rights. When it comes to civil and criminal law, there are rarely exceptions for religious communities. Cultural defense strategies rarely have much traction in court, except occasionally as mitigating circumstances. Polygyny, domestic violence, forced marriage of minors, honor killings, and genital mutilation are not excluded from prosecution on cultural or religious grounds. And for the most part, religious law and civil law coexist comfortably. This is particularly understandable as Biblical law has exercised a strong influence on American law.

Civil Law and Family Law

The United States, like all nations, has an interest in the solidity of family life. Marriage is a civil institution. There are a number of similarities between shari'a and halakha with respect to marriage. Marriage is a contract rather than a sacrament, forced marriage is impermissible, and women have rights in divorce and the division of marital property. Where religious family law and civil law are congruent, few issues arise. Both Islam and Judaism permit divorce, with regret. Both religions permit wives to initiate divorce under certain, though limited, circumstances. Both Islam and Judaism have complicated customary provisions for the support of women upon divorce. For Muslim women, there are several types of divorce. *Talaq*, divorce by triple verbal renunciation of the wife by the husband, is particularly loathsome to Muslim women and regarded as invalid in most liberal democracies and many Muslim states as well. Other forms of divorce are more equitable, requiring the husband to return the *mahr* bride gift, which belongs exclusively to the wife for her personal use during or after the marriage. If the woman initiates the divorce (*khul*), she may be forced to return the *mahr* to her husband in exchange for his agreement to the divorce. This is a form of extortion that may be invisible to the state. American family court judges, unfamiliar with the institution of *mahr*, may treat it as marital property and divide it between the husband and wife, contrary to the religious law. While informal Muslim mediators and arbitration boards will understand the idea of the *mahr* and the *khul*, woman-initiated divorce, they may take the part of the man and intimidate the wife into not turning to the civil courts for a remedy.

Muslim Law for Minority Communities

In academic circles, books, symposia, conferences, and academic programs have arisen to study Islamic family law. Of particular note are Harvard Law School's program and the Ford Foundation–supported law and religion program at Emory University.[83] The focus of these programs and studies is Islamic family law (IFL) as part of a rich, complex, widespread, and ancient system of Islamic jurisprudence, shari'a, that was codified for the most part in the eighth and ninth centuries CE. IFL governs issues related to marriage, divorce, spousal relations, maintenance, paternity, custody of children, and inheritance for more than one billion Muslims worldwide, making it the most widely applied and most varied system of family law in the world today. For instance, Sunni Islam produced four schools of thought (*fiqhs*), Shafi'a, Maliki, Hanafi, and Hanbali, and competing claims of the validity of their legal formulations based on Qur'an and Sunnah. As Islam spread through conquest or otherwise, it was influenced by local and regional culture, which were often absorbed into the fabric of Islam to the point where it was nearly impossible to discern the difference between the pure Islamic core and the cultural overlay. Many feminist legal scholars believe that many core provisions of Islamic law are fully compatible with US norms and family laws.

Professor of Law, devout Muslim feminist, and one of the founders of Karamah (Muslim women lawyers for human rights), Azizah Y. al-Hibri wrote extensively on traditional Islamic jurisprudence from a woman's perspective. She emphasized that the core principle of Islam is justice, from which flows all other jurisprudential secondary principles. "Thus, the *tawhid* principle provides the basis for the fundamental metaphysical sameness of all humans as creatures of G-d."[84] From this premise she concludes that Islamic family law must be based on divine logic as revealed in Qur'an and not some "hierarchical worldview foreign to it."[85] In this context, for decades, even centuries before issues rose to prominence, activists and scholars in diverse settings have been arguing for political and social rights for women.

"Despite their current crisis, Muslim women reject secular, Western-inspired feminists' views on reform. They remain attached to . . . their faith and cultures, while at the same time expressing frustration with traditional patriarchal views. This fact . . . confuses liberal feminists," but according to the organization of Muslim women lawyers, Karamah, the task is not to jettison Islam, but to reclaim it. Muslim feminists' work "exposes misogynist patriarchal claims for what they are—human prejudice, rather than divine decree."[86] Among Karamah's projects is their rich website of resources for women, including boilerplate marriage contracts and *The Muslim Marriage Contract in American Courts*.[87]

There are many sources of information on how to conduct family ceremonies from marriage to burial rights within the parameters of US law. Muslim organizations, as with Jewish organizations, provide downloadable marriage contracts that meet the standards of US civil courts. Many Muslim citizens and imams have no more judicial expertise with respect to either US law or their religious law than their non-Muslim counterparts.

Reform and Authority

The structure of religious authority complicates the picture for both Jewish and Muslim women. There is no unitary, official, or centralized authority to confer ordination or to certify individuals as expert voices. No single board, court or entity can impose reform across the community. Anyone in the Muslim community can claim credentials and seek to act as a community leader. There are no state-appointed muftis and no quality control.

However, some organizations have widespread credibility. For instance, there is a national board of Muslim legal experts, the Fiqh Council of North America, which includes a woman scholar, Zainab Alwani. She is a professor, a member of Karamah, and a community activist, and in her capacity as a member of the Fiqh Council, receives as many as a hundred inquiries each week from women who want clarification on Islamic law, especially pertaining to family law and such issues as divorce. Submitting a legal issue for consideration by this board is purely voluntary, and many self-appointed imams are the sole decisors for their local mosque.

Other imams issue fatwas on line, but may have no real expertise in Islamic law. Therefore, Muslims who have marriages officiated by imams may have documents and provisions of limited validity under US law. Some imams will officiate without an official civil marriage license. This may put at risk the couple and their children because there can be no state enforcement of inheritance, custody, health insurance, and, as has repeatedly been the case, immigration standing, one of the most potent threats a husband can hold over a wife's head. When it comes to guidance, advice, and rulings, the likelihood of congruence between US and Muslim legal rulings is slim because of the abundance of online imams issuing fatwas and offering advice from around the world.

According to shari'a, a Muslim woman is an independent legal entity. She retains rights before and within marriage to her own property and assets. She has the right to work and keep her salary, though many Muslim states may officially prohibit her work outside of the home or require the husband's permission. Patriarchal relations are often justified in terms of *qawwam*, which suggests that men are protectors and maintainers of women by dint of superior earning power. Many Muslim states still recognize the institution of *wilayah*, which is ideally a consultative role exercised by a guardian, usually the father or a close male relative. He must approve the marriage and make the arrangements on behalf of the bride. A man must support the women in his family, regardless of his own financial status. According to some Muslims, this situation is of greater value to a woman than Western notions of equality. It is, in their view, tantamount to affirmative action for women.[88] But in the United States, these norms are unenforceable by either the state or religious authorities.

Similarly, institutions such as *sadaq or mahr*, the obligatory gift from husband (money, orthodontia, jewelry, cars, and education are examples) by mutual agreement are reduced to norms in the United States. Often misinterpreted as dowry or bride price, the exclusion of the *mahr* from otherwise common marital property creates confusion in the civil court system. The rationale behind the gift is to allow a woman to ask for the full amount upfront, or delay a portion until a specified later date. If husband dies, *sadaq* constitutes a senior debt against his estate and can be more valuable than her inheritance. In case of divorce, *sadaq* is still hers, unless she initiates the divorce, in which case, the husband is often permitted to retain it. The *sadaq* or *mahr* constitutes a safety net in case of death or divorce. Patriarchal reality in Muslim countries means many fathers negotiate on the part of daughters to forego the *mahr* or *sadaq*. It is not uncommon for brothers to barter away their sisters' *mahr* in exchange with a friend for the marriage of his friend's sister. This negates the man's obligation at the expense of the sisters involved. Foregoing the gift or accepting a symbolic one is prestigious for the family, suggesting great wealth. Or, the father may use the *sadaq* to cover the wedding expenses. More commonly, the husband may borrow the wife's *sadaq* or pressure her to waive it. Women are highly vulnerable to such abuses of religious law.[89] All of this would be invisible to the civil courts in divorce proceedings.

Muslim marriage is a contract not a sacrament. Qur'an considers divorce to be the worst of the permissible acts, but recognizes that divorce will occur and admonishes believers to "separate in kindness."[90] Divorce may take several forms, which creates monumental confusion in the civil courts. Muslim men, women, and leaders may not know the ins and outs of either religious or civil divorce law. Many women do not know that a woman has the right to initiate divorce on several grounds such as lack of conjugal relations, domestic violence (which in Kuwait and Jordan include verbal abuse), and lack of financial support.

Civil Divorce Courts and Muslim Marriage Contracts

Jewish and Muslim marriage contract and divorce provisions are alien to US civil law though they constitute the bulk of cases that come before the civil courts. Muslims and Jews sign a contract before witnesses upon marriage. For the most part, the provisions of these documents do not conflict with civil law and do not, therefore, create legal controversies if the marriage dissolves. For Jewish and Muslim women, the snag may come before they ever get to civil court, or after civil law requirements have been met. For Jewish women, the snag is that a husband, under Jewish law, dissolves the marriage only when he grants his wife a get, a writ of divorce. If he refuses, for whatever reason, the marriage remains in force and the wife may not undertake a legal religious remarriage, even if she has obtained a civil divorce.

Despite Qur'anic injunctions to part charitably, most spouses do not. Often the husband refuses to pay the remaining portion of the *mahr*. Expert witness may be called into court to testify about the Islamic marriage contract in either the wife or the husband's behalf. But professors, lawyers, and imams may be insufficiently versed in Islamic marriage law. They may confuse culture, tradition, and Islam. Judges cannot be expected to discern who has and who does not have authority to speak for the community. Bar associations and judges are concerned about what can be done to make Islamic marriage contracts enforceable in US jurisdictions as the Muslim population grows.[91]

For Muslim women, as noted, the provision that is not part of the standard civil marriage license but is most central from the perspectives of the bride and groom and their families has to do with the *mahr* or *sadaq*. The amount of the dower is determined in advance as one of the terms of the marriage contract and is a central part of the marriage itself. It is usually negotiated by the father or a senior male relative of the bride on her behalf. The *mahr* is typically divided into two parts—one is an upfront payment, and the other is deferred until an agreed upon date or until the husband dies or divorces. While most Muslim marriage documents (especially the standardized, boilerplate contracts available through many mosques and online) contain a reference to the *mahr*, most judges have little or no familiarity with the concept.[92]

Moreover, most divorce judges and lawyers assume, in accordance with the US default position, that marital property is jointly held by a couple. This creates obvious problems for a Muslim wife, who may find that her *mahr* is counted as marital property and must be divided with her husband, or that she may have her *mahr* deducted from alimony or property settlements. The intention behind the *mahr* was to provide the wife with financial security, not to buy her for the husband's possession. Ironically, this protective custom can be an obstacle to the enjoyment of her rights, both civil and religious, if she is required to relinquish it as the price of her freedom. If the bride is farsighted and a good bargainer, she may enter any stipulations that she chooses in her marriage contract as long as she can get her groom to agree. This gives her the functional equivalent of a prenuptial agreement.

Muslim marriages officiated abroad may be of limited validity under us law. Even in the United States, there are problems of qualifying the officiate; a valid Muslim marriage does not even require that an officiate be present. Responses to Muslim divorce cases vary from state to state, and many judges have found some Muslim provisions to be either incomprehensible or unenforceable.

us courts are not hostile to premarital contracts or provisions based on religious law. Courts do not single out Muslim or Jewish premarital contracts as unenforceable because they are part of religious practice or because they emanate from a minority culture. Courts often draw parallels to secular prenuptial contracts and also to Jewish *kettubah* when adjudicating conflicts related to Muslim marriage provisions. When courts declare Muslim provisions to be unenforceable or void, it is often on grounds that these provisions are contrary to public welfare. For instance in the California case *Dajani v. Dajani*,[93] the couple had married in their native Jordan. The court regarded the *mahr* as unenforceable because they did not understand the concept of a deferred *mahr* and instead, interpreted it as a form of blackmail and profiteering.[94] The court understood the provisions of the prenuptial contract as creating a financial incentive for divorce, which goes against the state of California's policy of discouraging divorce in general.

Even Muslim lawyers are not of one mind when it comes to how to relate Islamic divorce law to secular divorce law. Just as there are problems about the status of Muslim marriages (or any marriages) conducted abroad, the rule of *lex domicili* assumes that the validity of a divorce is based on the laws of the country in which the couple lived and contracted the marriage. Some states recognize, others require, that the divorce be obtained under the jurisdiction of state law. In the Texas case *Seth v. Seth*, the court of appeal held that the couple could not be divorced under Texas law because the husband was already married when the second marriage was alleged to have occurred. The plaintiff (wife number two) claimed the husband had performed *talaq*, the unilaterally issued divorce by triple proclamation, by proxy to the first wife before marrying the second wife. The husband and the first wife argued that this had never taken place. The court found that the ceremonies had taken place but declined to give them any legal effect. The court said it would not apply Islamic law that would disenfranchise the first wife on such unfair terms.[95]

The civil court accordingly refused to recognize a *talaq* divorce carried out in Kuwait because there was no evidence of the divorce having been issued by any official state body. *Khul* divorces, even if extra-judicial, better qualify for recognition by US courts because they appear to be mutual and voluntary and fit the no fault model more closely. But the condition attached, that the wife forfeit her *mahr*, can be used by the husband as a form of blackmail, whereas the deferred *mahr* is more like insurance for the woman against an impulsive *talaq* declaration of divorce by the husband.[96]

"Based on the testimony of Wife Two's experts, the trial court could have found that Islamic law simply allows a non-Muslim man to convert to Islam by pronouncing a short phrase, and then divorce his wife through the ex parte procedure of talak. The harshness of such a result to the non-Muslim divorced wife runs so counter to our notions of good morals and natural justice that we hold that Islamic law in this situation need not be applied."[97]

In the case *Aleem v. Aleem*, Maryland's highest court refused to recognize a Pakistani divorce in 2008. The couple had become Maryland residents. The default under Pakistani law is that the wife has no rights to property titled in the husband's name, while the default under Maryland law is that the wife does have marital property rights in property titled in the husband's name. The Maryland court held "that this conflict is so substantial that applying Pakistani law in the instant matter would be contrary to Maryland public policy. . . . The *talaq* divorce of countries applying Islamic law, unless substantially modified, is contrary to the public policy of this state and we decline to give *talaq*, as it is presented in this case, any comity." In Maryland marital property is subject to fair and equitable division. "Additionally, a procedure that permits a man (and him only unless he agrees otherwise) to evade a divorce action begun in this State by rushing to the embassy of a country recognizing *talaq* and, without prior notice to the wife, perform 'I divorce thee . . .' three times and thus summarily terminate the marriage and deprive his wife of marital property, confers insufficient due process to his wife." *Talaq* divorce was ruled by the Maryland court to be an unconstitutional violation of provisions barring sex discrimination. It was not the court's lack of familiarity with Muslim marriage contract provisions, but its rejection of practices that conflicted with public welfare in general and the interests and rights of the wife in particular.

Muslim scholars who were asked to comment on the ruling agreed with the state appellate court: Abdullahi An-Na'im, a Muslim scholar and law professor at Emory University in Atlanta, said, "there can only be one law of the land." An-Na'im, author of *Islam and the Secular State: Negotiating the Future of Shari'a*, said, "if Muslims wish to influence what the law of the state says, they must do so through the normal political process and in accordance with civic discourse that is equally open for debate by all citizens, and not on the basis of religious beliefs."[98]

Muneer Fareed, secretary general of the Islamic Society of North America, said that if Aleem had traveled to Pakistan and invoked his *talaq* there, it might have been recognized in a US court under the concept of comity, under which nations accept the premise of a law in another country "whether or not we agree with the law or its spirit." But Aleem, he said, attempted to circumvent any such agreements. "There was a certain lack of faith here because the husband initiated the *talaq* after his wife had filed for divorce," Fareed said. "He was trying to defeat the ends of justice within the American legal system."[99]

Child Custody

For most mothers, regardless of faith, child custody represents the chief concern with respect to divorce proceedings. While Judaism is matriarchal in terms of defining a child's inclusion in the community, Muslim law permits a man to marry outside of the faith, but prohibits a woman from doing so, partly on the assumption that the father, in an Islamic divorce, would retain custody of the children (the difference between Sunni and Shi'a custody laws regards the age of the children at the time that the mother must surrender them to the father). If a Muslim man and non-Muslim woman divorce in the United States, Muslim law will not apply and the principle of the best interest of the child is likely to prevail. This principle will also apply in the event that both parents are Muslim, which often upends the man's customary expectations, and a few rare but dramatic kidnappings of children by fathers, who then flee to lands where Islamic law prevails, have provided grist for the media.

Jewish Family Law: The Case of Divorce

In order to dissolve a marriage in the United States, it is essential to get a civil divorce. Above and beyond that, one may desire a religious divorce if the religious community does not recognize a civil divorce as automatically nullifying the religious union. Most Jewish denominations require a get (a religious bill of divorce), particularly if either partner intends to ever remarry in the faith. This is particularly critical for women, because if they proceed into a new marriage without obtaining a get, the children born from the new union will be rendered *mamzerim*. This status is attached to the offspring of a relationship prohibited by the Torah (for example a woman who does not have a get who has relations with another man). The status imposes real costs on the child, who can only marry another Jew who is a *mamzer*. However, a man who remarries without a get does not suffer from this status, nor do his subsequent children because children of a bigamous marriage are not similarly stigmatized and other remedies are available. If the husband cannot persuade his wife to give a get, his rabbis may gather the signatures of a hundred rabbis and acquire a dispensation (*heternissuin*) permitting him to remarry. While a civil divorce is a requirement of most states, it is not a requirement of all Betai Din, who may accept the religious divorce as permitting remarriage even in the absence of a civil divorce. This is in part because Jewish law was purposefully designed so that Roman law (or the law of an adopted or imposed citizenship), if it violated Jewish law, would not be dispositive.

In earlier times, the problem of the *agunah*, a woman chained to a dead marriage, was not a common problem. There are no official figures on the number of *agunah* worldwide, but the Organization for the Resolution of Agunot, a New York–based group that organizes pickets in front of the houses and businesses of men who refuse to give their wives divorces, states that there are likely thousands of such women in New York alone, many of which may simply have given up their attempts to free themselves. Cases have been known to drag on for years and decades. The *agunah* problem is of fairly recent vintage. The problem of get refusal arises primarily when the woman has instigated a civil divorce that the man does not want. In no-fault states, the husband may not be able to prevent the civil divorce, but he has the power to scuttle the religious divorce and hold the wife or the children for ransom, and moral suasion is only effective when the man cares about his reputation.

Earlier in Jewish history, when Jews were forced to live in ghettos in Europe, or the *mellah* in Muslim countries, or in other insular communities by law or by choice, it was easier to pressure a husband into settling a divorce. In the shtetl, where there was no escape from the community, this was a powerful tool. The rabbis could order the community to shun the husband or his business, and publicity made his life miserable. But with immigration and dispersal of Jewish communities, it is often difficult for a rabbi or a congregation to bring a recalcitrant husband to heel. Men can change synagogue membership, move to another place, or simply ignore the pressure.[100] The Jewish Press, one of the nation's largest Jewish newspapers, each week runs the names of men who have divorce-related court orders against them in an effort to embarrass them. Internet distribution lists alert distant communities to the husband's infraction, but if the husband does not respond, everyone's hands are tied, including the rabbis'. A recent example is the Rosenbloom case, in which the husband simply ignored the summons from Baltimore's Beit Din and moved to a different town.[101] He also disregarded a ruling from the Beit Din holding him in contempt. This left his wife an *agunah*.

Informal Community Remedies

Jewish community lay leaders are not oblivious to the *agunah* issue. Neither are rabbis, who rightly fear that get withholding will lead to general disrespect for Jewish law, adultery, bigamy and a generation of *mumzerim*, in short, the possible unraveling of a coherent social fabric. There are numerous groups such as COLPA (the National Jewish Commission On Law and Public Affairs, which acts as the legal arm of observant Jewry), the Orthodox Union, Agudath Israel, JOFA, and many Orthodox rabbis of the RCA (Rabbinical Council of America) speak out on the need for redressing this injustice. Where they differ is on which remedies accord with halakha. The obstacle seems to be the issue of coercion not by, but of the husband, which, according to many readings of the law, invalidates a get. Jewish law requires that a man grant his wife a get of his own free will, meaning he cannot be coerced or threatened by the state, community, or his wife. Without a get or a *heter agunah* (permission by a halakhic authority based on a decision that her husband is presumed dead) she remains legally married.[102]

No one wants to rush straight into court, including Jewish feminists. Therefore, court is considered an option after all other remedies have been exhausted. With respect to the *agunah* issue, women have many allies. With few exceptions, rabbis have been decrying the situation for hundreds of years. Most, who claim that their hands are tied, sincerely believe that there are no remedies within halakha, even though dozens of scholars and rabbis have made proposals throughout Jewish history. All of them are halakhically deficient, argue some rabbis, even the proposal made by the great sage Maimonides. Even King David made his soldiers give their wives provisional *gittin* (pl. get) in the event the husband was killed and his body could not be retrieved as proof. Orthodox feminists argue that this is a clear case of interpretation and exegesis. It is abundantly clear that the intention of the get was never intended to keep a woman chained to a dead marriage. If anything, the *kettubah* (marriage contract) required the husband to pay his wife a large sum of money if he divorced her for no apparent reason.[103] Still in use today, the *kettubah* is publicly signed and handed to the wife's keeping during the marriage ceremony. It is seen by many Jews as representing the first bill of rights for wives.

In this context, it is not an issue of reinterpreting Jewish law in a contemporary context, but just the opposite. What is required here is that the contemporary interpretation be brought in line with the original intent of the law and divine purpose. According to a woman who heads an Orthodox association to solve the *agunah* problem (but chose not to be identified) the problem persists, in short, because of rabbis who are bent on retaining male prerogative. Additionally, the Batei Din are protective of their powers and fearful of courting too much government intervention. They are wary of rulings that might diminish the power of the Beit Din in the Jewish community. And as in any religious community, Judaism is not a uniform set of norms, practices, or interpretations. Therefore, when states legislate standards of kashrut or get laws, they typically favor Orthodox standards. This does not always sit well with non-Orthodox Jews and they, as well as the ACLU, have often been the most vocal challengers of state laws that accommodate public displays of menorahs, and the like. For instance a Conservative rabbi in Georgia is challenging the constitutionality of his state's kosher law, saying it favors Orthodox religious standards and constitutes state entanglement in religion by preventing him from "fulfilling his duties as a rabbi."[104] This struggle for authority within the religious community can be intensified when one group receives federal or state government recognition, distracting from the search for remedies to the situation of the *agunah*.

But most rabbis are principled and are open to halakhically acceptable remedies. Rabbi Irving Breitowitz, a University of Maryland law professor who wrote a book about *agunah*, said, "We are bound by the principles, but we can try to devise new mechanisms."[105] Many modern Orthodox rabbis will not perform a marriage without a prenuptial agreement that provides for divorce under Jewish law, naming a Beit Din as arbitrators. Many Orthodox rabbis frown on prenuptial additions to the marriage contract, nonetheless they have been gaining wide support in the United States. The purpose of the prenuptial agreement is to provide a measure of power for the wife by placing the punitive power of the state behind her. This takes the case out of the hands of the religious judges, but threatens with nullification by the rabbis any get thus obtained.

No obstacle provides as much shelter for rabbinic stalling as that of the "coerced" get. Coercion constitutes *meuseh* or a forced divorce, and this type of divorce is invalid and not recognized by Jewish law. Coercion does not simply refer to punishments or explicit threats, but includes, in some readings, even the implicit suggestion of duress. Yet sages such as Maimonides found it quite unproblematic to apply even physical force to a man who refused his wife a get. Today, among certain Orthodox communities, while the practice is unofficial, yeshiva boys have been enlisted to threaten recalcitrant husbands. The justification is subtle and suggestive of Maimonides' Aristotelian influence—it is permissible to help a person do what he really would want to do if his judgment were not clouded by an evil impulse.

Officially, most rabbis reject this line of reasoning. While rabbinical authorities are in wide agreement about the inadmissibility of coercion, a growing number are investigating and approving the use of prenuptial agreements as an addendum to the *kettubah*. There are several boilerplate forms that are acceptable to many Orthodox couples and their rabbis, because they commit both the bride and groom to a priori agreement to give or accept a get if the marriage dissolves. Some rabbis, however, reject the use of prenuptial agreements on halakhic grounds that are still disputed. For all of the controversy over prenuptials, they currently promise the most fruitful way to proceed in US civil courts. An addendum to the marriage contract that obligates the couple to abide by the Jewish courts' ruling in their divorce is enforceable in many state's courts under contract law, thus failing to trip the establishment clause wire. This possibility of looking to the state for enforcement of a Jewish legal document fills some rabbis with hope and others with dismay.

Halakhic Remedies: The Beit Din and the Civil Courts

The first stop for observant couples seeking a divorce is the often the Beit Din. The Rabbinical Council of America, the nation's largest Jewish Rabbinical network, handles more than three hundred divorces a year. Betai Din are established on a regional basis. There are several covering North America. Just as in Israel, some are known to be lenient and woman-friendly others stringent and rigid, but each Beit Din is answerable only to itself. The decentralized judicial legal and congregational system has added to the lack of consensus on the issue of Jewish divorce. If the biggest sticking point for the Beit Din in enforcing a get on a recalcitrant husband is running afoul of the halakhic prohibition against coercion, the biggest sticking point for US courts is running afoul of the establishment clause. Neither prove to be absolute obstacles.[106] The Union of Orthodox Jewish Congregations holds that a belief or worship issue does not automatically violate Lemon, the test used by the Supreme Court to determine establishment clause violations. It would be discriminatory against religious citizens. Gender equality is an important American norm that deserves to be legally enforced. A husband should not be permitted to shirk on grounds of religion. He broke the contract and is being held to it. When a man purposely subverts the workings of the civil divorce courts, the courts should take notice.

In Israel, religious courts have civil powers and can even put men in jail if they refuse to perform the divorce ritual. Unless the man gives the get, even in Israel, there is no divorce. Outside of Israel, governments have far less recourse. In the United States, if there is a prenuptial agreement that takes a contractual form, the state can enforce it as such. The other possibility, which has been used in Canada and some states in the United States, is to allow, with both parties agreement, arbitration by the Beit Din. They may impose punishments, generally a daily fine until the man delivers the get. "Unfortunately the Jewish religious courts in the Diaspora have extremely limited enforcement powers," said Nathan Diament, director of the Orthodox Union's Washington office. "If we're serious about trying to help these women, the way to do that is to get the secular courts to back this up."[107]

When religious courts and informal pressure fails, women have taken their claims to civil court. New York's legislature passed controversial laws in 1983 and 1992 designed to rectify the balance of power in favor of women whose husbands refuse to grant a religious divorce. In 1983, with the support of the largest Orthodox organization, Agudath Israel, New York State passed the "Get Law" or the Domestic Relations Law 253, which states that prior to the court granting a civil divorce, petitioning parties to the divorce will take all steps possible to remove any barriers to remarriage that the other party might encounter. The intention behind the law was to discourage the husband from withholding his wife's get. The court can avoid entanglement with religious issues by adopting a pure contract approach to law, assimilating the *kettubah* to civil contract theory, upholding equitable principles citing the unequal allocation of power between husband and wife seeking to terminate the marriage, and avoiding the infliction of emotional distress on the wife by the husband in withholding the get.[108] Nonetheless, the American Jewish Congress, Reform Jewish groups, and several civil liberties organizations regarded the New York law as an unconstitutional entanglement of state and religion. From the perspective of the wife who sought a civil and religious divorce, the law was of limited use. It only provided a remedy for a woman whose husband also wants the divorce. For husbands who do not initiate or want a divorce, the law was a blunt instrument. As legal scholar Lisa Fishbayn noted, "Indeed, it sometimes has the paradoxical effect of leaving a woman who is the respondent in the divorce petition doubly anchored, to a dead civil marriage as well as to a dead Jewish marriage."[109]

In 1992 New York introduced what was hoped to be a more effective remedy for the problem of get refusal. But its rabbinic opponents charged that the new legislation had bypassed them, and instead of relying on rabbinic authority, codified a principle derived from a New York Supreme Court case, *Schwartz v. Schwartz,* in which the court held that the husband's delay in issuing the get caused him to forfeit a portion of his interest in the division of marital property. The New York State amendment to the equitable distribution law would allow the court to take into account the failure of one party to remove barriers to religious remarriage of the other, as provided for in the 1983 Get Law. This law is of limited value, as many Orthodox women do not make use of it. The imposition of a financial penalty on the husband has been interpreted by some Orthodox rabbis to constitute a punishment, so the 1992 law is rejected as potentially coercive, rendering the get invalid, even if the Beit Din has grounds for rendering a compulsory order for the husband to issue the get before the divorce has reached the civil court. According to some Orthodox rabbis, the possibility that the husband may be complying in issuing the get in response to the threat of a financial penalty would invalidate the requirement of free will on his part. The subtext of the rejection of this sort of legislation is not exclusively halakhic, but goes to the core of Jewish communal autonomy in the United States. It is considered a bad idea to invite government involvement, as it constitutes a threat to the authority of Orthodox rabbinate, not just by women, but by other Jewish denominations.

In the case of New York's two most significant attempts to use legislation to remedy the plight of the *agunah*, the problem lay primarily with the rabbinical authorities, not with the civil authorities. But this was not the case in Maryland where, for four years in the late 1990s, lawmakers unsuccessfully introduced legislation designed to help women receive their *gittin*. In 2007 the Maryland State Senate failed to pass a similar law, Bill 533. The proposed bill had the backing of an unusual alliance of the Orthodox and the National Organization for Women. It also signaled a rare admission on the part of Orthodox rabbis that because of modern social conditions, they are no longer successful in applying internal measures and are now reaching out to the civil courts. Agudath Israel, an umbrella group representing Orthodox congregations, led the push in Maryland.

Under the proposed law, a husband who wanted a civil divorce would have to provide an affidavit that he had taken "all steps . . . to remove all religious barriers to remarriage by the other party."[110] This is very close to the language of the 1983 New York Get Bill that passed constitutional muster. The bill was defeated even though it had the support of a broad array of Jewish groups and Jewish proponents of the bill secured a letter from Maryland's assistant attorney general, stating, "although the proposed legislation presents a substantial issue under the Establishment Clause of the First Amendment, it would likely be upheld if challenged."[111]

To date, no state other than New York has get legislation. There is, however, case law in the statutory annotations of many states that means a judge can, if he or she deems it appropriate, create disincentives for the husband to withhold a get. The principles of contract law allow the court to compensate the harmed party by imposing damages on the party that fails to perform specific provisions of the contract, but it is not in the court's power to force someone to give a get.[112]

No matter how well meaning the legislatures and the courts are, they can only gently reinforce attempts by many Jewish activists—rabbis, feminists, lay leaders, and scholars—to rectify the harsh consequences faced by the *agunah* when an Orthodox rabbi refuses to make use of available halakhic and civil remedies.

Conclusion

When the state sets out to accommodate religious groups, it runs many risks, both to liberal and to constitutional norms. In the case of litigating Muslim and Jewish divorces, the risk is diminished because both religions treat marriage as contractual, meaning that the court can sometimes take on the divorce under the rubric of contract law. While the establishment clause tends to require the court to strictly scrutinize any state involvement in religious controversies, the laws protecting gender equality can often be used by the courts to trump establishment concerns. The ideal situation would be for religious and cultural groups to police themselves with regard to gender issues. But for the time being, women should be able to rely on the state not to thwart them by uncritically devolving partial sovereignty on these groups in the name of multicultural accommodation. Orthodox Jewish and Muslim feminists and lawyers in America are rapidly becoming political strategists. They have created an impressive array of national and local grass-roots organizations that disseminate information about women's rights within their religions and under American law. They have created shelters for abused women, raised funds, and raised voices in public protest. They have challenged religious authorities for greater participation in prayer and leadership. And they are raising their sons and daughters to carry these efforts forward. In this sense, the devout feminists have adopted the tried and true strategies of civil citizenship in the name of greater justice for all.

Conclusion

Women of faith in Kuwait, Israel, and the United States enrich our understanding of the connections between citizenship, religion, and feminism. They make use of the narrative of civic citizenship combined with what they take to be a more authentic, if alternative, reading of their faith tradition. They seek to recapture G-d's intention from which they believe the dominant interpretive insights and judgments to have strayed. Women in these settings are connected critics of their regimes and their religions.

In countries where they enjoy full rights of citizenship, both Muslim and Jewish feminists seek to align their religious equality with their political equality. Both groups have evolved, through struggle, strategies that are political and theological. Religious feminists in Israel, the United States, and Kuwait, though differently situated, have all made progress toward equality within their religions by enlisting civil law and constitutional promises to challenge male religious authority.

Feminists of faith, whether Jewish or Muslim, American, Kuwaiti, or Israeli, have more in common than they perhaps realize. Both emphasize that G-d is just and that men and women share in divine justice and mercy. Both emphasize that there is an irreducible element of human subjectivity in the act of interpretation required to understand these precepts. Education, principles of public discourse, and deliberation are the best antidotes to the fallibility of the individual exegete. Both understand that the right of exegesis belongs to all humans but that it has been monopolized by men, which has produced distortions of G-d's will through the ages. Both groups understand the necessity of disentangling religious principles from cultural accretions that have distorted divine intent. Both Muslim and Jewish feminists see their project as one of recovery, involving the reinterpretation of sacred texts according to their best principles, rather than as refracted through male perspectives and interests. Both groups engage in this process in full submission to G-d.

In Israel and Kuwait entrenched religious authorities are the most powerful opponents of equal rights for women. In deferring to these religious authorities, the secular governments of Israel and Kuwait risk sacrificing the guaranteed rights of their female citizens in the name of greater regime stability that they believe religious authorities can deliver or withhold.

In Kuwait religious critics of the established authority are no friends of feminists. They are primarily the Salafis and the Muslim Brotherhood, both of which have more in common with Islamists than feminists in terms of their agenda and goals. They promise, if they manage to become politically powerful in Kuwait, to upend the hard-earned reforms that feminists have achieved. Nonetheless, Kuwaiti women have made impressive political gains. They have been appointed to ministerial positions by two successive friendly amirs, and most recently, they have garnered grass-roots electoral support and had four women elected to the National Assembly. The election results signal a cultural shift reflected in public opinion in favor of women's political participation, but as in Israel, a determined opposition, backed by entrenched religious parties, still threatens these gains. Because Israel's voters are supportive of women's citizenship and civil rights, democracy poses no real threat of reversing women's gains. But Kuwait's fragile and tension-ridden sectarian democracy may actually prove the undoing of Kuwaiti women's gains. For the time being, Kuwaiti women still depend on the backing of the amir. Yet political challenges to this amir are increasing, and his popularity, though still widespread, may be ebbing. If he is replaced, there is no reliable predictor of the future of women's rights in Kuwait.

In Israel, where women achieved formal equal citizenship long ago, political culture reflects the popular habituation to women's public equality. Still, the religious parties threaten a different, but significant source of opposition. Real gains have been made by Israeli feminists, but a backlash by the religious authorities is a perpetual threat because of the dual legal system, which grants religious authorities a stranglehold over family law. While Israel's numerous internal critics of the religious authorities represent a more pluralistic, secular, liberal and democratic worldview, and are certainly friendlier to women's rights than the religious authorities, they are not necessarily embraced by Orthodox feminists who pursue reform within the Orthodox fold.

In the United States, where Jews and Muslims live as minorities in an overwhelmingly liberal Protestant culture, women are minorities within minorities. American law and a liberal democratic regime provide a different set of opportunities and challenges to feminists than the partly democratic and partly theocratic regimes of Israel and Kuwait. Ironically, the US hospitality to cultural diversity and its sensitivity to minority groups may actually compound the challenges for the women in Muslim and Jewish communities in its midst. The First Amendment principle of free exercise of religion and the informal principle of tolerance for multi-culturalism may find themselves at odds with the establishment clause and civil rights legislation that upholds gender equality. The United States provides the most sympathetic and fertile environment for women to acquire their rights in their religious communities in that neither charges of heresy nor calls for reform from within a religious community are enforced under US criminal law. Yet, ironically, the free exercise clause may also be applied in such a way as to unintentionally reinforce male religious authorities, as male leaders are most likely to represent the community's religious precepts before the judiciary and legislature. In such cases, American feminists may find themselves hobbled in their attempts to bring reformist pressures to bear against their religious authorities by the very sympathetic stance of Western societies toward minority cultures.

The adverse effect of a policy of multicultural accommodation, which unwittingly entrenches male power within religions and cultures, also applies in the international realm. Organizations such as the United Nations are squarely behind women's rights and gender equality. Nonetheless, the UN has made it a right to have one's culture recognized, respected, and preserved. As is the case at the national level, men speak for minority cultures and claim to represent their authentic values. The United Nations and the international human rights regime are relatively impotent in the face of national sovereignty. Unless national governments put forward women-friendly domestic legislation and allocate funds for adjudication and enforcement of these provisions, international treaties and documents remain mere paper.

Finally, the backlash against feminism is in full swing and should not be underestimated. Haredi groups in Israel have political leverage and a high birth rate. It is particularly alarming for Israel's future that many of the Haredi do not support Israel's statehood any more than they support full rights for women. Therefore, they have no real incentive to engage with the government in any area that appears to require religious compromises. They expect all of the compromises to be on the part of the state. Islamists, worldwide, while composed of diverse and sometimes adversarial factions, share a set of norms that are contrary to pluralism and toleration, and importantly, are contrary to the United Nations' norms favoring women's equality. Having harnessed religion to politics, Islamists reject political compromises as if they entailed religious compromises. In the realm of international relations, there are political solutions to political problems, but for groups that infuse politics with religion, no secular political solutions or compromises are worthy of consideration. Islamists have gained widespread credibility because of their resistance to the West and to modernity, which includes liberalism and women's rights. Where Islamists extend their political and military reach, women's rights and feminists are their first targets. My guess and my hope is that faithful feminists will stand strong against their opponents and that they will face down the manifold dangers with a determination rooted in a desire to see that G-d given justice prevails for our daughters.

Appendix

SURVEY INSTRUMENT FOR ISRAEL AND KUWAIT

B"H

Questions for My Israeli Colleagues:

1 What are the priorities and chief concerns of Orthodox Israeli women?
2 What is the relationship between civil law (law created through legislation) and religious law (halakha/jurisprudence) in Israel?
3 What is the relationship between women's personal status and citizenship in Israel?
4 How do you define feminism? What is the history of feminism in Judaism/Israel?
5 What do you accept and reject from the Western/secular feminist models?
6 How does the concept of human rights resonate in Israel? How about the concept of democracy?
7 Is there a difference between "Western," "secular," "Orthodox," and "Israeli" feminisms?
8 What practical measures are being taken by observant Israeli women activists that have a direct or indirect impact on promoting greater gender equality? For instance:
> Advocacy
> Education
> Entrance into professions
> Lobbying
> Court proceedings
> Voting rights campaigns and political participation
> Halakhic/jurisprudential training
> Outreach to less educated or non-elite women
> Internet or blogs
9 Is Judaism inherently patriarchal and discriminatory toward women or is gender-equitable, faith-based Judaism in keeping with the Torah?
10 By corollary, are traditional patriarchal interpretations of the oral and written Torah immutable and true to the texts, or do they reflect human prejudice of the interpreters?
11 What is the difference between Jewish culture and Judaism?

12 How do we separate divine decree from human interpretation?

13 How does textual analysis factor into gender issues? What counts as legitimate analysis/interpretation?

15 Who has or should have legitimate authority to engage in exegesis of the holy texts? Should there be a monopoly on the authority to interpret the law or to issue din/rulings in Israel?

Please accept in advance my gratitude to you and your colleagues for your willingness to engage some or all of these questions. Please feel free to ignore or modify any question that you find inappropriate.

Jan Feldman
Harvard University
John F. Kennedy School of Government
Women and Public Policy

B"H
Questions for My Kuwaiti Colleagues:

1 What are the priorities and chief concerns of Kuwait women?

2 What is the relationship between civil law (law created through legislation) and religious law (Islamic jurisprudence) in Kuwait?

3 What is the relationship between women's personal status and citizenship in Kuwait?

4 How do you define feminism? What is the history of feminism in Kuwait?

5 What do you accept and reject from the Western/secular feminist models?

6 How does the concept of human rights resonate in Kuwait? How about the concept of democracy?

7 Is there a difference between "Islamic," "Muslim," and "Islamist" feminisms?

8 What practical measures are being taken by Kuwaiti women activists that have a direct or indirect impact on promoting greater gender equality? For instance:
    Advocacy
    Education
    Entrance into professions
    Lobbying
    Court proceedings
    Voting rights campaigns and political participation
    Ijtihad
    Outreach to less educated or non-elite women
    Internet or blogs

9 Is Islam inherently patriarchal and discriminatory toward women or is gender-equitable, faith-based Islam in keeping with the Prophet's (peace be unto him) understanding?

10 By corollary, are traditional patriarchal interpretations of Qur'an, hadith,

Sunnah, and shari'a true to the texts or do they reflect human prejudice of the interpreters?

11 What is the difference between traditional Arabic culture and the holy texts?
12 How do we separate divine decree from human interpretation?
13 How does *ijtihad* factor into gender issues? What counts as legitimate *ijtihad*?
14 Who has or should have legitimate authority to engage in exegesis of the holy texts? Should there be a monopoly on the authority to interpret Islamic law or to issue fatwas within Kuwait?

Please accept in advance my gratitude to you and your colleagues for your willingness to engage some or all of these questions. Please feel free to ignore or modify any question that you find inappropriate.

Jan Feldman
Harvard University
John F. Kennedy School of Government
Women and Public Policy Program

Notes

Preface

1. Quoted in Judith R. Baskin, *Midrashic Women* (Waltham, MA: Brandeis University Press, 2002), 161.

Chapter 1. Women and Citizenship

1. Agence France Presse, "Kuwait MP Seeks to Scrap Sharia Controls in Election Law," *Khaleej Times,* October 12, 2009.

2. B. Izaak, "Freedom for Kuwaiti Women," *Kuwait Times,* October 21, 2009.

3. Margot Badran, "Ejected from G-d's House," *Al-Ahram Weekly* (Cairo), March 4–10, 2010.

4. Rana Foroohar, "Hear them Roar," *Newsweek.com,* April 9, 2010.

5. Max Weber, *The Protestant Ethic and the Spirit of Capitalism,* trans. Talcott Parsons (London: Routledge 1992).

6. Karl Marx, *The Marx-Engels Reader,* ed. Robert C. Tucker (New York: W. W. Norton, 1978).

7. Susan Moller Okin, "Is Multiculturalism Bad for Women?" *Boston Review* 22, no. 5 (October/November 1997).

8. Amina Wadud, *Inside the Gender Jihad: Women's Reform in Islam* (Oxford: Oneworld Publications, 2006).

9. Rational Citizen, January 29, 2007, commenting on Victoria Brittain, "Islamic Feminists on the Move," *The Guardian,* January 29, 2007, http://www.guardian.co.uk/commentisfree/2007/jan/29/islamicfeminismonthemove (accessed July 10, 2010).

10. This term, frequently used in political science, comes from the work of Albert O. Hirschman, who used the word "exit" as an alternative to the option of participation.

11. Tanya Goudsouzian and Fatima Rabbani, " 'Imported Values' Fail Afghan Women," *Aljazeera.net,* September 21, 2009.

12. "Afghans Rally Against Women's Law," *Aljazeera.net,* April 16, 2009.

13. Donna Abu-Nasr, "Report: Senior Saudi Cleric OKs Girls to Marry," *Jerusalem Post Online,* January 14, 2009.

14. Sean Yoong, "Malaysia Women's Group Sued Over 'Islam' in Name," *Yahoo! News,* March 22, 2010.

15. Robin Wright, "A Quiet Revolution in the Muslim World," *Time* magazine,

March 19, 2009, http://www.time.com/time/magazine/article/0,9171,1886539,00
.html (accessed July 10, 2010).

16. Jeffrey Gettleman and Waleed Arafat, "Sudan Court Fines Woman for Wearing Trousers," *New York Times,* September 7, 2009, http://www.nytimes.com/
2009/09/08/world/africa/08sudan.html (accessed July 10, 2010).

17. Ibid.

18. Omar Sobhani, "Afghan Women Attacked for Opposing Marriage Law," *USA Today,* April 15, 2009.

19. Okin, "Is Multiculturalism Bad for Women?"

20. Caryle Murphy, "Cleric's Support for Men and Women Mingling in Public Sparks Furor in Saudi Arabia," *Christian Science Monitor,* April 13, 2010.

21. John Dewey, *The Public and Its Problems* (New York: Holt, 1927).

22. *Jaringan Islam Liberal,* "What is Liberal Islam?" July 20, 2008, http://
islamlib.com/en/pages/about/ (accessed July 10, 2010).

23. Ahmad Sahal, "Free and Liberal," *Jaringan Islam Liberal,* August 8, 2006,
http://islamlib.com/en/article/free-and-liberal/ (accessed July 10, 2010).

24. http://web.archive.org/web/20061121024049/www.muslimwakeup.com/
bb/viewtopic.php2554

25. Al Islam: The Official Website of the Ahmadiyya Muslim Community, http://
www.alislam.org.

26. Ronald F. Thiemann, "Our Contemporary Dilemma in Historical Perspective: Religion Values, and the Framing of the Constitution," in *Religion in Public Life: A Dilemma for Democracy* (Washington, DC: Georgetown University Press,
2007).

27. Ayelet Shachar, "On Citizenship and Multicultural Vulnerability," *Political Theory* 28, no 1. (Feb. 2000): 76.

28. Barbara Swirski, "The Citizenship of Jewish and Palestinian Arab Women in Israel," in *Gender and Citizenship in the Middle East,* ed. Suad Joseph (Syracuse: Syracuse University Press, 2000), 314.

29. Haideh Moghissi, *Feminism and Islamic Fundamentalism: The Limits of Postmodern Analysis* (New York: Zed Books, 1999), 20.

30. Kecia Ali, *Sexual Ethics and Islam: Feminist Reflections on Qur'an, Hadith, and Jurisprudence* (Oxford: Oneworld Publications, 2006).

31. Shachar, "On Citizenship and Multicultural Vulnerability."

32. Johann Hari, "How Multiculturalism is Betraying (Muslim) Women: Congratulating Ourselves on our Tolerance of the Fanatically Intolerant," *The Independent,* April 30, 2007.

33. Michael Bryant, "Sharia Law in Canada," *Lecture,* Islamic Legal Studies Program at Harvard Law School and International Legal Studies. Co-sponsored with the HLS International Legal Studies Program. Pound Hall 335, Cambridge, MA,
March 31, 2008.

34. Paraphrased from Martha Minow, Keynote Address, "Is Pluralism an Ideal or

a Compromise?" "Untying the Knots: Theorizing Conflicts between Gender Equality and Religious Laws," Hadassah-Brandeis Institute Project on Gender, Culture, Religion, and the Law, Brandeis University, April 15, 2008.

35. "Sarkozy Speaks Out Against Burka," *BBC News*, June 22, 2009, http://news.bbc.co.uk/2/hi/8112821.stm (accessed July 27, 2010).

36. Attributed to Jonathan Sacks, chief rabbi of the United Hebrew Congregation of the Commonwealth, quoted by Susan Weiss, Lecture, "How the Tort of Get-Refusal Can Help Unravel the Israeli Version of the Multicultural Dilemma: Theory and Practice," Hadassah-Brandeis Institute Project on Gender, Culture, Religion, and the Law, Brandeis University, April 15, 2008.

37. Shachar, "On Citizenship and Multicultural Vulnerability."

38. Amr Hamzawy, "Kuwait: Interview with Dr. Badr Al Nashi, President of the Islamic Constitutional Movement (ICM)" *Arab Reform Bulletin*, 4, no. 3 (April 2006).

39. Lisa Hajjar, "Domestic Violence and Shari'a: A Comparative Study of Muslim Societies in the Mideast, Africa, and Asia," in *Emory University Islamic Family Law Project* (Louisville, KY: NISA Publications, 1995), 24.

40. The term gender jihad has been used by any number of feminists to describe the process of internal struggle for improvement and obedience to G-d's will. The struggle may be on the part of the individual or the community. By linking the concept of jihad with women's rights, the idea of a communal struggle to rectify injustices toward women is acknowledged as being on a par with other objectives of jihad. Amina Wadud's 2006 book, *Inside the Gender Jihad*, did a lot to popularize the term. See also Giles Tremlett, "Muslim Women Launch International 'Gender Jihad,' " *The Guardian*, October 31, 2005, and Asra Q. Nomani, "A Gender Jihad for Islam's Future," *The Washington Post*, November 6, 2005.

Chapter 2. Feminisms: Islam and Judaism

1. Asma Lamrabet, *Colloquia*, UNESCO, September 2006, cited in Karine Ancellin Saleck, "Europe's Muslim Feminism Renewal, Part I," *The WIP.net*, March, 2007, http://www.thewip.net/contributors/2007/03/europes_muslim_feminism_renewa.html (accessed July 27, 2010).

2. Victoria Brittain, "Islamic Feminists on the Move," *The Guardian*, January 29, 2007, http://www.guardian.co.uk/commentisfree/2007/jan/29/islamicfeminismonthemove (accessed July 27, 2010).

3. Margot Badran, "Islamic Feminism: What's in a Name," *Al-Ahram*, January 17–23, 2002, http://weekly.ahram.org.eg/2002/569/cu1.htm (accessed July 27, 2010).

4. Sue Fishkoff, "Women Kosher Supervisors on the Rise, Earning Respect," *Jewish Telegraphic Agency*, June 28, 2009, http://jta.org/news/article/2009/06/28/1006182/women-kosher-supervisors-on-the-rise-earning-respect (accessed July 27, 2010).

5. Farah El Alfy, "Muslim Woman Defies Male Dominance," *Aljazeera.net,* November 19, 2008.

6. Caryle Murphy, "Cleric's Support for Men and Women Mingling in Public Sparks Furor in Saudi Arabia," *Christian Science Monitor,* April 13, 2010.

7. Based on adult literacy rates from Dieter Berstecher, Cynthia Guttman, Michael Lakin, and Britt Sjöstedt, "Education for All Achieving the Goal," *Forum on Education for All,* UNESCO, June 1996, http://www.unesco.org/education/efa/ed_for_all/background/eworkdoc96.pdf.

8. Suroor, "Educating Muslim Women," *Nissa,* December 28, 2007, http://nisaa.ca/featurearticles/comments/educating_muslim_women/ (accessed July 27, 2010).

9. Ibid.

10. Azizah Yahia al-Hibri, "Muslim Women's Rights in the Global Village: Challenges and Opportunities," *Journal of Law and Religion,* 15, no. 1/2 (2000–2001), 109.

11. Khadeejah Abdul Hadi al-Mahmeed, "The Position of Women in the Islamic Political System," Ph.D. Diss., University of Sunderland, May 2006.

12. Ibid.

13. Interview with a Chabad Lubavitcher rabbi, who chose not to be identified. Cambridge, MA, April 2008.

14. Religious authorities claim that since the days of interpretation, there has been "closure of the gates of . . . reasoning." Naila Tiwana, "Islamic Feminism: Oxymoron or Reality? Barcelona Conference 2006," *MUW,* November 30, 2006.

15. Rabbi Shai Held, "Halacha and Innovation Are Not Mutually Exclusive: The Case for the Evolution of Gender Roles in Jewish Life. *The Jewish Week,* May 4, 2010.

16. Qur'an, 96:1, Yusef Ali, footnote 6203. Quotations from the Qur'an are taken from Abdullah Yusuf Ali, *The Qur'an Text, Translation and Commentary* (Elmhurst, NY: Tahrike Tarsile Qur'an, 2005).

17. Chantal Mouffe, 1995, 329. Quoted in Moghissi, *Feminism and Islamic Fundamentalism,* 142.

18. Haideh Moghissi, *Feminism and Islamic Fundamentalism,* 142.

19. Rabbi Shai Held, "Halacha and Innovation Are Not Mutually Exculsive."

20. "Understanding Orthodox Halachic Innovation: Rabbi Lopatin's Tribute to Rav Hershel Schachter, shli"ta," *Morethodoxy.com,* May 5, 2010.

21. "Understanding Orthodox Halachic Innovation."

22. Rabbi Shai Held,"Halacha and Innovation are not Mutually Exclusive."

23. Merkos L'inyone Chinuch, *Siddur Tehillat Hashem Annotated Edition with Tehillim* (Brooklyn: Chinuch Inc., 1978), 228.

24. Abu'l–al Mawdudi, "The Islamic Law," in *Princeton Readings in Islamist Thought,* ed. Roxanne Euben and Muhaamad Qasim Zaman (Princeton: Princeton University Press, 2009), 100–101.

25. Asma Barlas, *Believing Women in Islam: Unreading Patriarchal Interpretations of the Qur'an* (Austin: University of Texas Press, 2002), 8–9.

26. Asma Barlas, "Still Quarrelling over the Qur'an: Five Theses on Interpretation and Authority," Conference on Redefining Boundaries: Muslim Women and Religious Authority in Practice, Institute for the Study of Islam in the Modern World (ISIM), Amsterdam, June 24, 2007.

27. Azizah Y. al-Hibri, "The Muslim Marriage Contract in American Courts," Speech, Minaret of Freedom Banquet, University of Richmond, VA, May 20, 2000, http://www.karamah.org/articles_marriage_contract.htm. Paraphrased with thanks.

28. Ziauddin Sardar, "Rethinking Islam," *Seminar* 509 (January 2002), 48–52, http://www.ziauddinsardar.com/index.htm (accessed Sept. 5, 2010).

29. Ibid.

30. Qur'an 7:145.

31. Ibid.

32. Qur'an 39:18.

33. Yusef Ali, Qur'an, p.viii.

34. Yahya M, "Muslim Women Reclaim their Original Rights," *Islam for Today,* http://www.islamfortoday.com/womensrights.htm (accessed July 27, 2010).

35. Qur'an 33:35.

36. Muslim Women's League, "Gender Equality in Islam," *Muslim Women's League,* September 1995, http://www.mwlusa.org/topics/equality/gender.html.

37. Qur'an 4:1.

38. Qur'an 16:97.

39. Qur'an 3:195.

40. Qur'an 33:35.

41. Qur'an 16:97.

42. Qur'an 33:73.

43. Qur'an 57:12.

44. Qur'an 57:18.

45. Qur'an 4:15 and 24:2, Yusef Ali, footnote 523.

46. Qur'an 4:34.

47. Qur'an 2:187.

48. Qur'an 30:20, Yusef Ali, footnote 3526.

49. Abu'l al-Mawdudi, "The Islamic Law" in *Princeton Readings in Islamist Thought*, ed. Roxanne Euben and Muhaamad Qasim Zaman (Princeton: Princeton University Press, 2009), 99.

50. Qur'an 4:34 and 2:223, Yusef Ali, footnote 249.

51. Neil MacFarquhar, "Verse in Koran on Beating Wife Gets a New Translation," *New York Times*, March 25, 2007, http://www.nytimes.com/2007/03/25/world/americas/25iht-koran.4.5017346.html.

52. Qur'an 58:1.

53. Qur'an 33:32.

54. Qur'an 33:59, Yusef Ali, footnote 3764.

55. Yusef Ali, footnote 3766, applies to all women, not just those in the Prophet's household.

56. Qur'an 33:59, Yusef Ali, footnote 3761.

57. Haideh Moghissi, *Feminism and Islamic Fundamentalism*, 142.

58. Azizah Y. al-Hibri, "Qur'anic Foundations of the Rights of Muslim Women in the Twenty-First Century," in *Wanita Dalam Masyarakat Indonesia: Akses, Pemberdayaan dan Kesempatan* [Women in Indonesian Society: Access, Empowerment and Opportunity], ed. Atho Mudzhar et al. (Yogyakarta: Sunan Kalijaga Press, 2001).

59. Ibid., 11.

60. Amin Ahsan Islahi, "Fundamental Principles of Understanding Hadith," trans. Tariq Mahmood Hashmi, *Iviews, IslamiCity,* August 11, 2009.

61. Abul A'ala Maudini, "Sources of Islamic Law," www.mlwusa.org, September 1995.

62. Sardar, "Rethinking Islam."

63. Al-Hibri, "Global Village," Speech delivered before the International Women's Forum, Washington National Cathedral, October 15, 1999, 104.

64. Qur'an 81:8–9.

65. Ibid.

66. Islamvision, "Women's Rights," *Islamvision*, Islam Darshan Kendra, http://www.islamvision.org/women-rights.html.

67. Yusuf Al-Qaradawi, "The Status of Women in Islam," *Witness-Pioneer,* http://www.witness-pioneer.org/vil/Books/Q_WI/women_feminine.htm.

68. Ibid.

69. Ibid.

70. Ibid.

71. "Women's Rights," *Islamvision*, Islam Darshan Kendra, http://www.islamvision.org/women-rights.html.

72. Exodus 19:3. Talmud Mechilta Mishpatim. Adin Steinsaltz, *The Essential Talmud*, (New York: Bantam Books, 1976).

73. Ibid., 10.

74. Ibid., 3.

75. Ibid., 72.

76. Moses Maimonides, *The Guide for the Perplexed*, trans. Michael Friedlander (New York: Dover, 1956).

77. Talmud, Bavli Erucin 13b,"both are the words of the living G-d," Steinsaltz, *The Essential Talmud*, 6.

78. Ibid., 59b.

79. Judith R. Baskin, *Midrashic Women: Formations of the Feminine in Rabbinic Literature* (Waltham, MA: Brandeis University Press, 2002), 77.

80. Ben Sira 25:24, in Baskin, *Midrashic Women*, 33.

81. Ben Sira 42:12–14, in Baskin, ibid., 33.

82. Baskin, ibid., 41.

83. Genesis 18:10, Genesis 31:19, Genesis 34:1. All Torah references and citations come from *The Chumash: The Stone Edition*, ed. Rabbis Nosson Scherman and Meir Zlotowitz (Brooklyn: Mesorah Publications, Artscroll Series, 1993).

84. Baskin, *Midrashic Women*, 72, 75.

85. Ibid., 46. Genesis Rabbah 17:8.

86. B. Eruvin 100b R. Dimi. Quoted in Baskin, *Midrashic Women*, 75.

87. Baskin, ibid., 53.

88. Ibid., 110. B. Bava Batra 145b.

89. Proverbs 18:22.

90. Baskin, *Midrashic Women*, 42.

91. Jonathan Sarna, "The Future of American Orthodoxy," *Shma: A Journal of Jewish Responsibility* (February 2001), 2.

92. Michael Kress, "The State of Orthodoxy Today," *Jewish Virtual Library*, http://www.jewishvirtuallibrary.org/jsource/Judaism/orthostate.html (accessed January 15, 2008).

93. Sara Esther Crispe, "Chavah: Mother of All Life in Biblical Women," *Chabad*, Chabad-Lubavitch Media Center, http://www.chabad.org/theJewishWoman/article_cdo/aid/335943/jewish/Chavah-Mother-of-All-Life.htm.

94. *Muwatta*, Imam Malik ibn Anas.

95. CAIR Brochure on its website, www.cair.com, or at www.ijtihad/globalog/glocaleye, Muslim Women's League, "Muslim Women Meet in Morgantown, WV, to Create Historic New Women's Rights Group," June 4, 2004, http://www.mwlusa.org/news/muslim_women_meet_in_morgantown.htm. The Muslim Women's League, Morgantown, became a symbol of Muslim gender rights when activist, writer, and reporter, Asra Nomani and her supporters (including her father), began walking through the front door, reserved for men, of their local mosque and demanding to pray in the main hall, also reserved for men. They see themselves not as innovators—rather they are reclaiming rights bestowed upon women by G-d and by Muhammad in the seventh century. The board has reversed the male-only policy. Asra Nomani and her supporters also initiated two campaigns, "Take back your mosque" and "wedding night campaign," to better educate young brides about the issues related to married life.

96. Lamrabet, *Colloquia*. Sue Fishkoff, "Women Kosher Supervisors on the Rise, Earning Respect," *Jewish Telegraphic Agency*, June 28, 2009, http://jta.org/news/article/2009/06/28/1006182/women-kosher-supervisors-on-the-rise-earning-respect (accessed July 27, 2010). Modern Orthodoxy is becoming increasingly open to women-friendly reforms and leadership roles in the community.

97. Muslim Women's League, "Muslim Women Meet in Morgantown, WV."

98. Ibid.

99. Rabbinical Council of America, April 2010, Convention Resolution: "Women's Communal Roles in Orthodox Jewish Life."

1. The flowering of Torah study and teaching by G-d-fearing Orthodox women in recent decades stands as a significant achievement. The Rabbinical Council of America is gratified that our (members) have played a prominent role in facilitating these accomplishments.

2. We members of the Rabbinical Council of America see as our sacred and joyful duty the practice and transmission of Judaism in all of its extraordinary, multifaceted depth and richness—halakhah (Jewish law), hashkafah (Jewish thought), tradition and historical memory.

3. In light of the opportunity created by advanced women's learning, the Rabbinical Council of America encourages a diversity of halakhically and communally appropriate professional opportunities for learned, committed women, in the service of our collective mission to preserve and transmit our heritage. Due to our aforesaid commitment to sacred continuity, however, we cannot accept either the ordination of women or the recognition of women as members of the Orthodox rabbinate, regardless of the title.

4. Young Orthodox women are now being reared, educated, and inspired by mothers, teachers, and mentors who are themselves beneficiaries of advanced women's Torah education. As members of the new generation rise to positions of influence and stature, we pray that they will contribute to an ever-broadening and ever-deepening wellspring of *talmud Torah* (Torah study), *yir'at Shamayim* (fear of Heaven), and *dikduk b'mitzvot* (scrupulous observance of commandments).

100. "JOFA Reaffirms Commitment to Female Religious Leaders," JOFA Statement issued March 9, 2010, in preparation for its annual Conference, jofa.org.

101. "Understanding Orthodox Halachic Innovation."

102. Al-Mahmeed, "The Position of Women in the Islamic Political System."

103. Ibid., 24.

104. Ibid., 244.

105. *Alsyassah* (Kuwait), February 22, 2005.

106. Moghissi, *Feminism and Islamic Fundamentalism*, 385.

107. Al-Mahmeed, The Position of Women in the Islamic Political System, 101.

108. Ibid., 116.

109. Ibid., 53.

Chapter 3. Kuwait: Monarchy, Theocracy, and Democracy

1. Freedom House Press Release, "Freedom House Hails Election of Female Lawmakers in Kuwait," Washington, DC, May 18, 2009.

2. Agence France Presse, "Kuwait MP Seeks to Scrap Shari'a Controls in Election Law."

3. Hussain al-Qatari, "Opponents of Women, Freedom Under Fire," *Kuwait Times Website*, March 14, 2010.

4. Michele Dunne, "Interview with Dr. Rola Dashti, Member of the Kuwait Parliament," *Arab Reform Bulletin,* March 9, 2010.

5. Ibid.

6. B. Izaak, "Freedom for Kuwaiti Women."

7. Haya al-Mughni, "Kuwait," in *Women's Rights in the Middle East and North Africa,* ed. Sanja Kelly and Julia Breslin (New York: Freedom House, 2010), 225.

8. Lisa Hajjar, "Domestic Violence and Shari'a: A Comparative Study of Muslim Societies in the Mideast, Africa, and Asia," in *Women's Rights and Islamic Family Law,* ed. Lynn Welchman (New York: Zed Books, 2004), 237.

9. Judith Plaskow, *Standing Again at Sinai: Judaism from a Feminist Perspective* (San Francisco: Harper Collins Press, 1991). Also, Suzannah Heschel, "The Right Question is Theological," in *On Being a Jewish Feminist* (New York: Schocken Books, 1995), 223.

10. "Freedom House Hails Election of Female Lawmakers in Kuwait," Washington, DC: Freedom House Press, May 18, 2009.

11. Kuwait Public Authority for Civil Information, www.paci.gov.kw.

12. These figures do not count the expat foreign members of the workforce. The population of foreign workers is more than double the population of Kuwaiti citizens and has an impact on various aspects of Kuwaiti society, including the status of women. Kuwaiti feminists express concern about the situation of these foreign women workers, which is often deplorable, but this concern has not been translated into any appreciable remedies.

13. Kelly and Breslin, eds., *Women's Rights in the Middle East and North Africa,* 237.

14. Only 5 percent of the women registered and only .4 percent of women in the larger district turned out to vote. The newspaper blamed the poor showing on the hot weather. *Arab Times,* "Al-Baghli Wins Municipal Polls," June 26, 2008.

15. *Agence France Presse,* "Kuwait Heads for More Feuding," Gulf Research Center, June 1, 2008.

16. "Two Women Join Cabinet with Seven New Ministers," *Arab Times,* June 1, 2008.

17. The UN Charter Preamble affirms equal rights for men and women in article 1, " 'One of the Charter's aims is to emphasize and promote human rights and basic freedoms for all without discrimination on the basis of gender, language, religion and without differentiation between men and women.' Article 55 c also states that, 'The United Nations shall promote . . . universal respect for, and observance of, human rights and fundamental freedoms for all without distinction as to race, sex, language or religion.' " Ibtissam Ali Khamis, "Discrimination against Women through the Personal Status Law," *Karamah,* http://www.karamah.org/docs/Dis crimination_against_Women%20Bahrain%20Translation%202007.doc.

The text of the Universal Declaration of Human Rights, 1948, article 2, states, "Everyone is entitled to all the rights and freedoms set forth in this Declaration, without distinction of any kind, such as race . . . sex."

The United Nations has also sponsored conferences, protocols, congresses, and conventions on women's issues. The first Decade for Women, 1975–1985, initiated a pattern of national, regional, and international conferences on the progress of women. The First World Conference on Women (Mexico City, 1975), the Second World Conference on Women (Copenhagen, 1980), the Third World Conference on Women (Nairobi, 1985), and the Fourth World Conference on Women (Beijing, 1995) all focused attention on the discrepancies between stated goals and actual performance on a nation-by-nation basis.

Kuwaiti women accordingly held Women's Conferences in 1971, 1993, and 1999, all of which invited regional participation and focused, among other issues, on strategies to achieve the vote.

18. UN General Assembly, *Convention on the Elimination of all Forms of Discrimination Against Women*, December 18, 1979.

19. *The World's Women 2000: Trends and Statistics* (New York: United Nations Publication, 2000).

20. Hajjar, "Domestic Violence and Shari'a," 18.

21. Mohammad al-Naciri, "RCAR 2006—Kuwait," *United Nations Development Group*, United Nations, http://www.undg.org/rcar.cfm?fuseaction=RCAR& ctyIDC=KUW&P=490.

22. "Women in the Political Arena and the Indications of Their Success Therein," Report submitted to UNIFEM (United Nations Development Fund for Women), under the supervision of the Women's Cultural and Social Society of Kuwait, 2007.

23. Kuwait Parliament, "Voting Law No. 35," *Equality Now,* http://www.equality now.org/english/wan/beijing5/beijing5_personal_en.html.

24. *Board of Education of Kiryas Joel Village School District v. Grumet*, 114 S. Ct. 2481, 2485 (1994).

25. Okin, "Is Multiculturalism Bad for Women?" Shachar, "On Citizenship and Multicultural Vulnerability."

26. I am indebted to Haya al-Mughni for factual and historical data culled from her book *Women in Kuwait: The Politics of Gender* (London: Saqi Books, 2001) for this section.

27. Al-Mughni, *Women in Kuwait*, 15.

28. Ibid., 38.

29. A reference borrowed from a Qur'an verse, 2:249.

30. Al-Mughni, *Women in Kuwait*, 173.

31. Amira El-Azhary Sonbol, "Rethinking Women and Islam," in *Daughters of Abraham*, eds. Yvonne Yazbeck Haddad and John L. Esposito (Gainesville, FL: University Press of Florida, 2002), 119.

32. Henry M. Bowles, "Kuwait's Women's Rights Pioneer Talks Religion and the Future," *Kuwait Times*, November 30, 2007, http://www.kuwaittimes.net/read_ news.php?newsid=MTAxNzI5MDkwMw==.

33. Ibid.

34. Ibid.

35. Rola Dashti, "Kuwaiti Public Opinion Survey Report," 3 vols. Kuwait Economic Society (April 2006–June 2007).

36. "Kuwait Emir Dissolves Parliament," www.aljazeera.net, March 19, 2008.

37. "Kuwait Emir Warns Parliament," *Kuwait Times*, June 2, 2008.

38. Zahed Matar, "The Committee Should be Prevented from Forcibly Prying into Private Affairs of the People," *Arab Times*, June 26, 2008.

39. Ibid.

40. "Getting to Know You," *Arab Times*, June 17, 2008.

41. Abubakar A. Ibrahim and Ben Al-Arfaj, " 'She' Did It . . . She's In!; 4 Women Through in Historic Poll; Kuwait Punishes Islamists . . . Votes for Change," *Arab Times*, May 17, 2009, http://www.arabtimesonline.com/kuwaitnews/pagesdetails .asp?nid=32502&ccid=9.

42. Ibrahim and al-Arfaj, " 'She' Did It."

43. Riffat Hassan, "Women's Rights and Islam: From ICPD to Beijing," in Lisa Hajjar, *Interfaith Reflections on Women, Poverty, and Population: Essays on Global Population and Development Issues* (Louisville, KY: NISA Publications, 1995), 9–12.

44. However, many analysts will find problematic her preference for a shari'a based government and her regard for Iran as a model. Additional reservations among the majority Sunni population might be linked to her being a member of the Shia minority. But her minority status may be an advantage if it makes her sensitive to injustice. Al-Mahmeed believes that scholars, men and women, need to re-engage with the sacred texts and revive the traditional science of *ijtihad* or interpretation. She is convinced that much of the misogyny that is claimed to be inherent in Islam is the product of generations of male interpretation of Qur'an and hadith.

45. Al-Mahmeed, "The Position of Women in the Islamic Political System."

46. Ibid.

47. These findings are congruent with the data collected by Rola Dashti, "Kuwaiti Public Opinion Survey Report."

48. Cited in al-Mughni, "Kuwait," in *Women's Rights in the Middle East and North Africa*, ed. Kelly and Breslin, 233.

49. Eileen McDonagh, "Political Citizenship and Democratization: The Gender Paradox," *The American Political Science Review* 96, no. 3 (September 2002): 546.

50. "Women Played Key Role in Liberation of Kuwait," *Kuwait Times*, September 30, 2009.

51. Ibid.

Chapter 4. Israel: Divided Jurisdiction

1. Frances Raday, "A Free People in Our Land: Gender Equality in a Jewish State," Israeli Ministry of Foreign Affairs, April 1, 2005, http://www.mfa.gov.il/

MFA/Government/Facts+about+Israel-+The+State/A+Free+People+in +Our+Land-+Gender+Equality.htm.

2. Benedict Anderson, *Imagined Communities: Reflections on the Origin and Spread of Nationalism* (New York: Verso, 2006).

3. Ruth Halperin-Kaddari, *Women in Israel: A State of Their Own*, Pennsylvania Studies in Human Rights (Philadelphia: University of Pennsylvania Press, 2004).

4. Kobi Nahshoni, "Rabbinate to Discuss Civil Marriage for First Time," *Jewish World*, March 4, 2009, http://www.ynetnews.com/articles/0,7340,L-3680969,00 .html.

5. Berel Wein, "Defining A Jewish Democracy," *Jerusalem Post*, April 9, 2008.

6. Ibid.

7. Shahar Haselkorn, "Is Public Transportation on Shabbat a True Must?" *Ynet*, October 3, 2008, http://www.ynetnews.com/articles/0,7340,L-3601470,00.html.

8. The IWN brought suit before the Supreme Court using the case of *Brown v. Board of Education*, which overturned the "separate but equal clause." Halperin-Kaddari, *Women in Israel*, 171–172.

9. Peretz Rodman, "The Hopeless Irrelevance of the State Rabbinate," *Jerusalem Post*, August 31, 2009, http://www.jpost.com/servlet/Satellite?cid=1251145154693 &pagename=JPArticle%2FShowFull.

10. Ibid.

11. Haselkorn, "Is Public Transportation on Shabbat a True Must?"

12. Herb Keinon and Sheera Claire Frenkel, "Religious Services Ministry Created," *Jerusalem Post*, January 6, 2008, http://www.jpost.com/servlet/Satellite?cid =1198517306375&pagename=JPost/JPArticle/ShowFull.

13. Nathan Jeffay, "Livni's Rise Sparks Debate on Whether Orthodox Would Back a Woman," *Jewish Daily Forward*, June 26, 2008, http://www.forward.com/ articles/13671/.

14. Ruth Sinai, Mazal Muamin, and Haaretz correspondents, "New Anti-Livni Slogan Slammed for being Sexist," *Haaretz.com*, December 26, 2008.

15. Phyllis Chesler, "The Women of the Wall, Twenty Years On," *Jewcy*, Tilted Planet, November 30, 2008, http://www.jewcy.com/post/women_wall_twenty _years.

16. Phyllis Chesler, "The Women of the Wall."

17. "Kotel Rabbi Calls 'Women of the Wall' Prayer Provocation," *The Jerusalem Post*, November 18, 2009, http://www.jpost.com/servlet/Satellite?pagename =JPost/JPArticle/ShowFull&cid=1258489193852.

18. Clare Needham, "Following a Woman Arrest for Wearing Prayer Shawl at the Kotel, Women Feel a Spiritual Disconnect at the Wall?" *The Los Angeles Jewish Observer*, November 23–29, 2009, http://www.jewishobserver-la.com/Page.html.

19. Keinon and Frenkel, "Religious Services Ministry Created."

20. Albert O. Hirschman, *Exit, Voice, and Loyalty: Responses to Decline in Firms, Organizations, and States* (Cambridge, MA: Harvard University Press, 1970).

NOTES TO PAGES 118–130 ❧ 221

21. Shachar, "On Citizenship and Multicultural Vulnerability."

22. Pinhas Shifman, "The Status of Women in Israeli Family Law: The Case for Reform," in *Developments in Austrian and Israeli Private Law*, ed. Herbert Hausmaninger, Helmut Koziol, Alfredo M. Rabello, Israel Gilead (New York: Springer, 1999), 245–254.

23. 2000 Revision of the Women's Equal Rights Law of 1951, 168.

24. Halperin-Kaddari, *Women in Israel*.

25. Simon M. Jackson, "Jewish Law in Our Times," *Torah Mitzion*, Coda, March 13, 2005, http://www.torahmitzion.org/eng/resources/showLAW.asp?id=427.

26. Marcia Freedman, "Israeli Women, Thirty Years of Feminism in Israel: A Prognosis for the Future," *World Union of Jewish Students*, May 31, 2006, http://wujs .org.il/index.php?option=com_content&task=view&id=632&Itemid=198 (accessed July 27, 2010).

27. Lisa Hajjar, "Domestic Violence and Sharia: A Comparative Study of Muslim Societies in the Middle East, Africa and Asia," *Emory Law*, Emory University School of Law, 2002, http://www.law.emory.edu/ifl/thematic/Violence.htm.

28. "State of Israel," *Emory Law*, Emory University School of Law, 2002, http:// www.law.emory.edu/ifl/legal/israel.htm.

29. Sharon Shenhav, "The Human Rights of Jewish Women," *Jerusalem Center for Public Affairs*, Jerusalem Center for Public Affairs and the International Council of Jewish Women, http://www.jcpa.org/jcprg3.htm.

30. Zina Kalay-Kleitman, "Israeli Statement on Advancement of Women at the 59th UN General Assembly," *Jewish Virtual Library*, American-Israeli Cooperative Enterprise, October 14, 2004, http://www.jewishvirtuallibrary.org/jsource/UN/ women.html. Speaking before the Special Advisors on Gender Issues and the Advancement of Women by the Secretary General.

31. Ibid.

32. Ibid.

33. Brenda Gazzar, "MacKinnon: Much Yet to be Done to Achieve Gender Equality," *Jerusalem Post*, June 7, 2008, http://www.jpost.com/servlet/Satellite?cid =1212659681669&pagename=JPost%2FJPArticle%2FPrinter.

34. Sharon Shenhav, "Human Rights, Jewish Women and Jewish Law," *Justice*, no. 21 (Summer 1999): 29.

35. Gazzar, "MacKinnon."

36. Ibid.

37. Karin Kloosterman, "Judging By Israel, Women Have It All," *Canada-Israel Committee*, December 12, 2006, http://www.cicweb.ca/canections/dorit.cfm.

38. Ibid.

39. Ibid.

40. Phyllis Chesler, "The Women of the World."

41. Halperin-Kaddari, *Women in Israel*.

42. Psalms 45:14. Tractate Eruvin (100b).

43. Deborah Weissman, "Women's Suffrage: A Halakhic Perspective," in *Men and Women: Gender, Judaism and Democracy*, ed. Rachel Elior (New York: Urim Publications, 2004), 70–80.

44. Ibid., 73.

45. Ibid.

46. Ibid.

47. Ibid., 74.

48. Ibid., 75.

49. Ibid., 76.

50. Halperin-Kaddari, *Women in Israel*, 17.

51. Orit Kamir, "The Queen's Daughter is All Dignified Within" (Ps. 54:14): Basing Israeli Women's Status and Rights on Human Dignity," in *Men and Women: Gender, Judaism and Democracy*, ed. Rachel Elior (New York: Urim Press, 2004), 31–53.

52. Aristotle, *Metaphysics*, trans. Richard Hope (Ann Arbor: University of Michigan Press, 1960).

53. Halperin-Kaddari, *Women in Israel*, 21.

54. Chana Henkin, "New Conditions and New Models of Authority—the Yoatzot Halachah," *Nishmat*, Jeanie Schottenstein Center for Advanced Torah Study for Women, http://www.nishmat.net/article.php?id=160&heading=0.

55. Ibid.

56. Interview, Rabbanit Chana Henkin, December 17, 2007, Jerusalem.

57. Henkin, "New Conditions."

58. Interview, Rabbanit Chana Henkin.

59. Dina Kraft, "For Israel's Female Soldiers, Someone New to Provide Strength," *Jewish Telegraphic Agency*, March 9, 2009, http://jta.org/news/article/2009/03/09/1003575/ idfs-first-female-officer-in-the-rabbinate-corps.

60. Ibid.

61. Ibid.

62. Yuval Merin, "The Right to Family Life and Civil Marriage Under International Law and its Implementation in the State of Israel," *Boston College International and Comparative Law Review* 28 (2005), http://ssrn.com/abstract=1336074.

63. See Gidi Sapir and Daniel Statman, *Religious Marriage in a Liberal State*, Cardozo Law Review 30, no. 9 (2009): 2855, 2871.

64. Halperin-Kaddari, *Women in Israel*.

65. Susan Weiss, "Israeli Divorce Law: The Misdistribution of Power, its Abuses, and the 'Status' of Jewish Women," in *Men and Women: Gender, Judaism and Democracy*, ed. Rachel Elior (New York: Urim Press, 2004), 53–69.

66. Ibid., 57.

67. Ibid., 61.

68. Ibid., 63.

69. Edwin Freedman, *Divorce, Updated Israeli Style*, http://edfreedman.co.il/Downloads/Article 1007 l.pdf (p. 40).

70. Weiss, "Israeli Divorce Law," 67.

71. Hana Levi Julian, "Rabbinate Denies Decision on Civil Marriage," *Israel National News,* March 6, 2009, http://www.israelnationalnews.com/News/News.aspx/130306.

72. Susan Weiss, "The First Word: Sages of Israel—Take Modernity by the Horns," *Jerusalem Post,* November 5, 2006, http://www.jpost.com/servlet/Satellite?cid=1162378319817&pagename=JPArticle%2FShowFull.

73. Ibid.

74. Ruth Eglash, "Int'l Agunot Day: 'I Want Women to Know it's not a Mitzva to Suffer in Silence,'" *Jerusalem Post,* March 19, 2008, http://www.jpost.com/servlet/Satellite?cid=1205420721816&pagename=JPArticle%2FShowFull.

75. Sharon Shenhav, "Why We're Marching to Knesset Today," *Jerusalem Post,* March 18, 2008, http://www.jpost.com/servlet/Satellite?cid=1205420720546&pagename=JPost%2FJPArticle%2FShowFull.

76. Rabbi Shlomo Aviner, cited in Esti Keller, "Dancing on the Other Side of the Mehitza," *Jerusalem Post,* October 2, 2007.

77. Ibid.

78. Susan Weiss, "The First Word."

79. Sharon Shenhav, "International Jewish Women's Rights Project," *International Council of Jewish Women,* GlobalVisionsIsrael, December 2007, 2, http://www.icjw.org/UserFiles/File/NEWSLETTER%2022.pdf.

80. Ibid.

81. Ibid.

82. Ibid.

83. Sharon Shenhav, "Choosing Religious Court Judges in Israel: A Case Study," *Jewish Political Studies Review,* 18: 3–4, October 2006.

84. Eileen McDonagh, "Political Citizenship and Democratization: The Gender Paradox," *American Political Science Review* 96, no. 3 (September 2002): 653.

Chapter 5. The United States: Feminism Meets Multiculturalism

1. Attributed to Jonathan Sacks, chief rabbi of the United Hebrew Congregation of the Commonwealth, quoted by Susan Weiss, "How the Tort of Get-Refusal Can Help Unravel the Israeli Version of the Multicultural Dilemma."

2. Nick Madigan, "Court Denies Islamic Divorce," *Baltimore Sun,* May 07, 2008, http://articles.baltimoresun.com/2008-05-07/news/0805060427_1_aleem-divorce-wife/2.

3. Jan Feldman, *Lubavitcher as Citizens: A Paradox of Liberal Democracy* (Ithaca: Cornell University Press, 2003), 191.

4. "Court Backs Turkish Headscarf Ban," *BBC News,* November 10, 2005.

5. Robert C. Tucker, *The Marx-Engels Reader* (New York: W. W. Norton, 1978).

6. US Supreme Court, "Lemon v. Kurtzman," *Justia,* Justia Supreme Court Center, http://supreme.justia.com/us/403/602/case.html.

7. Shachar, "On Citizenship and Multicultural Vulnerability."

8. Charles Taylor, "The Politics of Recognition," in *Multiculturalism: Examining the Politics of Recognition*, ed. Amy Gutmann (Princeton: Princeton University Press, 1994).

9. Jon Meacham, "A Nation of Christians is not a Christian Nation," *New York Times Op-ed*, October 7, 2007.

10. Robert Bellah et al., *Habits of the Heart: Individualism and Commitment in American Life* (Berkeley: University of California Press, 1996).

11. Will Heberg, *Protestant, Catholic, Jew: An Essay in American Religious Sociology* (New York: Doubleday, 1955).

12. Pew Forum, "Pew US Religious Landscape Survey," *Pew Forum and Religion and Public Life*, 2008, http://religions.pewforum.org/reports.

13. Michael Sandel, *Liberalism and the Limits of Justice* (Cambridge: Cambridge University Press, 1998).

14. Sifra 25:36, 38.

15. Exodus 9:1.

16. Isaiah Berlin, "Two Concepts of Liberty," in *Four Essays on Liberty* (New York: Oxford University Press, 1969).

17. Max Weber, *The Protestant Ethic and the Spirit of Capitalism*, trans. T. Parsons (London: Routledge 1992). Aryei Fishman, "Religious Kibbutzim: Judaism and Modernization," in *Israeli Judaism: The Sociology of Religion in Israel*, ed. Shlomo Deshen, Charles S. Liebman, and Moshe Skokeid (New Brunswick, NJ: Transaction Publishers, 1995), 176.

18. Michel Foucault, *Madness and Civilization: A History of Insanity in the Age of Reason* (Oxford: Routledge, 2001), xii.

19. Jonathan Boyarin, "Circumscribing Constitutional Identities in Kiryas Joel," *Yale Law Journal* 106, no. 5 (1997): 1537–1570.

20. Jonathan Sacks, "The Law of the Land is the Law," *The Jewish Chronicle*, February 14, 2008, http://website.thejc.com/home.aspx?AId=58070&ATypeId=1&search=true2&srchstr=the%20law%20of%20the%20land&srchtxt=0&srchhead=1&srchauthor=0&srchsandp=0&scsrch=0.

21. *Bollenbach v. Monroe-Woodbury Central School District (1987)*.

22. Joseph Berger, "Milton Himmelfarb, Wry Essayist, 87, Dies," *New York Times*, January 15, 2006, http://query.nytimes.com/gst/fullpage.html?res=940DE3D8143FF936A25752C0A9609C8B63. Seymour Lipset, "Relating to Both Sides of the Partisan Fence," June 1997, http://findarticles.com/p/articles/mi_7214/is_199706/ai_n29903645/.

23. Pew Forum, "Pew US Religious Landscape Survey."

24. Cathy Lynn Grossman, "Tensions between Sunnis, Shiites Emerging in USA," *USA Today*, September 25, 2007, http://www.usatoday.com/news/religion/2007-09-24-muslim-tension_N.htm.

25. Ibid.

26. Ibid.

27. Ibid.

28. Ibid.

29. Home page, Council on American-Islamic relations, *www.cair.com.*

30. Marcia Pally, "Opinion: A Trans-Atlantic Divide Exists on Muslim Integration," *The Daily Star,* December 1, 2007, www.pewforum.org/new/display.php.

31. Pew, ibid.

32. Ibid.

33. Miriam Udel Lambert, "Born in the USA: A New American Islam Proves Devotion and Women's Liberation Do Mix," *The American Prospect,* December 8, 2000, http://www.prospect.org/cs/articles?article=born_in_the_usa_.

34. Abul Taher, "A Third of Muslim Students Back Killings," *The Sunday Times,* July 27, 2008, http://www.timesonline.co.uk/tol/news/uk/article4407115.ece.

35. Yahya Birt, "Discord and the Hope of Unity," *Altmuslim,* August 31, 2007, http://www.altmuslim.com/a/a/print/2589/.

36. Ulil Abshar-Abdalla, "Being a Muslim in the US: An Open Letter to a Friend," *Jaringan Islam Liberal,* November 11, 2006, http://islamlib.com/en/article/being-a-muslim-in-the-us/.

37. Ibid.

38. Samuel P. Huntington, "The Clash of Civilizations?" *Foreign Affairs* (Summer 1993), http://www.foreignaffairs.com/articles/48950/samuel-p-huntington/the-clash-of-civilizations.

39. M. A. Muqtedar Khan, "Should Muslims be Allowed to Impose Islam on Other Americans?" *Ijtihad,* November 2006, http://www.ijtihad.org/Impose-Islam.htm.

40. Lambert, "Born in the USA."

41. Martha Minow, "The Constitution and the Sub-Group Question," *Indiana JL* (Winter 1995), 71.

42. Feldman, *Lubavitcher as Citizens.*

43. Ibid., 192.

44. Clifford Geertz, "Thick Description," in *Interpretation of Cultures* (New York: Basic Books, 1973).

45. Robert Putnam, *Making Democracy Work: Civic Traditions in Modern Italy* (Princeton: Princeton University Press, 1994).

46. William Galston, *Liberal Purposes: Goods, Virtues, and Diversity in the Liberal State* (Cambridge: Cambridge University Press, 1991).

47. James Davis Hunter, *Culture Wars: The Struggle to Define America* (New York: Basic Books, 1991).

48. Ronald Dworkin, *Taking Rights Seriously* (London: Duckworth, 1977).

49. John Stuart Mill, *On Liberty* (London: John W. Parker and Son, 1859).

50. John Rawls, *Political Liberalism* (New York: Columbia University Press, 1993).

51. Ibid., 146, 198.

52. John Locke, *A Letter Concerning Toleration* (London: Awnsham Churchill, 1689).

53. Michael McConnell, "Believers as Equal Citizens," in *Obligations of Citizenship and Demands of Faith: Religious Accommodation and Pluralist Democracies*, ed. Nancy L. Rosenblum (Princeton: Princeton University Press, 2000), 90–110.

54. Robert Cover, "The Supreme Court 1982 Term—Forward: Nomos and Narrative," *Harvard Law Review* 97, no. 4 (1983): 1–12. Rawls, *Political Liberalism*, 176.

55. Iris Marion Young, *Justice and the Politics of Difference* (Princeton: Princeton University Press, 1990).

56. Brian Barry, *Culture and Equality: An Egalitarian Critique of Multiculturalism* (Cambridge: Harvard University Press, 2001), 12.

57. Young, *Justice and the Politics*.

58. Will Kymlicka, *Finding Our Way: Rethinking Ethnocultural Relations in Canada* (Toronto: Oxford University Press, 1998).

59. Shachar, "On Citizenship," 57.

60. Ibid., 80.

61. Robert Cover, "The Supreme Court 1982 Term—Forward: Nomos and Narrative," *Harvard Law Review* 97, no. 4 (1983): 1–12.

62. Ibid. Abner Greene, "Kiryas Joel and Two Mistakes about Equality," *Columbia Law Review* 96, no. 1 (January 1996). Jonathan Boyarin, "Circumscribing Constitutional Identity in Kiryas Joel," *Yale Law Journal* (March 1997), 1537–1570. Nomi Stolzenberg, "He Drew A Circle That Shut Me Out: Assimilation, Indoctrination, and the Paradox of A Liberal Education," *Harvard Law Review* 106, no. 3 (January 1993): 581–667.

63. The Supreme Court in *Board of Education of Kiryas Joel Village School District v Grumet, 114 S.Ct. 2481, 2496 (1994)* overturned a New York State law that permitted a community of Satmar Chassidim in upstate New York to create a school district that tracked the boundaries of the Village of Kiryas Joel. The goal of the Satmar was to be able to qualify for New York State special educators that their special needs children were otherwise entitled to as residents, had they attended public rather than religious schools. The Satmar petitioned the state for the school district after a disastrous attempt to bus their disabled and non-English speaking students to the public high school of the adjoining Woodbury/Monroe school district. While the parents testified that their children had been harassed and traumatized in the public high school, the court feared that by acceding to the Satmar request, the state would not only be violating the establishment clause, but would be drawn into giving its imprimatur to gender-based and religious-based segregation. Critics claimed that the Satmar were really after self-segregation and were engaging in "defensive huddling." It was also asserted that Kiryas Joel was a poor candidate for grants of partial sovereignty because of its lack of internal democracy, gender inequality, and its high probability of "constitution flouting." Ira C. Lupu,

"Uncovering the Village of Kiryas Joel," *Columbia Law Review* 96, no. 1 (January 1996): 104–120.

64. Christopher Eisgruber, "The Constitutional Value of Assimilation," *Columbia Law Review* 96, no.1 (January 1996): 87–103.

65. Yasemin Soysal, "Changing Parameters of Citizenship and Claims-making: Organized Islam in the European Public Sphere," *Theory and Society* 26 (1997): 511.

66. Fourth Conference of European Muslims, July 1990.

67. Edward W. Said, *Orientalism* (London: Routledge & Kegan Paul, 1978).

68. Haideh Moghissi, *Feminism and Islamic Fundamentalism*, 53–4.

69. Seyla Benhabib, *The Claims of Culture: Equality and Diversity in the Global Era* (Princeton: Princeton University Press, 2002). Kwame Anthony Appiah, *The Ethics of Identity* (Princeton: Princeton University Press, 2005). Anne Philips, *Multiculturalism without Culture* (Princeton: Princeton University Press, 2007).

70. Feldman, *Lubavitcher as Citizens*, 65.

71. Okin, "Is Multiculturalism Bad for Women?"

72. Ibid., 30.

73. Ibid., 8.

74. Blu Greenberg, "Women of Valor: How American Jewish Women Made Contributions to Jewry and the World," March 12, 2004, http://www.jewishvirtuallibrary.org/jsource/Judaism/valor.html.

75. Shachar, "On Citizenship and Multicultural Vulnerability."

76. Faisal Kutty, "Ontario Report Affirms Right to Use Islamic Principles in Arbitration," Washington Report on Middle East Affairs, March 2005.

77. Submission by B'nai Brith, "Canada Review of the Arbitration Process in Ontario," September 2004, Beis Din of Toronto.

78. Homa Arjomand, "Report of Meeting with Marion Boyd Regarding Shari'a Court in Canada," July 15, 2004.

79. "Dispute Resolution in Family Law: Protecting Choice, Promoting Inclusion," Executive Summary of Report Prepared by Marion Boyd, December 2004.

80. This section draws heavily for its factual material upon Pascale Fournier, "The Reception of Muslim Family Law in Western Liberal States," Written for the Canadian Council of Muslim Women, Shari'a/Muslim Law Project, September 2004.

81. Rowan Williams, Archbishop of Canterbury, "Islam in English Law: Civil and Religious Law in England," Lecture given at Lambeth Palace, February 7, 2008, http://news.bbc.co.uk/2/shared/bsp/hi/pdfs/07_02_08_islam.pdf, cited in Ayelet Shachar, "Privatizing Diversity: A Cautionary Tale from Religious Arbitration in Family Law," *Theoretical Inquiries in Law* 9, no. 2 (July 2008), article 11, Berkeley Electronic Press, http://ssrn.com/abstract=1151234.

82. Shachar, "Privatizing Diversity."

83. Asifa Quraishi and Najeeba Syeed-Miller, "No Altars: A Survey of Islamic Family Law in the United States," *Emory Law*, Emory University School of Law, http://www.law.emory.edu/ifl/cases/USA.htm.

84. Azizah Y. al-Hibri, "An Introduction to Muslim Women's Rights," in *Windows of Faith: Muslim Women Scholar-Activists in North America*, ed. Gisela Webb (Syracuse: Syracuse University Press, 2000), 52.

85. Ibid., 53.

86. Karamah, "Projects," *Karamah*, TriVision Studios, http://www.karamah.org/projects.htm.

87. Azizah Y. al-Hibri, "The Muslim Marriage Contract in American Courts," Speech, Minaret of Freedom Banquet, University of Richmond, VA, May 20, 2000, http://www.karamah.org/articles_marriage_contract.htm.

88. Ibid., 111.

89. Al-Hibri, "The Muslim Marriage Contract," refers to "patriarchal Western women," 67.

90. Qur'an 2:229.

91. Eugene Volokh, "Maryland's Highest Court Refuses to Recognize Pakistani (Islamic Law) Divorce," *The Volokh Conspiracy*, May 7, 2008.

92. Azizah Y. al-Hibri, "Family Law Issues Affecting American Muslim," Speech, NGO Forum, United Nations Fourth World Conference on Women, Huairou, China, September 7, 1995, http://www.islamfortoday.com/familylaw.htm.

93. *Dajanai v. Dajani (1988) 204C.A. 3rd 1387.*

94. Al-Hibri, "Family Law Issues."

95. I am grateful to Professor Lisa Fishbayn for this reading of the case.

96. Quraishi and Syeed-Miller, "Family Law Issues."

97. *Seth v. Seth 694 S.W. 2nd 459; 1985 Tex. App. LEXIS 6918.*

98. Madigan, "Court Denies Islamic Divorce."

99. Ibid.

100. Michelle Boorstein, "Ancient Divorce Laws' Modern Quandary," *Washington Post*, February 5, 2006, http://www.washingtonpost.com/wp-dyn/content/article/2006/02/04/AR2006020401007_pf.html.

101. Eric Fingerhut, "Unchaining Women," *Washington Jewish Week*, February 1, 2007.

102. The specific process of the get is explained in detail in Marc Feldman, "Jewish Women and Secular Courts: Helping a Jewish Woman Obtain a Get," *Berkeley Women's Law Journal* 5:141.

103. Ibid.

104. Sue Fishkoff, "Conservative Rabbi says Georgia's Kosher Law Unconstitutional," *Jewish Telegraphic Agency*, August 10, 2009, http://jta.org/news/article/2009/08/10/1007159/conservative-rabbi-says-georgias-kosher-law-unconstitutional.

105. Irving Breitowitz, quoted in Boorstein, "Ancient Divorce."

106. "OU Joins With Other National Jewish Organizations in Circumcision Court Case," Institute for Public Affairs, Union of Orthodox Jewish Congregations of America,September 17, 2007, http://www.ou.org/public_affairs/article/29309.

107. Nathan Diament, quoted in Nathaniel Popper, "Divorce Bill Leaves Feminists and Ultra-Orthodox in Bed Together," *Jewish Daily Forward*, February 2, 2007.

108. This is treated extensively by David M. Cobin in "Jewish Divorce and the Recalcitrant Husband: Refusal to Give a 'Get' as Intentional Infliction of Emotional Distress," *Journal of Law and Religion*, jstor.org/stable/1051005.

109. Lisa Fishbayn, "Gender, Multiculturalism and Dialogue: The Case of Jewish Divorce," *Canadian Journal of Law and Jurisprudence* 21, no.1 (January 2008): 86.

110. Popper, "Divorce Bill Leaves Feminists and Ultra-Orthodox in Bed Together."

111. Ibid.

112. I am indebted to Professor Lisa Fishbayn for this insight.

Index

Sonbol, Amira El-Azhary, 95

Soysal, Yasemin, 174

St. Augustine, 170. *See also* Catholicism

Sufi, 51, 163. *See also* Shi'a; Sunni

Sullivan, Kathleen, 154

Sunnah, 37, 40, 42–43, 48, 50–52, 185. See also *ahadith*; Muhammad; Qur'an; shari'a

Sunni: family law of, 192; family law court of, 76, 80, 85; majority in Kuwait, 18, 82; politics of, 94–95, 102; presence of in United States, 163–164; schools of thought, 185; views of women, 69. *See also* Shi'a; Sufi

Sura 4:34, 10, 15, 31, 46, 48, 56. *See also* Qur'an

Swirski, Barbara, 12

Talaq, 7, 47, 181–182, 185, 190–192. *See also* bride price; family law; get; *khula*

Talmud, 55–57; availability to women, 128, 134, 136, 139, 140; reinterpretation of, 35, 41; understanding of gender, 59–61, 148. *See also* halakha, midrash

Toanot halakhah, 138–140

Tocqueville, Alexis de, 168

Torah, 26; communal necessity for, 32–37, 41, 173; comparison with Qur'an, 2, 43; controversy at Wall, 65, 115–116; feminine learning of, 67–68, 128, 131, 134–136, 140; feminist critique of, 59–60; feminist views of, 2, 33, 63; openness for reinterpretation of, 29–30, 57–58; oral versus written, 55; and divorce law, 193. *See also* Moses; Qu'ran; Sinai; Talmud

Tzniut. *See* modesty

United Nations: Charter, 20, 85; Commission on Status of Women, 126, 149; Universal Declaration of Human Rights, 20, 124

US Constitution: free exercise clause and establishment clause, 16–17, 154–155, 162, 203; relation to religious minorities, 167, 200; and religious divorce, 198. *See also* Federalist Papers; Kiryas Joel; Lemon test

Uziel, Rabbi Ben-Zion Meir Hai, 130–132. *See also* Kook, Rabbi Avraham

Wadud, Amina, xi, 3, 45, 66

Wahabi Islam, 28, 34, 51, 81, 89. *See also* Hamas; Islamists; Muslim Brotherhood; Salafi

Weiss, Susan, 144, 146

Women's Cultural and Social Society (WCSS), 89, 91–93, 96–97, 105

Women's Equal Rights Law, 122, 124, 133, 135

Women of the Wall (WOW), 65–66, 115–116

Yemen, 4

Yishuv, 18, 130–132

Yoetzet, 137–140. *See also* halakha

Young, Iris Marion, 171–172

Zionism, 68, 124, 133

Library of Congress Cataloging-in-Publication Data
Feldman, Jan L. (Jan Lynn), 1955–
Citizenship, faith, and feminism: Jewish and Muslim
women reclaim their rights / Jan Feldman.
    p. cm.—(Brandeis series on gender, culture, religion
and law)
Includes bibliographical references and index.
ISBN 978-1-58465-972-3 (cloth: alk. paper)—
ISBN 978-1-58465-973-0 (pbk.: alk. paper)—
ISBN 978-1-61168-011-9 (e-book)
1. Feminism—Religious aspects—Judaism 2. Feminism—
Religious aspects—Islam. 3. Jewish women—Political
activity—Israel. 4. Muslim women—Political activity—
Kuwait. 5. Women's rights—Israel 6. Women's rights—
Kuwait. 7. Multiculturalism—United States. I. Title.
BM729.W6F44   2011
296.082—dc22   2010051581